THIRSTY, AND YOU GAVE ME DRINK

THIRSTY,
and
YOU GAVE ME DRINK

HOMILIES AND REFLECTIONS FOR CYCLE C

EDITED BY

Deacon Jim Knipper

PUBLISHED BY :

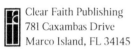

Clear Faith Publishing
781 Caxambas Drive
Marco Island, FL 34145

ISBN: 978-1-940414-35-5

Cover & interior design by Doug Cordes
Cover art & interior illustrations by Br. Mickey O'Neill McGrath, OSFS

The mission of Clear Faith Publishing is to spread joy, peace and comfort through great writing about spirituality, religion and faith that touches the reader and serves those who live on the margins. Portions of the proceeds from this book are donated to organizations that provide clean water, shelter, and counsel for those in need. For more information, please visit us at: www.clearfaithpublishing.com.

CONTRIBUTING AUTHORS

William J. Bausch

Margaret Blackie, PhD

Greg Boyle, SJ

Mark Bozzuti-Jones, DMin

Margaret Bullitt-Jonas, PhD

L. Patrick Carroll

John Chaffee

Rory Cooney

David A. Davis

Becky Eldredge

Robert Ellsberg

John Fisher, OSFS

Michelle Francl-Donnay

Kyle Haden, OFM

Cassidy Hall

Luke Hansen

Fr. Jan Michael Joncas

Deacon Greg Kandra

Anna Keating

Deacon Jim Knipper

Michael Leach

Richard G. Malloy, SJ

James Martin, SJ

Shirin McArthur

Megan McKenna

Brian McLaren

Penny A. Nash

Jan Richardson

Richard Rohr, OFM

Tim Schenck

Annie Selak

Timothy Shriver

Mary Sperry

Fran Rossi Szpylczyn

Patrick Wenrick

John Whitney, SJ

Phyllis Zagano, PhD

DEDICATION

*For all who have the courage to
Believe what you read,
teach what you believe,
and practice what you teach.*

"It is no use walking anywhere to preach unless our walking is our preaching."

—ST. FRANCIS OF ASSISI

"Either you allow Holy Scriptures to change you, or you will normally try to use them to change and clobber other people."

—RICHARD ROHR, OFM

"Christ has no body now on earth but yours, no hands, no feet but yours. Yours are the eyes with which Christ looks out his compassion to the world. Yours are the feet with which he is to go about doing good. Yours are the hands with which he is to bless us now."

—TERESA OF ÁVILA

"The strategy of Jesus is not centered in taking the right stand on issues, but rather in standing in the right place—with the outcast and those relegated to the margins."

—GREG BOYLE, SJ

CONTENTS

PREFACE

LITTLE DID I KNOW THAT WHEN WE STARTED
Clear Faith Publishing, years ago, with the goal of issuing just one book of homilies, that we would be entering our tenth year with our latest release, *Thirsty, and You Gave Me Drink*. Our mission has been to provide homilies and reflections which feed the heart and soul of our readers. From our first book, which contained fifteen authors from a wide base of Christian clergy and laity, we have expanded our base of contributors to over thirty-five, providing greater depth and diversity in the ways these gospels can be broken open for our readers. Many of us have heard these gospels time and time again over the years, possibly missing the ways that they can open our eyes, our hearts, and our souls to the great love God has for all of us—and how to share that love with those in our lives.

The secondary goal of these award-winning books has been to financially support charities that do the work of feeding, sheltering, and providing counsel for those in need. Now, in the middle of the second series of books, which follow the Roman Catholic Liturgical Cycle, we have donated over $100,000 across the charities listed in the back of our books.

We hope you will enjoy these homilies and reflections and that they feed and challenge you to see Christ in a new way—in the faces of those in your life who are hungry and thirsty and seek to be fed. Finally, may the love of Christ, which dwells within each of us, without exception, encourage us to spread the Good News to a country and a world that cry for healing and forgiveness as we go forth to care for one another, especially for the least of our sisters and brothers.

DEACON JIM KNIPPER
01 NOVEMBER 2021
FEAST OF ALL SAINTS

Advent

1ˢᵀ SUNDAY *of* ADVENT

RICHARD G. MALLOY, SJ

"Stand erect and raise your heads because your redemption is at hand."

1ST READING	2ND READING
JER. 33:14-16	1 THESS. 3:12-4:2
PSALM	**GOSPEL**
25:4-5, 8-9, 10, 14	LUKE 21:25-28, 34-36

BIG JOHN BIGGER AND HIS WIFE, JANE, HAVE a baby. Who's bigger, big John Bigger or the new baby? Answer: the baby. Why? Because the baby is (wait for it...) a "little Bigger."

Anyone who has had a baby, anyone who has been in a family anticipating a birth, knows the joy and suspense of awaiting the arrival of a newborn. A new baby is so wonderful! The baby's smile is beautiful and their laugh is one of the most incredibly joyous sounds you will ever hear (well, unless it's 4:00 a.m. and you've got to get up, again, to feed the little one).

Today, we begin Advent. We await a child. We anticipate our God, who will once again be born among us: baby bald and vulnerable, needing our love and care, calling us to become our deepest, truest selves—men and women who will respond in love, generously, to those in need.

Today's Gospel speaks of ominous signs, signs of upheaval and difficulties. Infants wrapped in swaddling clothes also turn everything upside down. Babies can cause difficulties: diapers, feedings at all hours, loss of sleep, trips to the emergency room. Luke's Gospel tells us, "when these signs begin to happen, stand erect and raise your heads because your redemption is at hand." Redemption—*Apolutrosis* in Greek: deliverance, emancipation, liberation. When you see these signs, when you see this baby lying in a manger, know that God is doing something good. God is birthing something, someone, wonderful.

Several years ago, I had a deep and consoling Christmas prayer experience. For many years, on Christmas Eve I'd celebrate two Masses. Christmas Day, I'd join with elderly Jesuits for Mass in the infirmary, then go on to visits of four or five families, the last with my elderly mother. We'd go to the home of family friends, who always welcomed us for their big meal, a characteristically raucous and loving Irish celebration.

A couple of years ago, my mother had died, and one family I usually visited was out of town. All of a sudden, it was 1:00 p.m. on Christmas Day, and I had nowhere I had to be until later in the afternoon.

I went into the house chapel and settled down. Slowly, I read Luke 2:1–20, lingering on the words: Caesar Augustus. David. Mary and Joseph. The time came. She gave birth to her firstborn son. Shepherds. Great fear. "Do not be afraid!" trumpets the angel. Good news. Great joy. A savior has been born for you. An infant. Wrapped in swaddling clothes. Glory!

Entering into the classic Ignatian method of contemplation, I imagined myself in the Gospel scene. My imagination was filled with the quiet rustling of the barn. An ox and donkey snort, their breath visible in the frigid air. A few mice dart around in the straw. The musty smell of earthen floor. A small charcoal fire reminds me of the same in John 18 and 21.

I gaze on Mary holding Jesus. She looks tired, really exhausted. She's far from home, no gal pals to help her. Joseph too looks weary. He seems a bit awed and almost fearful. How is he going to care for these two? Does he already sense the horror of Herod's persecution?

As I just sit there, being present to the moment in my imagination, suddenly, unexpectedly, Mary turns to me and asks, "Do you want to hold him?"

She gently places the sleeping baby Jesus, wrapped in swaddling clothes, in my arms.

As I hold the savior of the world, all tiny and baby bald, smaller than a loaf of bread, I don't do anything, or say anything. Silence is often the best conduit of God.

There isn't any tremendous grace given, nor any startling insight into the mystery and majesty of divinity. What pervades my consciousness is a sense of peace, a deep realization: Again, He has come. He is here, here to love us, to save us. He is here to love me, to save me.

A deeper realization of the vulnerability of God dawns on me. A welling up of gratitude for the gift of faith, and hope for our world, moves in me. Love for Jesus, and a sense of connection to Mary and Joseph as they accept their mission, surges within me. The reality of Emmanuel, God with us, takes hold in my heart.

Carl Sandburg once wrote, "A baby is God's opinion that life should go on."[1] This baby is God's pledge and promise that life will go on forever. Hold on to him.

Christmas in the chapel, holding the baby Jesus. What did the experience mean?

In the years since then, the grace of that prayer has deepened. Holding the baby Jesus teaches us to hold and handle with care the vulnerable and weak, those who are threatened with abortion or the death penalty, those who fear deportation or forced immigration to flee danger and war, and those who do not have the necessities of life: the unemployed, the hungry, and the homeless. Such people are like our vulnerable God, a sign for us in this baby born of Mary.

Greg Boyle, SJ says we are a loving and healthy community when we stand in awe of the courage and grit it takes poor people to carry the burdens of poverty. We should stand in awe of them, rather than stand in judgment of the ways they bear the burdens placed upon them.

Do we desire to hold the baby Jesus? Do we want to hold the poor and needy? Do we give of ourselves to care for the vulnerable and for those who cannot care for or defend themselves? This Advent, let us open our minds and our hearts, our wallets and our checkbooks, to those in need. This Advent, let's find ways to be a little bigger by giving a lot more.

To do that, we ask God to come close and help us. Let us pray.

---

1   Carl Sandburg, *Remembrance Rock* (New York: Harcourt, Brace, 1948), 7.

2ND SUNDAY *of* ADVENT

THE REV. JAN RICHARDSON

Those who sow in tears will reap with cries of joy.

1ST READING
BAR. 5:1-9

2ND READING
PHIL. 1:4-6, 8-11

PSALM
126:1-6

GOSPEL
LUKE 3:1-6

ON THE SOUTHWEST COAST OF IRELAND, there is a town that holds my heart. I visited it briefly with a group of friends during my first sojourn to that country. Through some strange and wondrous occasions of synchronicity, I have had the opportunity to return there to spend stretches of time writing. The town's beauty and hospitality have made it a place of remarkable solace and good cheer, a particular gift as I have worked to dream my way into a new life following the unexpected death of my husband just a few years after we were married.

If you are familiar with Ireland, you know that its landscape has held tremendous suffering. The town I visit bears witness to this in its Old Cemetery, where there is a Famine Plot containing the remains of thousands who died during the Great Famine in the nineteenth century.

There is something about Ireland that can stir deep sorrow for me. I suspect it is simply the nature of the country, that its terrain has a way of inviting whatever grief we carry to come to the surface. I can get sad in Ireland like nowhere else. When I first experienced this, it prompted dismay and a sensation of guilt: *I'm in Ireland! How dare I be sad?* And then one day it occurred to me, *Ireland! What a fantastic place to be sad!* because, for all the sorrow that Ireland can evoke, it also knows a vast amount about what to do with that sorrow.

I was talking one evening with a friend who lives in the town, and I asked him about this sense that Ireland has a tremendous capacity to absorb grief and to create from it. He nodded vigorously. Poetry, literature, song, art: This country that has held great suffering has also somehow developed an astonishing range and depth of practices that have helped transform its pain. This kind of transformation does not attempt to explain away the trauma or to hide its lingering effects; it does not romanticize pain or seek to turn it into something noble. Instead, Ireland's long devotion to well-honed creative practices has enabled it to enter into its collective and personal tragedies, to work with them, and to clear space within them for something else to come through—something that rises up as celebration, as fierce connection, as joy that, though often complicated and haunted by history, endures even in the midst of ongoing grief.

Ireland has been a place that has helped me engage in those practices in my own life, those ways I work on my ability to hold what comes—the sorrow and loss as well as the wonder and gladness that so often inhabit the same space. It has been a place that reminds me that our capacity for joy relies on more than a particular mood or disposition over which we do not always have much control. Opening to joy means being willing to let the world enter us, to let it break our hearts, but not to remain over-whelmed by the breaking. It asks that, instead of turning away, we find those places where we can engage, can create, can offer what is uniquely ours to offer—those places where we learn to sing amid the brokenness, in celebration of all that goes deeper still.

BLESSING TO SUMMON REJOICING

When your weeping
has watered
the earth.

When the storm
has been long
and the night
and the season
of your sorrowing.

When you have seemed
an exile
from your life,
lost in the far country,
a long way from where
your comfort lies.

When the sound
of splintering
and fracture
haunts you.

When despair
attends you.

When lack.
When trouble.
When fear.
When pain.

When empty.
When lonely.
When too much
of what depletes you
and not enough
of what restores
and rests you.

Then let there be
rejoicing.

Then let there be
dreaming.

Let there be
laughter in your mouth
and on your tongue
shouts of joy.

Let the seeds
soaked by tears
turn to grain,
to bread,
to feasting.

Let there be
coming home.

3ʀᴅ SUNDAY *of* ADVENT

PHYLLIS ZAGANO

"Whoever has two tunics should share with the person who has none."

1ST READING	2ND READING
ZEPH. 3:14–18A	PHIL. 4:4–7
PSALM	**GOSPEL**
ISA. 12:2–6	LUKE 3:10–18

WE ARE MORE THAN HALFWAY THROUGH
Advent and the days are crowding upon us. We are more than busy. There
is less time to prepare. There is less time to shop. Christmas will be upon
us soon, and so we say, "Rejoice"!

Somewhere in our memories of past Advents we have stored the Latin
Introit, the opening words, for today's liturgy: "*Gaudete in Domino semper:
iterum dico Gaudete.*" "Rejoice in the Lord always: again, I say, rejoice."

And that we do.

The readings for this day are more than happy readings. They are excit-
ing and excited reminders to carry us through the week. Zephaniah tells us
to "Shout for joy." Why? Well, if we hear the words addressed to ourselves
(they are said to Israel), then we can know and feel the excitement when

the prophet says, "The Lord has removed the judgement against you [and] has turned away your enemies."

That is very good news at any time, especially now as we fear the growth of the pandemic, the possibilities of economic instability, and even the coming change of seasons.

But Zephaniah is clear: "You have no further misfortune to fear." He also tells us, "Do not be discouraged!"

Discouragement is a big part of the Christmas season, and so it creeps its way into Advent. Even though the bells are jingling all around us, whether in the subway or the mall, we tend to fret as we make lists of our lists and juggle our responsibilities with wants and needs. It seems there never is enough time.

Let's take a breath. Isaiah asks us to "Shout with exultation."

But why?

Well, there is a saying: "Jesus is the reason for the season."

That indeed is what it is all about. That indeed is what we too often forget.

It is about Jesus. Is there nothing more worthy of rejoicing?

We see gifts and gilt in every store window. We hear cheery songs on every radio station. But we quite probably do not see many images of the nativity. We quite probably do not hear many hymns to Mary and to Joseph and to the Child.

Yet, unto us a Child is born—or, at least, unto us a Child will be born—this December 25, just as last year and the year before. The promise is that next year and every year to come will be the same. We will know that Jesus will come as a babe, to be born in a simple place, and that he brings with him the promise that he will birth his life within our hearts.

That is why Isaiah tells us to "Shout with exultation."

And the result of the Incarnation, the promise of salvation, allows us to listen calmly to the Letter to the Philippians and to believe what we are told: "Have no anxiety at all, but in everything...make your requests known to God."

What do we want? What do we need?

Of course, we want peace, and we need it, too. We want peace in our hearts, in our families, in our neighborhoods, in our world. We want a peace that will carry us through the pre-Christmas frenzy. We want the peace that will bring our families together for the holidays. We want the peace that will keep our neighborhoods quiet and safe. We want the peace that will heal our troubled world, that will stop all war, that will cure all illness, that will feed all during famine.

Can the birth of Christ bring all these?

I think so. The answer to any question we may have is in the Gospel. Luke tells us today about the crowds that surrounded John the Baptist. Of course, the story is not quite where it belongs in the chronology of the life and death of Jesus, but it can answer that strong question: Can the birth of Christ bring peace in our hearts, in our families, in our neighborhoods, and in our world?

The answer is yes. Luke has John the Baptist tell us how.

The crowds asked John, "What then should we do?" and, as Luke explains, John said: "Whoever has two tunics should share with the person who has none. And whoever has food should do likewise."

John had advice for tax collectors, too: "Stop collecting more than what is prescribed." And so, with soldiers, whom he told not to extort, or falsely accuse, or grumble about their pay.

John preached kindness.

I think we first must be kind to ourselves. We can only do what we can do; we can only give what we can give. That helps us gain peace of heart.

We must be kind to our families. We cannot rehearse old arguments; we cannot maintain a grudge that has separated us in one way or another.

The same with neighborhoods—some rich, some poor, some in between. Every neighbor has a need. Many, if not most of them, we cannot fill. But we can be kind. It costs nothing to pick up the newspaper on a rainy day and put it on someone's porch. It is easy to wave and send a smile across the street or over the fence.

And then there is the world: our fragile, suffering planet. In too many places it is ailing, from fires, floods, or extremes of the weather. We can do our small part to keep the Earth safe, by all the simple measures that we heard about in school. We conserve water. We recycle materials. We don't pollute.

That is being kind, to ourselves, our families, our neighborhoods, and our world. And that kindness lets us welcome the peace the season promises. Then, and only then, will we know St. Paul's promise deep in our hearts. "Then the peace of God that surpasses all understanding will guard [our] hearts and minds in Christ Jesus."

Rejoice! Again, I say, rejoice!

4TH SUNDAY *of* ADVENT

PATRICK WENRICK

"Blessed are you who believed."

1ST READING
MICAH 5:1-4A

2ND READING
HEB. 10:5-10

PSALM
80:2-3, 15-16, 18-19

GOSPEL
LUKE 1:39-45

ROWAN WILLIAMS, FORMER ARCHBISHOP OF Canterbury, states in his book *Where God Happens* that we need to pay attention and learn from the Desert Fathers and Mothers to heal the experience of alienation that has become endemic to our age. They hold the keys to this healing. Though I agree with Rowan, I would say that we must return to the Gospels' figures to discover the importance of rootedness in healing alienation.

Over the past year, a global pandemic, a humanitarian disaster in Haiti, and the fall of a government in Afghanistan have brought forth severe isolation and lack of connectedness. This isolation is seen in many neighborhoods of our cities and towns, where people lack food and resources for a better life. Many have lost trust in others and long for healing, though they don't know how to establish it. Such international and local situations exacerbate the recovery needed—not by some, but by all of us.

In today's first reading, we hear the prophet Micah prophesy that the Messiah would come from a little out-of-the-way place called Bethlehem.

In this isolated, out-of-the-way place, God chose to go into the world in the person of Jesus.

As one looks at the destruction and alienation in our world, think of how alienated and isolated Mary, Elizabeth, Joseph, and Zechariah must have felt when they realized what was happening to them, all because they were open to the presence of God in their lives. In particular, when forced to travel to Bethlehem for the census, the isolation and lack of connectedness with relatives and friends were very pronounced for Mary and Joseph.

Mary, a young girl of fourteen and a virgin, is asked by an angel to be the mother of the Messiah. Joseph, not even married to Mary, is told that Mary is pregnant—and not by him. Zechariah finds it hard to believe that his wife, at ninety, is pregnant, and he cannot speak until the child is born and Zechariah writes on a tablet that the baby's name would be John. Talk about turning people's lives upside down. Yet, watch what they do with the upheaval that affects their lives. Mary travels to see Elizabeth. The two of them become support for each other. Mary initiates a visit that draws Elizabeth out of her anxiety and isolation. Eventually, Zechariah becomes more grounded in his faith and trusts that his experience is from God. He communicates, through writing on a tablet, that the child to be born shall be called John. His faith brings him out of his isolation as he begins to communicate with others.

In troubled times today, many are confined to their homes, longing for a phone call, a visit, or a conversation. Many suffer isolation and lack acceptance because they are not entirely welcome at our worship houses—despite the fact that we profess to believe in a God who accepts all people unconditionally. These people, as you know, live in our neighborhoods, assisted living facilities, and hospitals. Some are sitting next to us in our churches and places of worship. These places are the Bethlehems of today. This is where alienation happens, but where Christ beckons us to visit and communicate God's love for all.

Isn't it about time that our churches became more about inclusion than exclusion? We indeed profess a belief in a God who accepts all, regardless of race, color, creed, sexual orientation, or marital status. Yet, our actions in and outside some of our churches speak less of inclusion and more about division and isolation. Mary didn't let herself or Elizabeth remain in isolation after God visited. God didn't allow Zechariah to remain without a voice or Joseph to go to Bethlehem alone. God is present, even when we insist that all are not welcome at our tables and in our Bethlehems.

Often, we need to travel to a strange place to realize the importance of belonging. If you have ever been to a country where English is not spoken, then you know the sense of inclusion that I am referring to. A simple thing like asking for directions or recommendations for a place to buy food becomes a very frustrating endeavor.

Let our prayer become more like Mary's. She visits Elizabeth and draws her into the mystery of God's presence. Let our prayer become more like that of Joseph and Zechariah, who trusted during crises, even though they did not understand what God was doing. Let us connect with our brothers and sisters who feel alienated from our churches and life together. Let us be known for inclusion rather than exclusion. Amen!

Christmas

NATIVITY *of the* LORD: NIGHT

FR. KYLE HADEN

"I proclaim to you good news of great joy that will be for all the people."

1ST READING
ISA. 9:1–6

2ND READING
TITUS 2:11–14

PSALM
96:1–3, 11–13

GOSPEL
LUKE 2:1–14

AS A FRANCISCAN, I ADMIT THAT ONE OF MY favorite places to visit is the little town of Assisi, the home of my father Francis. I have visited the town several times over the years. The first few times that I visited, I rented a car so I could wander around Umbria, the beautiful region where Assisi is located. On one occasion, I decided to drive to the town of Bagnoregio, birthplace of St. Bonaventure, patron of the university where I teach. After spending a few hours in the village, perched on what look like the plateaus of Arizona, I began my drive back to Assisi.

As I was driving, I saw a road sign that indicated that the town of Greccio was only a few miles away. For a Franciscan, this village holds a deep affection, as it was the place where Francis celebrated the nativity of the Lord using live animals. I decided to visit the town. As I entered the church, I was deeply moved with what I saw. The interior of the church was filled with nativity sets made from peoples around the world. Each of the sets reflected the culture from which they came. It is an artistic reminder of the catholicity/universality of the Church.

Francis of Assisi was profoundly drawn to the historical human Jesus he read about in the gospels, so much so that he tried to literally imitate Jesus's words and actions. Today, we might find some of his behavior a bit odd. However, it was his attempt to be completely conformed to the image of Jesus he read in the holy gospels. In the nativity, Francis saw something that many failed, and still fail, to see in the Christ child. He perceived the great truth that almighty God, creator of heaven and earth, who sustains all of creation through his omnipotence, had chosen to empty himself of his divinity, to impoverish himself and enter into our human existence as a vulnerable, fragile human being.

While Francis is known to have had a radical view of poverty, it was this impoverishment of the Godman that he wanted to replicate—to empty himself in order to more fully embrace the other, regardless of the other's social status. This included lepers, those he previously despised and held in contempt. As God in Christ embraced us in our poverty and sickness, so Francis wanted to embrace the broken and sick in his own time and place.

We hear in the first reading from the prophet Isaiah, "For a child is born to us, a son is given to us; upon his shoulder dominion rests. They name him...Prince of Peace" (Isaiah 9:5). Francis took seriously that Jesus was prince of peace. In fact, he would regularly greet people with the phrase, "May the Lord give you peace." When there was a conflict between the mayor and the bishop of Assisi, a conflict that could easily lead to violence, Francis added the phrase to his Canticle of Creation, "Happy those who endure in peace; by you, Most High, they will be crowned," and had one of the brothers recite it in the presence of the two men. It had the effect of bringing a reconciliation between them, who, we are told, wept, and embraced each other.

Christ came into the world to bring us into the peace of God's kingdom. As disciples, we are called to imitate Jesus's ministry of peace, as exemplified in Francis's own ministry of peace. In a divisive world of competing ideologies, competing political agendas, ours is a ministry of reconciliation. This in turn calls us to a vulnerability, an emptying of all

that keeps us from being able to embrace the other, regardless of ideological or political differences.

In the letter of Titus, we read that "The grace of God has appeared,
saving all and training us to reject godless ways and worldly desires and to
live temperately, justly, and devoutly in this age" (Titus 2:11–12). So often
in Christian history, there has been a great deal of emphasis given to the
conviction that salvation is some form of fire insurance—a get-out-of-
hell-free card. The focus of Christian discipleship in this way of thinking
is centered on the next life, while life in the here-and-now is something
one simply endures.

In the nativity of the Lord, Francis saw the reality of God's deep interest in our life on earth, in our social relationships. How we live with one
another, care for one another, love one another, and recognize the divine
image in one another—these are things Francis took seriously as he saw
them lived out in the life of Jesus. It was this insight that drew Francis to
live a life that rejected godless ways and worldly desires. It was this that
formed in him the desire to live temperately, justly, and devoutly in this
age. It was also what broke him out of the cultural mindset that viewed
human society in rigidly hierarchical and stratified categories. No longer
did he see the poor, the excluded, or the powerless as being lower on
the social ladder. Rather, these people were the beloved of God, equal in
dignity with the highest prince, bishop, or pope. And as such, they were
to be treated according to their God-given dignity.

Christ, Immanuel, God with us, emptied himself, becoming a lowly
human being. In the poor and the lowly, in the broken and sick, Francis saw
the face of the crucified. In the vulnerability of the baby Jesus, Francis saw
our own vulnerability. Christ descended into our powerlessness and took
this risk in order to convey his deep and abiding love for us. In his desire to
be completely conformed to the image of Christ, Francis descended from
his social rank, giving up his status and wealth in order to be fully present
to those consigned to the lowest status of society. While Francis did not
reject those of higher social status, he was not afraid to remind them of
their call to care for the poor.

Though most are not called to embrace the radical poverty of Francis,
each of us are called to be conformed to the image of Christ, not simply
in the next world, but in the here-and-now. In this light, let us hear the

words Francis spoke to his brothers after years of ministering to the poor and abandoned: "Let us begin again, for up until now, we have done little or nothing."

May the Lord give you peace.

NATIVITY *of the* LORD: DAY

THE REV. JAN RICHARDSON

The light shines in the darkness.

1ST READING
ISA. 52:7–10

2ND READING
HEB. 1:1–6

PSALM
98:1–6

GOSPEL
JOHN 1:1–18

WHEN I THINK OF MY ARTISTIC ANCESTORS—
the creative people whose lives and work have inspired and informed my own—I trace my lineage back to the Middle Ages. My artful family tree includes the medieval monks and nuns who labored at their desks with paint and ink, working by hand to create sacred books: gospel books, prayer books, psalters. I think of scribes who traced each letter upon the vellum, artists who saturated pages with their pigments, so often adding the shimmering gold that would give rise to the name for such manuscripts: *illuminated.*

> In the beginning was the Word,
> and the Word was with God,
> and the Word was God.

Many illuminated manuscripts required months or years to create, involving what might strike us as a staggering amount of time and expense. We may wonder why these books warranted such extravagance when they could have been fashioned more simply. Yet for the artist and the scribe, creating an illuminated manuscript often became a lavish act of devotion, a response to the God who created us and came among us with such extravagant love.

> What came to be through him was life,
> and this life was the light of the human race.

I am continually enchanted and inspired by those who poured them-selves out in creating these luminous books that became a form of prayer, of proclamation, of sacrament. These artful ancestors understood how a book could become what the Celtic tradition has called a *thin place*—a space where heaven and earth meet, and we perceive more clearly the presence of the God who is always with us.

> The light shines in the darkness,
> and the darkness has not overcome it.

Those medieval scribes and artists well knew that there are kinds of darkness we need. The seed in the ground, the child in the womb, the body and soul in rest and in dreaming: we must have times of shelter from the light in order to grow in the ways God calls us to grow. Yet with their pages, these manuscript makers bore witness to the ancient longing for light that is built into our bones, the hankering we carry for a place of warmth and welcome. For all that God can do in the darkness, there is no escaping this penchant for illumination, this desire simply to see.

We find this same longing at work in the passage from John's Gospel that we read on Christmas Day. In this gorgeous prologue, John forsakes genealogies, biographical details, and even the conventions of narrative. His version of the Incarnation makes no mention of a baby, of Mary, of Joseph; he gives us no shepherds, no angels, no far-traveling, gift-bearing Magi wafting in on the fragrances of frankincense and myrrh. Instead, John tells us a story about light: the light that was with God from the beginning, the light through whom all life has come. John pares away the Christmas story to its essence.

> And the Word became flesh
> and made his dwelling among us,
> and we saw his glory . . .
> full of grace and truth.

Oh, my friends, it is Christmas Day. In these hours and always, may we turn ourselves toward that Word, that grace. May we lean into the light that begins in the deepest dark, bearing itself into this world for us. May we open our eyes, our hands, our hearts to the mysterious ways it comes.

HOW THE LIGHT COMES

I cannot tell you
how the light comes.

What I know
is that it is more ancient
than imagining.

That it travels
across an astounding expanse
to reach us.

That it loves
searching out
what is hidden,
what is lost,
what is forgotten
or in peril
or in pain.

That it has a fondness
for the body,
for finding its way
toward flesh,
for tracing the edges
of form,
for shining forth
through the eye,
the hand,
the heart.

I cannot tell you
how the light comes,
but that it does.
That it will.
That it works its way
into the deepest dark
that enfolds you,
though it may seem
long ages in coming
or arrive in a shape
you did not foresee.

And so
may we this day
turn ourselves toward it.
May we lift our faces
to let it find us.
May we bend our bodies
to follow the arc it makes.
May we open
and open more
and open still
to the blessed light
that comes.

DEACON GREG KANDRA

"Son, why have you done this to us?"

1ST READING
1 SAM. 1:20-22, 24-28

2ND READING
1 JOHN 3:1-2, 21-24

PSALM
84:2-3, 5-6, 9-10

GOSPEL
LUKE 2:41-52

ON THE FEAST OF THE HOLY FAMILY, WE ARE challenged to think about what it means to be a family, and how we can be more like the one we call "holy."

It isn't easy. Nowadays, the most common adjective you might hear before "family" isn't "holy," but "dysfunctional." So many of us are living with divorce, separation, alcoholism, addiction, and abuse. More families are coping with unemployment, economic hardship, and uncertainty.

Chances are, every person in this church this morning has been affected by all of these in one way or another.

How can we try to live as a holy family in times like these? We encounter this feast, just days after Christmas, and wonder: What do we have in common with those prayerful people in that Nativity scene?

After all, in that family, one of them was born without sin, and the youngest member happens to be the Son of God.

All families here today who fit that description, raise your hand.

But then, there is the *other* member of that family: the quiet one, the one who is, in fact, most like us. I'm speaking, of course, of St. Joseph.

In 2020, Pope Francis declared a Year of St. Joseph. The pope wrote: "Each of us can discover in Joseph—the man who goes unnoticed, a daily, discreet and hidden presence—an intercessor, a support and a guide in times of trouble. Saint Joseph reminds us that those who appear hidden or in the shadows can play an incomparable role in the history of salvation."[1]

This Sunday, I think Joseph has much to teach us about faith, about fortitude, and yes, about family.

Joseph, of course, is the patron of the universal church, the patron of workers, and the patron of fathers. Since he found a place for Mary and Jesus to live, realtors will tell you he's also the patron for finding or selling a home.

But I think his role is so much greater than that. Joseph is a man for us all.

First, he is the patron for all of us who want to learn how to listen. Joseph has no lines in the Bible; there is no Magnificat attributed to him, no prayer, no words of wisdom, no catchy quotes. Instead, he is famous for his silence. He is most notable for what he heard and did.

He listened. He dreamed. He waited. He followed the advice of angels. He went where God led him. He is a figure of holy trust. He teaches us that silence is golden—that the quiet ones, the shy ones, can sometimes change the world.

Secondly, he is the patron of all who need to trust in God. "Let go and let God" could have been his motto. Faced with an unexpected pregnancy and the possibility of scandal, he trusted God's will and cared for the woman he loved.

Thirdly, he is also the patron of people who end up being sent where they may not want to go. Joseph had to travel with his pregnant wife to Bethlehem, then flee to Egypt, then return to Nazareth, and then, years later, retrace his steps in Jerusalem when it seemed his son was lost.

He is a patron for all who might be fearful about the future, and for all who are forced to take a difficult and dangerous journey. He is an intercessor for refugees, for migrants, for soldiers. He stands before

---

1   Pope Francis, *Patris Corde*, December 8, 2020, https://www.vatican.va/content/ francesco/en/apost_letters/documents/papa-francesco-lettera-ap_20201208_patris- corde.html.

God's throne for anyone who is anxious or worried about how to face what is coming. In so many ways, he is a saint for our times.

Finally, he is the patron for all who feel unworthy or unready or unprepared. Joseph was chosen for an extraordinary role in salvation history. Scripture describes him as "righteous." There is no doubt he was a good and holy man. But how could he possibly have been ready to be the foster father of the Son of God?

He was a man unafraid to surrender himself to the will of God.

Our former pastor, Msgr. Joe Funaro, had a great devotion to St. Joseph, but also liked to remind us that he was, first and foremost, just like us. He wasn't perfect. He was someone who struggled with temptation, doubts, and difficulties.

But, across a lifetime of obstacles and problems, Joseph became what God intended him to be. And, in the end, he helped raise the savior of the world.

What did it take? It took patience, attention, trust in God, and prayer. It took the ability to have faith in times of uncertainty and courage in times of doubt.

When we are facing some insurmountable problem, maybe we should ask ourselves: WWJD? What Would *Joseph* Do? You don't need to be a husband, father, or carpenter to seek his example.

He's a saint for all of us.

In a world where so many families are more dysfunctional than holy, more broken than whole, we might find help and hope by asking for advice from the silent partner of the holy family, that *other* carpenter from Nazareth.

Ironically, the quiet one has much to say, if we are willing to listen. The one who taught Jesus to measure and cut and build can teach us, as well. Joseph can teach us how to measure our lives. How to cut off what is unneeded. And how to build families of faith and perseverance and trust.

SOLEMNITY *of the* BLESSED VIRGIN MARY

Mary kept all these things, reflecting on them in her heart.

1ST READING
NUM. 6:22-27

2ND READING
GAL. 4:4-7

PSALM
67:2-3, 5-6, 8

GOSPEL
LUKE 2:16-21

"*WHEN MARY SHOWS UP, PAY ATTENTION!*" These are words I hear come out of my mouth when I listen to others in spiritual direction and they begin to mention that Mary is showing up in their prayer. I have learned, through my own prayer life and in listening to others, that when Mary shows up in our prayer it is something to pay attention to. And why wouldn't it be important? Mary *is* the Mother of God.

In his book *The Gift of Spiritual Intimacy*, Monty Williams, SJ defines spiritual intimacy as our "truest sense of ourselves as inseparably rooted in God."[1] Mary understood what this gift of intimacy looked like in a real and personal way. As she sheltered Jesus within her, she was inseparable from him. At the same time she was sheltering Jesus within her, Mary

---

1   Monty Williams, *The Gift of Spiritual Intimacy: Following the Spiritual Exercises of Saint Ignatius* (Toronto: Novalis, 2009), 11.

was also experiencing the gift of being inseparable from God, who was with her in ways we cannot imagine as she physically carried Jesus within.

Mary's witness to us is that she knows how to create space in life for intimacy with God. She literally created space in her body for Jesus. After his birth, she mothered him and noticed many things that revealed the intimacy between her son, Jesus, and God. As the Gospel tells us today, "she kept all these things, reflecting on them in her heart."

What I know from walking with people in spiritual direction is that one of Mary's many roles in our lives is to accompany us to her son. She is our great intercessor, who seeks to draw us deeper into a relationship with her son. She desires for us to have that same intimacy she had with Jesus and God.

I cannot count the number of times I have witnessed Mary showing up as the "God-bearer" in someone's life, inviting someone to a deeper intimacy with her son. Sometimes this is through the invitation to turn to the rosary in prayer. Other times it is seeking the intercession of one of her many devotions or turning to her in conversation through imaginative prayer.

I have noticed Mary appearing in moments that are like moments of birthing, as God sought to come to life in new calls and expressions of love in people's lives. Mary appears as a midwife in people's prayer, encouraging people to say "yes" to the incarnate moment of God's expression of love in their lives that is seeking birth. I have watched parents come to understand Jesus's humanity in a new way as they understand Mary's role as earthly mother in similar acts of love that they do as parents. They ponder things in their hearts, such as holding babies in their arms, bringing them to their community of faith to be received, and nurturing their children along in the fullness of their development.

I see Mary's presence appear when the Holy Spirit is seeking to create more space in a person's life through healing or through freeing a person from sin or brokenness. Her motherly presence seems to be there as an encouragement to let the other person know intimacy with God is possible through letting go of what might hold us back from sharing ourselves fully with her son. I witness her appear at a Wedding at Cana-type moment, where God is inviting the other person forward to use their gifts and there might be hesitancy. Just as she did with Jesus, she stands by, perceiving

God's presence in our lives, encouraging us to use the very gifts we have. She is people's strength in moments of suffering, bearing witness to God's presence despite hardship or darkness.

Mary continues to be the God-bearer in our lives. She is here for us. She is ever accompanying us and inviting us into a deeper relationship with her son. She seeks for us to open and make room in our lives for her son the same way she opened herself to make room for Jesus within her. This opening can happen through spending time both with her and her son in the abundant number of ways our faith offers us: prayer, the sacraments, the Eucharist, and in sharing our gifts with the world.

I often imagine Mary's desire, prayer, and posture of accompaniment in our lives are offering us a blessing, like what we hear in the first reading:

> The Lord bless you and keep you! The Lord let his face
> shine upon you, and be gracious to you! The Lord look
> upon you kindly and give you peace!

On this day that honors and celebrates Mary, may we remember that she stands with us, praying for us to not only know her son, but to also become God-bearers in the world through our words and actions.

EPIPHANY

DEACON GREG KANDRA

They opened their treasures.

1ST READING	**2ND READING**
ISA. 60:1-6	EPH. 3:2-3A, 5-6
PSALM	**GOSPEL**
72:1-2, 7-8, 10-13	MATT. 2:1-12

FOR THOSE WHO MAY BE KEEPING TRACK, this marks the twelfth day of Christmas—so there is still time to go out and get those twelve drummers drumming. I think Macy's is having a sale.

This is Epiphany Sunday, and the star of the gospel is—literally—the star. It is the original GPS device, guiding the magi from the east toward Christ. One of my favorite Christmas symbols here in New York is that massive snowflake that resembles a star hanging over 57th Street. Nothing symbolizes the hope and serenity of this season more beautifully.

Of course, it may be significant that if the wise men were to follow that star today, it wouldn't lead them to a stable and the Christ child.

It would lead them to Trump Tower and Tiffany's.

But that star, and all that it represents, captures the imagination. The very word Epiphany means "manifestation." I looked in Webster's this morning and the dictionary elaborates: "An intuitive grasp of reality through something simple and striking."

Imagine that: something as simple as a child.

Something as striking as a star.

History is silent about just who or what the magi in the gospels really were. In some translations, they are astrologers; in others, they are kings or "wise men." And, in fact, we don't know exactly how many of them there were. But because they brought three gifts—gold, frankincense, and myrrh—tradition has held that there were three of them.

It is, of course, a meaningful number. Three is the number of the Trinity. It is the number of days Christ spent in the tomb.

But it also signifies something even more meaningful and, for us this morning, much more important: It represents to us community.

Again and again, when Christ is revealed to the world, he doesn't show himself to just one person at a time.

Think of Christmas night, when the news was announced to shepherds—another group, another kind of community.

And now, with the three magi, the Incarnation is announced to another community.

This will happen repeatedly. Next week, at Jesus's baptism, there will be a crowd of witnesses. When he preaches, he will speak to multitudes. When he performs his first miracle, it will be at a public gathering: a wedding. When he reappears after his resurrection, it will be to a roomful of believers. Even on the road to Emmaus, he presents himself not to one person, but to two.

That is part of the great message of Christianity. We are meant to receive the good news together, to live it together, to celebrate it and share it with one another.

The simple fact remains: Christianity is not a solitary experience.

Thomas Merton put it beautifully. "Love is our true destiny," he wrote. "We do not find the meaning of life by ourselves alone—we find it with another."[1]

The other important thing to remember about the magi is that they didn't come empty handed.

The gospel tells us, "They opened their treasures."

Like the magi, each of us has a treasure to offer Christ, to offer the world.

The prayerful question we should ask ourselves this Sunday is: What is it? What do we have to give?

---

1   Thomas Merton, *Love and Living* (San Diego: Harvest, 1979), 27.

I recently heard a story told by a marketing expert named Barbara Glanz. She gave a talk to a group of supermarket employees on the subject of customer loyalty: How to get people to keep coming back. She told those in her audience, "Every one of you can make a difference and create memories for your customers that will keep them coming back." And she challenged them to think about that.

One of the people in the audience was a nineteen-year-old grocery bagger named Johnny. He had Down Syndrome. And he thought very seriously about what she told him and went home and talked to his father about it. How could a bagger make the shopping experience special for people? He decided that every night after work he would find a thought for the day. If he couldn't find a thought for the day, he'd just make one up. And he had his father type it on the computer and make copies. Johnny then would cut up the sayings and put one in each bag.

Barbara Glanz was impressed by that idea and didn't think much of it until a month later, when she got a call from the store manager. He said he couldn't believe what had happened: Every day, Johnny's checkout line got longer and longer. People who normally shopped once a week were coming back more often, sometimes every day, just to get Johnny's thought for the day. He'd never seen anything like it. Eventually, other parts of the store started looking for ways to make their experience for customers unique—and the whole place was transformed.

No matter who we are, or where we come from, or what we do, each of us has a treasure to offer, a gift to give.

As we celebrate today Christ manifesting himself to the world, think of what that manifestation has meant to each of us, to *this* community. And let's ask ourselves what we can give in return—to God, and to one another.

What are your treasures?

The Christmas season may be drawing to a close, but the season of giving goes on.

BAPTISM *of the* LORD

PHYLLIS ZAGANO

"He will baptize you with the Holy Spirit and fire."

1ST READING
ISA. 40:1-5, 9-11

PSALM
104:1B-4, 24-25, 27-28, 29B-30

2ND READING
TITUS 2:11-14; 3:4-7

GOSPEL
LUKE 3:15-16, 21-22

IT IS A NEW YEAR. IT IS TIME FOR A NEW START.

It is time for us to gather our thoughts and set out into the world that needs the Gospel more than ever before. Drought, firestorms, floods, and pollution still trouble our fragile earth. Wars, famine, disease, and political unrest still plague its people. But we need to pick ourselves up, dust ourselves off, and, as the song recommends, start all over again.

We can do this if we remember our baptism. Better, we can do this if we remember our baptismal promises. Today, we repeat the promises someone else most probably affirmed for us when we were infants.

Do we reject Satan? Yes. His works? Yes. His empty promises? Yes. These are essential to living the Christian life. As the minister will say when placing ashes on our heads in a few months, "Turn away from sin and be faithful to the Gospel." That is the key, you know. The key to the Christian life is the Gospel. Not the prosperity gospel, not the political gospel, not even the "Gospel" too many angry bloggers attempt to spread with social media, much to the detriment of the life of the Church.

The Gospel to which you and I are faithful is the Gospel that teaches us how to answer the questions asked in the baptismal promises. We must infuse our lives with the Gospel. Only then can we say, personally and communally, that, yes, we believe in God the Father Almighty, creator of heaven and earth. Only then can we say we believe in Jesus Christ, his only Son, our Lord, who was born of the Virgin Mary. Only then can we accept the fact that, as Scripture attests, he was crucified, died, and was buried, and rose from the dead. Only then can we believe that Jesus the Christ is now seated at the right hand of the Father. Only then can we say these things and mean them intentionally, deeply, personally.

I think it is important to remember our baptismal promises today, as we start out in this new year, and every following day. The promises tell us who accompanies us, who will help us as the winter turns to spring, then to summer and to fall. If we believe in the Holy Spirit, we can believe in the Spirit's inspiration. If we believe in the communion of saints, we can believe that they, too, can guide us and give us examples for our own lives. If we believe in the forgiveness of sins, we can walk anew into the world knowing we are loved, and loved deeply, by God.

And, knowing we are so loved, we can believe in the resurrection of the body. We can believe in life everlasting.

The sum and total of our Christian commitment is reflected in the ways we live the Gospel. Christianity is not only for Sundays, but rather it is the bedrock of our ways of living every day, at work, at school, in the family, in the community. The Gospel, in fact, gives the answer to every question in every situation, whether at work or school or in the family or the community.

The important part about living our baptismal promises is that we cannot confuse the law with the Gospel. Law, and here I speak of Canon Law, does in fact reflect the Gospel and the Church's doctrinal teachings. But living the Gospel is not so much about obeying the law as it is finding in every situation when and how the "law of love" can be applied. We must love God above all, with our entire minds and all our strength. And we demonstrate that love in concrete situations. Do we love our neighbors as ourselves? Remember, Jesus said he did not come to abolish the law or the prophets, but rather to fulfill them.

So, at work and at school, are we paying attention to the fact that we must love the other, and that we must love ourselves? Are we honest with others in our transactions and do we pay attention to what we do? Do we take the time for our personal rest and for leisure?

Then, in our families and communities, do we love the other and ourselves? Are we backstabbers and gossips? Are we caring for ourselves physically and emotionally, so we can be present to those with whom we live?

If you think about it, our baptismal promises are not just for the day of baptism or only for today's feast. They are with us every day we profess to be Christians. We have the right—indeed, we have the duty—to recognize the dignity we gained at baptism. And, we have the equal right and duty to live in that dignity within the Church, as full and equal members of it, with full and equal voices in it.

The law tells us that we are free to make our needs and desires known to the hierarchy. In fact, according to what the Code of Canon Law calls our "knowledge, competence, and prestige,"[1] we have both the right and often the duty to pass our opinions along to the hierarchy and to the rest of the Christian faithful. If we solely go along to get along, we will not be carrying the Gospel openly; in fact, we might be hiding behind it. The fulfillment of our baptismal promises is to live and work in ways that, Canon Law points out, are "attentive to common advantage and the dignity of persons."[2] That means us and everyone around us. That means today and every day. That means being Christian.

---

1   *The Code of Canon Law,* Can. 212 §3

2   Ibid.

Lent

ASH WEDNESDAY

FRAN ROSSI SZPYLCZYN

"And your Father who sees in secret will repay you."

1ST READING
JOEL 2:12-18

2ND READING
2 COR. 5:20—6:2

PSALM
51:3-6, 12-14, 17

GOSPEL
MATT. 6:1-6, 16-18

TODAY IS ASH WEDNESDAY; LENT BEGINS. THE readings remain very clear; this is not the first or the last time we will hear these words in our lives. Perhaps we can walk together this Lent, and help each other to stay on the path?

In our first reading from Joel, we hear these words. They sound so powerful, don't they?

> Even now—oracle of the LORD—
> return to me with your whole heart,
> with fasting, weeping, and mourning.
> Rend your hearts, not your garments,
> and return to the LORD, your God.

Return. Whole heart. That's right—rend heart, not garments. Can we, a people who live in a culture focused intensely on the exterior, truly do the interior work of God? What a challenge we face because we all receive many messages intended to influence the lives we choose to live. Even if we are focused on God, many of us avoid fasting, weeping, and mourning. Maybe we can ask ourselves the following questions to guide our Lenten journey, as we choose to live differently—even if only for these forty days. God invites us to think about the choices before us today, as illustrated in this reading.

- What does fasting mean to us? Do we get caught up in fasting from food or Facebook, but forget to fast from inner elements of life, such as busyness, desire for productivity, a drive for success, or from simply trying to be "more holy" (whatever that means!)?

- How do we "rend our hearts"? Are we willing to tear open our hearts in order that we might truly change, or, better yet, allow God into our open hearts so that God may change us?

When we think about fasting or letting go, when we practice those things, we are acting in defiance of a culture that functions on being more, doing more, or getting more. How can we square that with our Christian faith? Jesus is inviting us into the desert to empty out and relinquish, which are very hard to do. That is one element of Lent for us to pray and walk with.

Today's psalm, Psalm 51, can offer us some help along these lines—and offers us some questions for reflection.

> A clean heart create for me, God;
> renew within me a steadfast spirit.
>
> Do not drive me from before your face,
> nor take from me your holy spirit.

- Here we are with hearts again. What does it mean to have a clean heart? Where does our own willingness emerge—or lack of it?

- What would it mean to have the Holy Spirit taken away?

By asking God to create a clean heart, we are in fact asking God for help with that emptying process and recognizing that this will energize our desire. We are also being reminded that we do not want to be separated from God. To remain close, we must continue letting go.

In 2 Corinthians, we read these words and consider further questions of the season that we are beginning.

> Behold, now is a very acceptable time;
> behold, now is the day of salvation.

- Can we experience God's invitation in every moment?

- How can we enter into the present moment as the acceptable time—which means every moment?

- Are we afraid of the door closing, or an offer with an "expiration date"?

I don't know about you, but I'm often one to say, "When the time is right, I will… [fill in the blank]." Save money, donate more, volunteer consistently, listen more deeply, and so forth. Yet, when is that time? That time is always right now—especially today, on Ash Wednesday. There is no expiration date that we are aware of, but there is no reason to delay either. God calls us closer each moment of each day.

The Gospel presses more deeply than ever with questions for our hearts, questions that prepare us for death and ultimately new life.

"And your Father who sees in secret will repay you."

- With this sentiment appearing three times in the Gospel, how do we understand our relationship with God?

- Are we fearful or hopeful of how we will be repaid? Do we think of it at all?

What does being "repaid" by God draw up in you? It might bring a shudder of fear, if you can only imagine a scary God who is waiting for us to slip up. Might this be a time for us to re-envision that God as one of compassion, who will repay us with loving compassion? God asks us to be humble and to be small—again, in a world that does not appear to value either. Yet, taking this on by letting go of what the world's norms might direct us to do will bring us the great reward of a loving God in our hearts.

As we go forth, these are just a few questions that we might all hope to pray with as we begin our Lenten pilgrimage. It is easy to get caught up in our own perceptions, but perhaps we can pray for one another to live these and other questions more fully. My prayer is that we all trust God to lead us on this Lenten path and that we follow in hope and humility.

Perhaps that is the key to starting and to moving ahead—consider this a journey, not a punishment; an adventure, not an obligation. There are "luggage limits" if we pay attention; there is a great deal of wisdom to not making emotional pack mules of ourselves. Let go, shake off, move freely! Oh, how easy to say, how hard to do.

I can't do this alone. I need God and I need you. We need one another. Shall we go? Shall we go together with Jesus? The desert beckons; let us set forth!

1ˢᵀ SUNDAY *of* LENT

DEACON JIM KNIPPER

Filled with the holy Spirit, Jesus returned from the Jordan and was led by the Spirit into the desert.

1ST READING
DEUT. 26:4-10

2ND READING
ROM. 10:8-13

PSALM
91:1-2, 10-15

GOSPEL
LUKE 4:1-13

GONE ARE THE WHITE VESTMENTS OF Christmas and the lively green of Ordinary Time. Gone are the flowers that adorned our sanctuary. Gone are the ashes that marked our foreheads and gone are the alleluias and the Glorias we sang with praise in our liturgies—as we gather at the threshold of our penitential Lenten Season on this first Sunday of Lent. It is this Sunday, each year, in which the Church gives us the passage of scripture that recounts the Holy Spirit leading Jesus into the desert for forty days, where he was tempted by the devil.

But to realize the significance of this, we have to look at where this piece of scripture appears. For, up to this point in Luke's Gospel, Jesus has not yet begun his ministry: no healing, no cures, no miracles, and no disciples. Rather, Jesus breaks from his Jewish tradition and heads to the Jordan River to participate in what was then a pagan ritual, and is washed in the River Jordan by his cousin John. Whereupon the heavens opened up and the Holy Spirit descended upon him in the form of a dove and a voice from above called him the "beloved son" of one who "is pleased." Then, from there, the Holy Spirit led Jesus into the desert wilderness.

My wife and I head out to Albuquerque a few times each year to see our son and beautiful daughter-in-law. And that high desert area is an incredible land. The surrounding mountain ranges and vast sky serve as God's canvas as each sunrise and sunset paints an incredible scene. During the day, you must be careful to carry water with you, for dry, arid air at altitude can leave you parched and thirsting for water. In the desert, you can just walk a short distance and nothing looks familiar. Walk farther into the wilderness and it becomes a dangerous land.

But it seems clear that before Jesus could begin his ministry, he needed time in such space. He needed to go to a place, in solitude, that was without distractions. Being fully human, he needed to wrestle with the same temptations we face: those of power, possessions, and prestige. It would seem that only after all that—and more—during those forty days of fasting and prayer, does he have the focus, maturity, and clarity to head back to Galilee and begin teaching in the synagogues, where all came to listen to him.

And so, once again, for forty days, we head into our individual and personal deserts, where we are called to that space where we are barren... where we hunger and thirst...and where we are called to take the time to look around—to identify our own emptiness and to answer the mantra of Jesus to "Repent, for the kingdom of heaven is at hand."

Repent? *Repent* doesn't mean that you need to walk around in sackcloth and ashes while beating upon your breasts in order to show everyone how mournful and contrite you are for your sins. Rather, we are being called to do something much more difficult than that. We are called to move beyond the mind that we have by focusing on our prayer life—not saying prayers to try to change God's mind, but prayers that change our capacity to see who God is within ourselves. For the "repent" that Jesus talks about means to turn ourselves around, to change our viewpoint, to change the way we think, to rid ourselves of our ego.

For the three temptations that were recorded (Luke implies there were others) are really fed by our *sense of self*. We are tempted to fill our emptiness with "stuff" by gathering more and more possessions, hoping that our thirst, our pain, and our barrenness will go away. We focus on power, control, and self-satisfaction, for "if it feels good, it must be good." And we foster and nurture a society that holds in esteem those who have climbed to the heights of what society has defined as "success."

Indeed, we are tempted to play games with what we say versus what we do—where we speak of our love for God, but are focused on what is in it for us first. Where we come for the ashes on Wednesday and by today are already not interested in doing the necessary desert work. Where we are tempted to go climb the social ladders we deem necessary in an attempt to reach our personal pinnacles, versus staying grounded and facing a process that converts and redeems and transforms us completely.

But keep in mind: Christ came, not to start a new religion, but to end the status quo. He did this by challenging us to move away from the addiction we have to the way we think and the way we judge; away from the temptations we have—the same temptations that he had. But all that is not easy, and today's gospel teaches us that such transformation requires us to spend time with the desert and the wilderness, and the barrenness we find in our lives.

And what does that transformation sound like? Later in this chapter of Luke, we hear the first words of Christ after he came out of the desert: "The Spirit of the Lord is upon me, because he has anointed me to bring glad tidings to the poor...liberty to captives...sight to the blind, and to let the oppressed go free."

He was defining his ministry. He was defining what we are called to do. And it had to have sounded as radical then as it does today.

So, we have begun our forty days of Lent. Some of us will build an artificial desert by what we "give up for Lent," thereby creating the needed empty space and time, while others may already find themselves in their own personal desert—perhaps through dealing with an illness, the death of a loved one, loss of a job, a divorce, facing addictions, and the list goes on. Either way, we have this incredible gift of time called "Lent" to examine our lives, our direction, and our struggles, and the chance to use the gifts of the Holy Spirit to take the time necessary in order to focus on turning ourselves around.

Over the next forty days, God's grace through nature will feed that drab desert ground in Albuquerque and by Easter it will be ablaze with life and color. Likewise, Lent is a time and an opportunity for renewal and fresh growth to take place in our own hearts and souls.

So, guided by the Holy Spirit, may our Lenten journeys be filled with desert space and time so that we may be open to hear God's nurturing call.

May we have the grace and wisdom to face the same temptations of power, prestige, and possessions that Christ faced in the desert and be open to transformation.

And during this Lent, may we have the courage to face ourselves: to see our weak places...to touch our wounds...and be determined to repent, to turn around and indeed believe the good news—that the kingdom of God is truly at hand!

2ᴺᴰ SUNDAY *of* LENT

MICHELLE FRANCL-DONNAY

Your face, Lord, do I seek!

1ST READING
GEN. 15:5-12, 17-18

2ND READING
PHIL. 3:17-4:1

PSALM
27:1, 7-9, 13-14

GOSPEL
LUKE 9:28B-36

"COME," SAYS MY HEART, "SEEK HIS FACE."

These are the words that open today's liturgy, which we hear again in the psalm:

> "Come," says my heart, "seek his face";
> your face, Lord, do I seek!
> Do not hide your face from me.

PSALM 27:8-9A

Luke tells us that Jesus took Peter, James, and John up a mountain to pray. And, before their eyes, Jesus was transfigured, wrapped in glory, luminous, his very face changed. He was deep in conversation with a long-dead prophet and a patriarch. What their hearts had known, what they had surely prayed for in this psalm, was no longer hidden from them. And they weren't sure what to do. Ought they to build something? I can sympathize, for I too was bewildered when I chanced to encounter the transfigured Christ.

Five years ago, I was in Rome for a series of meetings. My walking route took me past Sant'Agostino, the fifteenth-century basilica that is the mother church of the Augustinian order. I planned to duck in to light a candle in front of St. Monica's tomb—and frankly, to escape the heat for a few minutes. Rome was in the middle of a brutal midsummer heat wave. But when I arrived, the church had just closed for the midafternoon *riposo*. I wandered over to the shady side of the piazza to check the bulletin board for when it would reopen, hoping to stop on my return.

As I peered at the board, I realized there was a young man lying asleep in the shadows of a doorway a few feet away. He was shirtless, a sleeping bag wrapped around his middle, his bare legs crossed at the ankle. The reflected light from the ivory marble facade of the church made him almost glow. He looked like Christ, just taken down from the cross and laid on the rough stones. And, just like that, he was transfigured: Christ crucified lay at my feet.

I stood there for what seemed a very long time. Like Peter, James, and John, I was stunned to see before me so clearly what my heart had told me so often—that we are each the image and likeness of God, that each of us is clothed in Christ, that each of us is called to tend the wounded Body of Christ. I had prayed the words of that psalm again and again in the Liturgy of the Hours: *Do not hide your face.* And now, face to face with this reality, like Peter, James, and John, I was uncertain of what to do. In my creaky Italian, I asked a nearby shopkeeper who was closing up whether there was some place I could call for help. He gestured at a sign with the hours when the church would have food for the hungry and walked off.

When I returned to Sant'Agostino later that afternoon, the shadows had crept to the other side of the piazza and the young man was gone. I went inside, lit my candle, and prayed with St. Monica. There was a box for the care of the poor at the entrance of the church, into which I emptied all the Euros I had with me, hoping that the young man had found respite. All these years later, I still wonder what became of him. I still pray for him. *Your face, Lord, do I seek.* And I still wonder what else I might have done.

Are we willing to seek the face of the Lord—not just on the altar, but in the least among us? And what should we do when we encounter him? Peter, James, and John wanted to hold onto that moment, to enshrine it in time and space. Sixteen centuries ago, preaching on the Gospel of Matthew, St. John Chrysostom, the fourth-century bishop of Constantinople, reminded his congregation to seek the face of God outside the church walls, to learn to recognize Christ in the hungry, the wanderer, the homeless. Before you build shrines and adorn the altars inside the churches with cloths of gold, counseled Chrysostom, be sure that Christ at the gates outside is not shivering from the cold, or going hungry, or lacking a place to sleep. The saint's advice is often pithily summarized as, "If you cannot find Christ in the beggar at the church door, you will not find Him in the chalice."

When I remember that day at Sant'Agostino, it is not the beauty of the Caravaggio in the side chapel, or Monica's stately marble tomb that takes my breath away, but the memory of Christ lying transfigured in a doorway that calls to my heart. Peter, James, and John were taken aback by their unexpected vision, but just as we prepare to encounter Christ in the Eucharist at Mass, we can prepare to meet him outside the church walls. *Your face, Lord, do I seek.* The Gospel tells us what to do when we find him: feed the hungry, clothe the naked, welcome the stranger. Open your hands wide and give to the poor. *O Lord, do not hide your face from me.*

3ʀᴅ SUNDAY *of* LENT

FR. KYLE HADEN

"If you do not repent, you will all perish as they did!"

1ST READING
EXOD. 3:1–8A, 13–15

2ND READING
1 COR. 10:1–6, 10–12

PSALM
103:1–4, 6–8, 11

GOSPEL
LUKE 13:1–9

ONE OF THE DIFFICULT ASPECTS OF MINISTRY

is dealing with the tragedies that occur in people's lives. In many cases, one simply doesn't know how to respond to the question, "Why did this happen?"

I recall one day when a couple came to the parish, asking to speak with me. The look on their faces indicated great pain. The young woman showed signs of advanced pregnancy. When we sat down to talk, the husband told me that they had just come from the hospital, where they were given the news that the baby in his wife's belly was dead, and the next day she would have an induced stillbirth. They came to me to ask if I would be willing to have a funeral Mass for the child. That I could do, but I found myself struggling, with them, around the questions, "Why did this happen? Why did God allow this?"

One of the realities of being human is the need for meaning, for purpose. A lack of meaning in a person's life has debilitating effects. It can lead to depression, a feeling of hopelessness, and a withdrawal from relationships. We form the meanings of our life through the many relationships we develop over time. The ones we love become part of our souls, part of our identities. These relationships shape our vision of the world, for better or worse. Over time, the meanings we form become normalized, and we become comfortable with them. They give order to our world, both inner and outer. Humans need and desire a sense of order.

The loss of order can be quite painful. For example, one day you are with your loved one and all seems fine, normal. You almost take for granted their being in your life. Then, tragically, you get a call that your beloved has been killed in an accident, or through an act of violence. Suddenly, the world you found so comforting is thrown into chaos. After the shock of realizing your beloved is gone, questions begin to bombard your mind and emotions. "Why, why, why? Did God do this? Did God allow it? Did I do something to offend God?" We ask these questions in an attempt to bring order back to our heart and mind, to dispel the chaos tearing at our emotions.

The individuals in today's gospel were not so different from us, despite living in a very different culture from our own. Many of the people in Jesus's world suffered, as we suffer, numerous tribulations, whether due to poverty, social exclusion, political and military oppression, disease, or the simple fragility of life. The two tragedies narrated in this passage cover the poles of human suffering. In one case, suffering comes about through human intent, while the other is due to the accidents that occur while living in the material world.

Notice that, like ourselves, these individuals want to know the meaning behind these tragedies. The Jews in Jesus's time took as certain that God, who is supremely just, metes out reward and punishment according to a person's or nation's actions. They were convinced that suffering was the result of sin. Didn't the book of Deuteronomy state that God rewarded those who kept his law and punished those who did not? This belief shaped their understanding of the world. It shaped the meaning of their lives.

Jesus's response is probably not what they expected. In fact, it was religiously countercultural. He ignores the implication that God was behind these two tragedies. Jesus instead turns the focus away from God, to the people.

Many people over the years have interpreted these verses allegorically. God is the orchard owner, and Jesus the gardener who both cares for the trees and protects the fruitless plants against the owner's (God's) anger. An attentive read through the gospel of Luke should dispel such a portrait of God. The God that Jesus proclaims is in fact depicted as a loving father who deeply desires to save his lost children who have strayed from God's will. Recall Jesus telling us that "there will be more joy in heaven over one sinner who repents than over ninety-nine righteous people who have no need of repentance" (Luke 15:7).

Despite our need to understand why there is suffering in the world, the reality is, reasons for suffering as an intrinsic part of human experience— whether due to the evil intentions of others or the accidents that occur in life—elude our comprehension. It is a mystery that will not be fully answered this side of eternity. Jesus seems to indicate this by ignoring the question concerning God's culpability in the sufferings of others. Having emptied himself of his divinity and immersed himself in the fullness of human experience, Jesus also was unable to answer many of the questions concerning life's mysteries.

Instead of answering the question of God's culpability, Jesus instead turns the conversation toward our culpability. We have been called to produce fruits. St. Paul tells us that these fruits consist of love, joy, peace, forbearance, kindness, goodness, faithfulness, gentleness, and self-control (Galatians 5:22–23). In our failures to produce such fruit, Jesus tells us to repent. Most of us have heard this call to repentance many times in our lives. In many cases, repentance has been described in moralistic categories, with the threat of punishment for bad behavior. God is portrayed as vindictive. And yet, the God that Jesus portrays in Luke's Gospel does not manifest such vindictiveness.

I remember, while taking a class on the Gospel of Matthew in my doctoral program, asking the professor, "Does God punish us because of our sins?" I was recalling how I was taught to believe this to be the case. The professor's response was, and I paraphrase, "God does not punish us in the way we usually think of it. Rather, God has created the universe in such a way that, intrinsic to the very nature of reality, there are consequences to actions." For example, if I run as fast as I can headfirst into a wall, there will be a messy and painful consequence to this action. Likewise, if a spouse cheats and has an affair, there will be consequences.

Suffering many times turns into bitterness, which can, in turn, create in us a desire for revenge against the one we blame for our suffering. We create scapegoats upon whom we project our pain and anger. Sometimes we blame God. Suffering has led many people to abandon God. Many times, we blame an "other" for our pain. Such blaming has resulted in the demonization and dehumanization of the other, or others. No doubt we have been caused to suffer by another's malice. While there is justification for a society to hold criminals to account for their crimes, we are called to resist the desire to demonize or dehumanize such individuals. "Love your enemies, and pray for those who persecute you" (Matthew 5:44). The gospel calls us to seek restorative justice as opposed to retributive justice.

Jesus is calling on us to look more deeply into our own souls, and our hearts, and discern the sources that shape the meanings of our lives. Are love, forgiveness, and reconciliation informing our meaning and purpose in life? Do they order our affections? Are they producing acts of kindness, mercy, and regard for the other? If not, it is we who in fact put the axe to our own roots. It is we who cut ourselves off from the life of love, the love that sustains the universe and our very souls. And so, let us repent our failings to produce, and endeavor to produce the fruit that gives life and love to the world and ourselves.

4ᵀᴴ SUNDAY *of* LENT

FRAN ROSSI SZPYLCZYN

The father ran to his son, embraced him and kissed him.

1ST READING
JOSH. 5:9A, 10–12

2ND READING
2 COR. 5:17–21

PSALM
34:2–7

GOSPEL
LUKE 15:1–3, 11–32

WE HAVE REACHED THE FOURTH SUNDAY OF Lent. Traditionally, this is celebrated as Laetare Sunday, a day of rejoicing, a reminder that Lent will soon conclude. Today we hear the story of the Prodigal Son as told in Luke's Gospel, and we are reminded of the mercy that God offers to all who will return.

We have been focused on our fasting and other Lenten practices up to this point. For me, fasting is difficult, but recently I was reminded that mercy can be much more challenging—both giving it and receiving it. This short tale from the Desert Fathers offers some insight:

> Abba Mios was asked by a soldier: "Father, God then accepts the repentance of the sinner?" The Elder, after counseling him with many instructive words, suddenly asked him:
>
> "Tell me, my beloved, when you tear your uniform, do you throw it away?"

"No," the soldier answered, "I sew it and use it anew again."

Then Abba Mios also thoughtfully told him:

"If you take pity on your clothing, will not God take pity on His own creation?"

In case I needed any reminding of that, today's is a clear message about what God wants. God wants us.

In reading the short anecdote about our desert father, Abba Mios, I really had to pause and think about how the ethos of repair in our culture works its way into the theme of reconciliation.

We live in a "throwaway" culture—a culture of planned obsolescence. There could be another whole series of reflections about just that. Today, let's examine what a throwaway culture can mean in terms of lived mercy.

Things are designed to run out of usefulness and break more quickly than they should. My old kitchen range was thirty years old and going strong, but the oven was beyond repair. We got a new stove, and the expected lifespan is under ten years. Things malfunction or break, and we easily get rid of them to get new stuff that will need to be replaced sooner rather than later. This ranges from clothes and shoes to appliances—large and small—houses, cars....

What about people?

Well, there is a lot that I could say about people, but I will focus on one aspect, and that is forgiveness.

It is so hard to forgive and to be forgiven. What a burden it carries. There is something to be said about going out and just getting some new people. Well—not really, but it does seem that way, doesn't it? And even if we don't get some new people, we can certainly find numerous ways to sustain the energy that is required for keeping those that we are angry or hurt.

That's why I think the Abba Mios story is so interesting. It may be harder to comprehend in an era in which our cloak does not get repaired, our sock does not get darned, our torn seam does not get re-sewn—we just get a new one.

There are other things that we might expend energy in trying to restore and keep, but, either way, the emphasis is on things. Our things, our stuff, mean a lot to us.

But what about people?

In the parable of the Prodigal Son, a story so well-known, we see a story of truly radical reconciliation. It is important to have some understanding of Jesus' time—this kind of event did not happen lightly.

The father is clearly out there, waiting for his son. He sees him in the distance! Typically, the scorned father would be waiting inside and might not be all that concerned. This father, who is Our God, is anxiously anticipating our return!

He throws his arms around his son, another socially unimaginable moment from that time. The son would, if anything, have to pay the father homage and then maybe get the father's attention.

No—this father, Our God is elated to embrace us and welcome us back.

I could go on and on, but you get the picture.

We are not thrown away; we are never thrown away. There is no planned obsolescence for us. Each of us is God's unique and loving creation and God treasures each and every one of us.

So, I would simply ask you to consider all the things—and people—that you might otherwise throw away. Especially with the people, this might mean:

- a friend who has offended you so deeply that you will never speak to them again
- a spouse who has hurt you beyond imagining
- a son or daughter who has not quite lived up to your expectations for them
- a relative who has brought, in your estimation, shame upon the family
- anyone who disgusts or annoys you
- yourself

Yes—yourself. We are all called into this radical reconciliation moment by our God, who loves us. If we can't give ourselves the forgiveness needed, if we can't accept God's outrageous attempts at such deep love and welcome, we may miss the moment on the road when our own prodigal person returns.

Especially since it might be yourself! We never really know who we will be called on to forgive...and we really can't imagine how radical God's forgiveness is. But we can try, and that might mean being merciful and forgiving to ourselves first.

So, bear this in mind: You may have to recycle your old iPod, but don't do it with your people, or with yourself.

God is always waiting.

5TH SUNDAY *of* LENT

RICHARD G. MALLOY, SJ

"Let the one among you who is without sin be the first to throw a stone at her."

1ST READING
ISA. 43:16–21

PSALM
126:1–6

2ND READING
PHIL. 3:8–14

GOSPEL
JOHN 8:1–11

THE OLD JOKE GOES THAT JESUS STOOD before the crowd of angry, self-righteous men, poised with stones in hand. "Let the one without sin cast the first stone!" This big rock comes flying out of the mob and almost hits the woman in the head. Jesus looks over, rolls his eyes, and says, "Ah, Mom, come on, give me a break."

This section of John's Gospel is startling on many levels—as startling as the idea of Jesus's mother Mary casting the first stone.

We need to note that the account of this incident was added late to the Gospel of John. In earlier versions, it isn't there. The community that formed around the beloved disciple produced a way of thinking about and telling the story of Jesus which was different from that of the communities of Matthew, Mark, and Luke. And the Johannine community must have thought this moment, when Jesus stood up for this woman threatened by the zealous bullies, was really worth telling and remembering.

The way Jesus dealt with the woman caught in adultery, and the way he challenged the enraged, self-appointed, self-righteous enforcers of orthodoxy, has much to teach us today. Let me firstly say something about the power of shaming; secondly, something about rigid and fundamentalist approaches to religious meanings and practices that are devoid of discernment; and thirdly, suggest something startling about who today are the persons "caught in adultery" and who are those with "stones in hand."

Firstly, in a culture based on shame and honor, the culture of Jesus's first-century world, a woman engaging in adultery was shameful. Shame can so conquer and possess us—both those shamed and those doing the shaming. Note, only the woman here is shamed and potentially stoned, not the man who also engaged in adultery.

Shame seems able to keep us from God and separate us from community. Our alcoholic father, our inability to pay our bills, our not having a high school or college degree, our addiction to X, Y, or Z (the demons of addiction truly are Legion)—so much can make us hide, cower, and suffer in shame. Into this situation comes the power of Jesus, accepting us as we are and restoring us to right relationship with community and God.

Secondly, religious rules and cultural norms interact and embody spiritual meaning(s), sometimes flexibly, wisely, and well; sometimes rigidly, harshly, and hatefully. Jesus here is calling for compassion and care for the person to be put in proper place, above simplistic and fundamentalist readings of religious laws and cultural expectations.

In his short and profound book *Let Us Dream*, Pope Francis calls us to engage in dialogue and discernment. He analyzes the dangerous deficiencies of people "who are allergic to uncertainty and want to reduce everything to black and white. And it [discernment] is quite impossible for ideologues, fundamentalists, and anyone else who is held back by a rigid mindset. But discernment is vital if we want to create a better future."[1]

Jesus here discerns the truth of the situation. He bends down to think and doodle in the dirt. Then he straightens up and speaks truth. Yes, the

1   Pope Francis, *Let Us Dream: The Path to a Better Future* (New York: Simon & Schuster, 2020), 54.

woman is in error, but so are those who want to murder her. The enforcers of the Law are blind to their own sinfulness. They are so willing and ready to stone the woman, but cannot, will not, realize the fact that their own infuriated response to her is separating them from God. Her desperate need for divine assistance opens her to Jesus's call to repentance. The stunning truth of Jesus's challenge to the crowd forces them to see the error of their ways.

Pope Francis writes, "discernment...allows us to navigate changing contexts and specific situations as we seek the truth. Truth reveals itself to the one who opens herself to it."[2] Truth here is that the woman and those who want to stone her are not all that different. All stand in need of God's mercy and compassion: all of us, everyone. We all are called to extend mercy and compassion to one another, to realize we are sinners: sinners loved by God, sinners embraced like the prodigal son, sinners who stand before Jesus like this woman in need of mercy and the power of grace to transform us.

Thirdly, we need to ask ourselves, who are those we want to stone today? Who are we if we want to stone people?

We have become so polarized and pitted against one another. We can be so rooted in our indignation and anger against those who are just WRONG! We need to reconceive our social relations and see one another more in the light of the wisdom contained in the vision of the Reign of God that Jesus preached and inaugurated.

Jesuit George Murry (1948–2020), the Bishop of Youngstown, Ohio, described the heavenly banquet in his commencement address to the University of Scranton in 2018:

> Imagine pulling people in from every neighborhood, from every walk of life, compelling them to sit down and share a meal together. You would have black and white and brown all together, rich and poor, gay and straight, progressive and conservative. Everyone's mind would be blown when a vegan found a way to share a meal with a carnivore rancher, when a Black Lives Matter activist chuckled at the joke told by a Confederate flag-wearing Harley rider,

2 Francis, *Let Us Dream*, 55.

and when a Trump enthusiast asked an undocumented immigrant to pass the tortillas.

Somewhere in all of the mixing and relating, the Holy Spirit moves! God's blessed community looks like a smorgasbord of humanity, in heaven and on earth. That's not to say that it is OK to hold onto our biases, even our moral failings, but we grow past them together. In relationship with one another, we live into what connects us while learning a great deal about one another's life and individuality.[3]

Finally, I raise this question gently and gingerly: Does our love and compassion extend not only to victims, but also to victimizers? Our Church has suffered from the shame of clerical sex abuse. Let me be clear. One kid abused is one kid way too many. Anyone abused must be treated with respect, compassion, and love. The Church must always put victims' needs and care first and foremost. The Church has apologized again and again. Billions have been paid. But the sad and sinful fact is that Church leaders grievously failed when confronted with priests abusing children.

Yet I hear so much rage and anger directed at our bishops, as if you or I, as a bishop in 1953 or 1964 or 1972, would have done differently. As if bishops could have known better than did Penn State with Jerry Sandusky, or the Boy Scouts when their organization dealt with the sin, compulsion, and crime of pedophilia. Such a perspective does not justify the failures, but it may help explain them a bit.

And is hatred and disdain for our bishops justified? Can bishops ever be forgiven? Was there really a coverup, or were bishops woefully unprepared to deal with sex abuse? Do we really think bishops were totally uncaring, asleep at the switch, urging priest pedophiles to go get another kid? Or was it more that bishops were ashamed of the conduct of the priest, were told by mental health professionals that pedophiles could be treated for their condition, and were too willing to give a sinner another chance?

---

3   George V. Murry, SJ, "2018 Commencement Principal Address," *The University of Scranton*, May 29, 2018, https://news.scranton.edu/articles/2018/05/news-grad_U2018_BishopMurry_Speech.shtml.

Even more challenging, do we have any sympathy and compassion for the abuser? Can abusers ever be forgiven? The TV show *Chicago Med* told a story of a pedophile so suffering from his distorted desire that he refused treatment in the emergency room. Even though he had never abused a child, he wanted to die rather than continue to live with "an itch he could never scratch." How often have we seen sympathy expressed for a pedophile?

It is so easy to pick up the stone. That rock feels hard and jagged and deliciously deadly in our hand. The rock makes us feel powerful and consoled as our fist tightens around it. We feel so righteous and right in our condemnation of the "other," who is wrong and whom we condemn in the name of God. We need to discern such disordered and distorted desires to stone and pummel one another.

This Lent, let's realize that such desires to condemn do not lead us to the place where God wants us to be. Let's recognize our own sinfulness and need for repentance. Let's drop our stones. Let's hear Jesus's challenge to us today. He does not condemn anyone. He simply says, "Go, and...do not sin any more."

In order to have compassion and be merciful, in order to discern how and where and when and whom to forgive, in order to reconcile, we need God's help. And so, let us pray.

PALM SUNDAY

MEGAN McKENNA

"Father, into your hands I commend my spirit."

1ST READING
ISA. 50:4-7

2ND READING
PHIL. 2:6-11

PSALM
22:8-9, 17-20, 23-24

GOSPEL
LUKE 22:14—23:56

THIS IS THE LAST WEEK OF JESUS'S LIFE ON earth. This is the week about life in the face of death. This is the week of the Truth in the face of lies. This is the week of Jesus's incarnation, compassion, and humanity in the face of violence, hate, and inhumanity. This week is about the fragility and vulnerability of life in the face of horrendous evil.

This week we call Holy is a week of dangerous memories of the passion, death, and raising to new life of Jesus. This is the week we, as friends, companions, and disciples of Jesus, walk the last days of his life with him. We walk in solidarity and in communion, at one with the Light, with the fierce Darkness (which is the unknown mystery of God), all the way to the cross, and then on to the glory of the resurrection. It is not just Jesus's way, but it is our way of the cross, carrying and bearing one another's cross with others. This is a week of liberation and freedom, of facing death and bearing one another's burdens, and resisting all that is evil and in opposition to God's life.

We bear the mark of Jesus, the sign of the cross, and we sign ourselves with this gesture that both shatters our lives and gives us new life. We gather our lives, our struggles for justice and peace, and all that is laid upon us by others' injustice, betrayal, rejection, and violence, and walk with Jesus, sharing our burdens passionately and living deeply all our joys and anguish, handing them over with Jesus, in his Spirit, to our Father, in a moment of giving ourselves back to God.

This is the week we try to live under no sign of power but the sign of the cross, the sign of God as Three and One, binding all of us together in communion. This is not just about Jesus and his handing over his life; it is also about our lives being handed over, and of all people who suffer and seek everlasting life, but especially in solidarity with the poor, the least among us, our sisters and brothers, Jesus's beloved friends.

Our Gospel provides us an account of Jesus's passion written by Luke. We begin at table with Jesus in the upper room as he "eagerly desire[s] to eat this Passover with you before I suffer." He takes the bread and the cup, gives thanks, and shares them among his friends. It is food that is "given for you; do this in memory of me." It is not just bread and wine that are taken and given to us; it is his body, his life, and all he is, that is given—even his death—as gift to us.

But it is immediately refused in some ways. The one who betrays him makes his move and then the others begin to argue about who's the greatest in the group, ignoring Jesus, the servant, who is serving them at the table and with his whole life. And then he tries to warn Peter than he too will deny him, reject him, and refuse even to acknowledge that he knows him. Jesus prays for him, but Peter will not heed Jesus's words even now.

Then Jesus goes out to pray in the garden, asking them to pray with him, keep him company as he agonizes over what he must face. "Father, if you are willing, take this cup away from me; still, not my will but yours be done." His prayer is so intense, he sweats blood, but he finds them asleep and ignoring him. The crowd arrives, with Judas intent on kissing him as the sign that he's the one to seize and arrest. Jesus is the Son of Man, and in the melee, Peter uses his sword and attacks one of the high priest's servants. He heals the servant and rebukes Peter and the disciples. There is to be no violence.

He is led away to the house of the high priest. Peter follows at a distance, careful of not being seen, but he is caught out. Three times he is recognized or associated with Jesus and three times he vehemently declares he does not know Jesus, he is not one of Jesus's disciples, and finally, that he doesn't even know anything about Jesus. Jesus sees Peter, who remembers Jesus's words and goes out and weeps bitterly.

Then the torture begins, with Jesus's captors taunting him, slapping him, mocking him as a prophet, and insulting him. At daylight, he is taken before elders and leaders, and Jesus declares they won't believe him, but "from this time on the Son of Man will be seated at the right hand of the power of God." They twist his words and condemn him.

Then he's taken to Pilate. When questioned now, he says only, "You say so." Pilate can't find anything to use as the basis for a crime, so sends him to Herod. Jesus won't even speak to Herod, so they treat him with contempt and drag him back to Pilate. Jesus is accused of "inciting the people" and the crowd demands that Pilate free Barabbas, a murderer and thief, instead of Jesus. The cry goes up from the crowd to "Crucify him!" and eventually Pilate "handed Jesus over to them to deal with as they wished."

Jesus begins walking the way of the cross and soon the soldiers "took hold of" a Cyrenian, Simon, and forced him to bear the cross on his shoulder, carrying it behind Jesus. There are women who wail and weep for him, but Jesus warns them to weep for themselves and their children, for all the people who are suffering and will suffer terribly all too soon.

He's crucified with two criminals. It is almost as though the telling is seen from a distance, but Jesus speaks three times. The first is most telling of Jesus, the Son of Man, the servant of the least and the poorest: "Father, forgive them, they know not what they do." His thought is for others, for all of us, to be reconciled with him; for care for all of us, even as he is being torn away from life.

Jesus is the poor man, embracing all human beings and always looking for the poorest among us. He rejects earthly power for the power of mercy, dying as he lived, among thieves, murderers, the unjust, and those who do evil and reject God's goodness and the Good News. The one who lived as a beggar, among the poorest, continues to bless the poor, dying with nothing. Even his garments are given away in a dice game. Then Jesus is mocked by all those around him, and he is offered soured wine, which he refuses.

Then, those on the crosses on either side of him speak. One blasphemes him, telling him to save himself and them. But the other turns toward Jesus and aligns himself with him, defending him. "Jesus, remember me when you come into your kingdom." And Jesus assures him: "Today you will be with me in Paradise." Even now, Jesus grasps at any small gesture or word and responds generously, giving away life forever to the thief.

And then, as the day drags on and Jesus hangs in agony, trying to breathe, he speaks his last words: "Father, into your hands I commend my spirit."

Jesus's living and dying serves to demand that we, who believe in him, must do everything to rescue others from injustice and violence, relieve others' pain, and give solace to those who suffer—but especially we are called to serve and attend to the poor, to be their servant as Jesus was, giving even his life so that all might have life. The cross is about inflicted suffering and death, not what comes naturally, as a part of life.

And we must, with Jesus, resist anything that harms anyone's body and soul. Jesus's love and devotion to us is stronger than death, based in hope that he dwells in God and shares all as gift with us. With Jesus, we must learn to humbly resist power and be friends with the poor. We, with Jesus, must seek words that rouse others to life, and humbly resist injustice and anything that harms others. We, with Jesus, must live to set the poor free and liberate all so that they might live in God's grace, with life to the fullest.

Our lives, our actions, our relationships must all be works of justice, mercy, and solace, bearing others' burdens and lifting people up who are bowed down; do no harm to anyone; and do for others what Jesus does for all of us. We too must share his cross, and seek to un-crucify others, take up our cross, and come after Jesus. What we would do for Jesus, we are to do for others: the suffering, poor, crucified ones among us.

There is an amazing scientific reality recently discovered during the Human Genome Project. It is an odd molecule in the human body: laminin. It is a protein adhesion molecule, responsible for holding together the human body. It's the rebar, the glue which literally holds on our skin, holds all the linings of our organs, and keeps us from being a pile of bones and flesh that lacks substance. If you research laminin on the Internet, you can see that we are held together by thousands of tiny crosses. We are signed with the cross throughout our entire body, flesh, and organs, within and outwardly, through our skin. The tissues that hold us together, our scaffolding that provides structure, are cell-crosses.

God has signed us with the sign of the cross. When we sign ourselves and bless others with the cross, we are seeking to make God's image within us ever stronger. Our bodies too are formed in the sign of the cross, as we stand up, rising toward our God, and with arms outstretched, reaching across to touch and be bound to all the earth, all the poor of God. This week, may we remember Jesus living, suffering, and dying with us, and being raised up as God's sign of the cross, etched deep in our bodies, hearts, minds, and souls.

HOLY THURSDAY

DEACON GREG KANDRA

"So that as I have done for you, you should also do."

1ST READING
EXOD. 12:1–8, 11–14

2ND READING
1 COR. 11:23–26

PSALM
116:12–13, 15–18

GOSPEL
JOHN 13:1–15

EARLY IN THE MUSICAL *HAMILTON*, THERE IS A
scene where four key characters meet: Alexander Hamilton, Marquis
de Lafayette, a slavery abolitionist named John Laurens, and a tailor's
apprentice by the name of Hercules Mulligan. Poised at a pivotal moment
in history, they share their dreams of a better future in a song called "The
Story of Tonight":

> Raise our glass to the four of us.
> Tomorrow there'll be more of us
> telling the story of tonight,
> the story of tonight.

It is that way, I think, with this evening.

I don't think the apostles, on that long-ago night in the Upper Room,
had any ideas quite that grand. They could not have known what was about
to happen, how their world was about to change.

And yet, two thousand years later, here we are, telling the story of that night, the story of tonight. The story of the Last Supper.

It is a night that reaches across history—a night when our hearts are lifted one last time before they are broken.

As one of the apostles put it at another time, at another pivotal moment: "It is good that we are here." It is good that we gather to tell this story again.

So much of what we heard from scripture a few moments ago offers us this simple but insistent message: What is happening here matters.

Pass it on.

The reading from Exodus, marking the great Jewish event of Passover, concludes: "This day will be a day of remembrance for you, which your future generations will celebrate with pilgrimage to the Lord; you will celebrate it as a statute forever."

Pass it on.

In his letter to the people of Corinth, St. Paul wrote the earliest account of the Last Supper and stated: "I received from the Lord what I also handed on to you."

It was passed on to him. He passed it on to them. He is saying, "Here it is."

Pass it on.

And in St. John's Gospel, Jesus tells his followers, after he has washed their feet: "I have given you a model to follow."

This is our model and our mission: Pass it on.

But what is it, really, that we are passing on?

To begin with, there are two great events that we commemorate this evening: the institution of the Eucharist and the institution of the priesthood.

At the Last Supper, we are reminded that Jesus gave us himself—body and blood, soul and divinity—and gave us, as well, the way to keep giving us himself, through the priesthood.

We can't let this night pass without expressing gratitude to Almighty God for the men who give us, again and again, the immeasurable gift of the Eucharist—and who give us, as well, the gift of their lives. They continue what Jesus began.

They pass it on.

But there is something else Jesus asked his apostles to carry forward, something else to pass on. This is our great charge, our great challenge: to do what Jesus did.

Daniel Berrigan famously said, "If you want to follow Jesus, you better look good on wood."[1]

This account from John's Gospel tells us where that really begins. It begins on the ground, on our knees, as slaves to one another. To paraphrase Berrigan: If you want to follow Jesus, you better look good with a basin and towel.

The one who received "all power in heaven and on earth" humbled himself not just before his friends. He humbled himself before those who would betray him and deny him and run away in fear.

He did it for this simple purpose: to show them, visibly and beautifully, how to love. This is our model to follow.

This is where the great work begins. We need to serve one another, helping wash away the dirt and the pain and the dust of the world, the residue of life.

We hear it asked often: "What would Jesus do?" Here is the answer. Even on the last night of his life, the greatest teacher continued to teach. Before his own death, he showed us how we have to die to ourselves.

In some places, this day is known as "Maundy Thursday." Maundy is derived from the Latin word *Mandatum*, meaning "mandate." What is our mandate?

It is there in the verse that was sung before the Gospel, and it comes from words Jesus speaks just after this scene: "I give you a new commandment: love one another. As I have loved you, so you also should love one another."

Love one another.

Pass it on.

In a few moments, the elect from RCIA will come forward to have their feet washed. My brothers and sisters, try to remember this night, this event, because it reaches beyond just getting your feet wet.

Remember the words of Jesus. Remember our call, our command, our *mandate*: "Wash one another's feet. I have given you a model to follow, so that as I have done for you, you should also do."

---

1   As quoted in Jim Forest, *At Play in the Lion's Den: A Biography and Memoir of Daniel Berrigan* (Maryknoll, NY: Orbis, 2017), frontispiece.

Remember what this means. Cherish what is about to happen here. That includes the rest of this beautiful evening—even the way it ends. This, too, is part of the story of tonight.

Tonight, like the apostles, we will walk with Jesus to a garden—that tabernacle surrounded by fresh flowers in the middle of the church.

So often, Jesus has walked with *us*. Tonight, we walk with *him*.

We stand watch. We pray with him and pray for one another. We pray for our broken and wounded world.

And there, amid all the flowering signs of life, we remember that humankind's fall began in a garden named Eden. And we remember anew that Jesus began his Passion—what brought about our redemption—in a garden named Gethsemane.

At his Last Supper, Jesus told us to celebrate the Eucharist with these simple words: "Do this in remembrance of me."

Well, all of what we share tonight is an act of remembrance, and adoration, and faith. It has been this way since the beginning, since that night in an Upper Room when history was made, and everything changed.

Soon there will be more of us, telling the story of this night, the story of tonight.

This is our story: a story of humility and hope, a story of sacrifice and salvation, a story of love.

This is our story.

Pass it on.

GOOD FRIDAY

BECKY ELDREDGE

"*Everyone who belongs to the truth listens to my voice.*"

1ST READING
ISA. 52:13—53:12

PSALM
31:2, 6, 12-13, 15-17, 25

2ND READING
HEB. 4:14-16; 5:7-9

GOSPEL
JOHN 18:1—19:42

A FEW YEARS AGO, I ACCOMPANIED AND helped take care of my grandfather, who had brain cancer. Throughout his journey, he and I would discuss suffering and pain. The most poignant conversation came during one of his last weeks of life. It was a day that he was asleep for most of my visit. As I leaned in to kiss his forehead goodbye, he awoke, looked at me with his bright blue eyes, and said, "I am glad you are here because I need to talk to you about something." Not knowing what in the world he was about to ask me, I said, "Ok, Boppy. What's on your mind?" His response: "Suffering and Jesus."

I was initially caught off guard at the depth of what he began sharing, but quickly understood the profound moment that was unfolding before me as I listened to his thoughts and questions about Jesus's suffering, his suffering, and Jesus's companionship with him during his journey. I fought back tears as long as I could, as my heart expanded with love for both my grandfather and Jesus. It felt as if Jesus was affirming everything I had come to understand through my own experiences of hardship and pain, through the words of this man I loved deeply and who loved me deeply: Jesus's amazing gift of companionship in our suffering. The relief and awe I had in hearing how intimately Jesus was with him was so overwhelming I could no longer hold back my tears, nor could he, and we both wept at the gift of Jesus's relationship with us.

What my grandfather shared with me that day is the good news of our faith. We are never alone, not even in our suffering. While we are not promised a life free from suffering, we are promised companionship through whatever we are facing.

Over a decade ago, I made the *Spiritual Exercises of St. Ignatius of Loyola.* Since making them, Good Friday has never been the same. A focus of the *Spiritual Exercises* is growing a deep friendship with Jesus that includes walking with him through his passion and death. This experience of walking so closely with Jesus's suffering changed me. It changes all of us when we draw near to Jesus's suffering. Praying with Jesus's suffering helps us understand his humanity and the fact that he gets the breadth and depth of suffering that we go through. As Jesus's suffering touches our own, profound healing begins.

What does the promise of Jesus's companionship in our suffering look like?

Jesus's companionship offers us five gifts:

> *I'm here.* God was with Jesus throughout his passion and death. Jesus was not abandoned by God. We, too, are promised the enduring presence of Jesus as we face suffering in our own lives.

> *Tell me.* We see Jesus going to God in prayer in the garden. We can only imagine how Jesus continued to go to God in prayer throughout his passion and death. Jesus invites us to tell him about the suffering we are going through and to remember that it matters to Jesus.

> *Fix your eyes on me.* Jesus continued to fix his eyes on God throughout his passion. Jesus invites us to fix our eyes on him as we endure suffering in our lives. His presence can steady us and help us find a center and still point.

Let me draw near. God drew near to Jesus in his suffering. God also sent others to draw near to Jesus in his suffering: Veronica to wipe his face, Simon the Cyrene to carry his cross, Mary and the beloved disciple to stand with him at the foot of the cross. Jesus seeks to draw near to us when we are suffering and comfort us the way God comforted him, and the way others comforted him.

Do as I have done. As Jesus offers us the gift of companionship in our suffering, we are invited to offer what we receive to others who are suffering. Like Jesus does to us, we can remind people that we are here for them and that they can tell us about what they are going through. We can help people find a still point in Jesus. We can also draw near to others' suffering.

My grandfather understood that day that he was not alone and that he was held in the light of Jesus's gift of accompaniment. He knew that Jesus offered him a place to voice his needs and prayers, a place to be comforted, and a place of strength and hope.

As our conversation ended, and I leaned in once again to kiss him on his forehead, he told me, "Becksa, please, go tell people what we understand." With a conviction I felt in the depths of me, I promised him I would, and I am. I invite you to do the same.

Easter

BRIAN McLAREN

Then the other disciple also went in...and he saw and believed.

1ST READING
ACTS 10:34A, 37–43

2ND READING
COL. 3:1–4

PSALM
118:1–2, 16–17, 22–23

GOSPEL
JOHN 20:1–9

WE OFTEN THINK OF PETER AS THE CHIEF OF the disciples. He may indeed have been loudest, or most confident, or even the most dedicated, but apparently, he wasn't the *fastest*.

There was a faster disciple, widely believed to be John, who outran Peter on Easter morning, the Gospel tells us. That faster disciple reached the tomb first and waited outside. True to form, as soon as Peter arrived, he plunged right in and looked around. He saw...nothing—no body. No corpse, and no risen Christ or angels either. He saw nothing but the linen wrappings that had covered Jesus's corpse. Stand with him for a second and see it too: nothing. Nothing but empty wrappings. Do you feel the emptiness of the moment? The despair? The heartbreak?

Eventually, the unnamed disciple joined Peter inside. And that disciple, it seems, was not only faster than Peter at running. He was also faster than Peter when it came to belief. He believed, even though he didn't understand.

Many of us, if we're honest and brave enough, can admit that we feel like that disciple: *We believe Easter is important. We believe something truly significant happened. But we're not sure we understand what the point is.*

Theologians and preachers often tell us Easter *proves* something—perhaps the victory of Christ over sin and death, or the power of God, or the reality of our own resurrection someday. But then we respond, "Just a minute. If the resurrection proves something, how do we prove the resurrection? How do you prove something based on something else that you can't prove?"

Maybe, instead of *proving* something, the Easter stories are supposed to *show us* something, something that has always been true, but we often do not see. If that's the case, what might the stories of Easter be trying to show us today, this morning, at this moment?

In his 2020 encyclical *Fratelli tutti*, Pope Francis gives us a possible answer in his closing prayer:

> Grant that we Christians may live the Gospel,
> discovering Christ in each human being,
> recognizing him crucified
> in the sufferings of the abandoned
> and forgotten of our world,
> and risen in each brother or sister
> who makes a new start.[1]

This beautiful prayer suggests at least part of what the crucifixion and empty tomb are trying to show us. First, in the crucifixion, we see that God is suffering in and with us humans as we suffer—in all our human crucifixions of racism, injustice, poverty, oppression, violence, abandonment, misunderstanding, mean-spiritedness, and hate. And then, in the resurrection, we see that God is rising with every brother or sister whenever they rise and make a new start.

About ten years after running to the tomb and plunging in like the proverbial bull in a china shop, Peter took another trip. This time, he wasn't so confident. You might say he dragged his feet the whole way,

---

1   Pope Francis, "An Ecumenical Christian Prayer," *Fratelli tutti*, October 3, 2020, https://www.vatican.va/content/francesco/en/encyclicals/documents/papa-francesco_20201003_enciclica-fratelli-tutti.html.

or, at the very least, he was filled with second thoughts. He, an observant Jew, entered the home of a Gentile, a Roman centurion named Cornelius. Once inside, he looked over a room full of Cornelius's family, servants, and associates. He realized that he used to think of all Gentiles like these as second-class citizens, as outsiders, as the other, as the dirty and unclean and unacceptable. But now, he is beginning to see them differently. He realizes that when Christ died and rose, Christ died and rose for and with them too, for and with all people—no discrimination, no partiality, no favorites, no exclusion, no exceptions.

Back at the tomb that Easter morning, he didn't see this yet. He didn't "get it" all at once. It took time. Gradually, over many years, Peter came to understand what we are being shown every Passion Week: that God is with us, and not just with *some* of us, but *all* of us, all of humanity. God truly cares for all of us. All of us: Those who sleep on streets and those who live in mansions. Those in Congress and those in prison. Those dressed in gowns and tuxedos at an exclusive restaurant and thirsty refugees in rags being held in detention at a border. Whatever our race. Whatever our religion. Whatever our politics. Whatever our gender or occupation or education or age. The brave and the timid. The rich and the poor. The fast and the slow.

So, this Easter, perhaps you can stop worrying yourself about what Easter proves. Instead, consider what it shows. Consider what it is trying to help us see. And then, perhaps you can pray as Pope Francis suggested:

> Grant that we Christians may live the Gospel,
> discovering Christ in each human being,
> recognizing him crucified
> in the sufferings of the abandoned
> and forgotten of our world,
> and risen in each brother or sister
> who makes a new start.

Could it be that God is trying to show us, not just that Jesus rose back on that first Easter morning, but that in all of humanity Christ is rising again, making a new start for humanity, always, everywhere, even here and now, in me and you?

2ND SUNDAY *of* EASTER

THE REV. PENNY A. NASH

"Blessed are those who have not seen and have believed."

1ST READING
ACTS 5:12-16

2ND READING
REV. 1:9-11A, 12-13, 17-19

PSALM
118:2-4, 13-15, 22-24

GOSPEL
JOHN 20:19-31

ONE OF THE NURSES ON THE WONDERFUL PBS
show *Call the Midwife* is Lucille Anderson, who came from Jamaica to serve the poor in London's East End in the 1960s. She first arrived at Nonnatus House, the home and headquarters of the order of nuns and nurses among whom she would work, by walking for miles through a snowstorm after her train got stuck.

She very quickly fell ill, her fever diagnosed not by a thermometer, but by the compassionate touch of hand to forehead by one of the nuns.

Lucille herself knew the power of touch. When racism reared its ugly head as she went about her work, and her colleagues tried to find the words to express their outrage and sorrow, Lucille reminded them that this was not the first time she had been rejected. There was a cost to her calling. Often, she said, white patients did not want her to touch them, as if they were afraid that the black might rub off onto their own skin.

Touch is such an intimate and powerful thing that some shrink from it, even as others, like Thomas in the Gospel today, crave it. There is no doubt that touching something makes it real to us in a way that nothing else does.

For Thomas, it is touching that transforms his understanding of Jesus from a man he considered his teacher into his Lord and God.

As a result of that touch, Thomas comes to believe—but not necessarily in the thing called resurrection. That's the wrong image. Now he believes that Jesus is God, not just a special friend who did wonderful works. Now Thomas sees Jesus in a way that he did not see him before. He believes *in* Jesus, which might be different from saying he believes in a difficult physical concept. Their relationship is transformed and a new intimacy is established, one in which Thomas, with the help of the Holy Spirit, is empowered to carry on Jesus's work.

The writer of the Gospel of John was particularly interested in belief. All through the Gospel, people have met Jesus, had intimate experiences with him, and, as a result, believe in him. They don't just believe he exists. They believe he is who he says he is. They believe that Jesus shows us who God is. The whole Gospel is the testimony of those who were with him and believed in him—and is written to help others believe, too.

That testimony of John and his cohort, however, is not all there is to belief. Later, John tells the story of how Jesus encounters Peter on the beach and asks him, "Do you love me?" and Peter says, "Yes, Lord, you know that I love you." Then Jesus responds: "Feed my lambs...tend my sheep...feed my sheep."

John's story tells me the truth—Jesus is one with God, Jesus himself is the truth—and shows me his power. Jesus brings about healing and restoration to those who encounter him and reminds us that there must be a response to that truth. My believing needs to have something to do with my own body, in connection with my heart and my mind.

So, the question now, today, on this Sunday after the Day of Resurrection, is this: How am I going to respond to the truth of Jesus? We don't have a physical Jesus to touch now. So, we must grapple with the stories and the difficult concepts in a way that his followers did not. We are trying to understand resurrection in a world in which disaster is still happening, where people are still dying and staying dead.

For me, a response needs to include actual physical experience, an expression of the transformative power of love in the world. And, as I think about that today, in this place, at this time, I offer my favorite prayer from the New Zealand Prayer Book—the collect for today, in fact. It says: "Living God, for whom no door is closed, no heart is locked, draw us beyond our doubts, till we see your Christ and touch his wounds where they bleed in others."[1]

The response to the truth of Jesus is to touch others' wounds with compassion. This is how resurrection is lived out, whatever we are able to believe about the concept. It is by first seeing those wounds, and then by loving the wounded the way the Good Samaritan loved the man from another tribe who had been beaten and left for dead by the side of the road: by binding up his wounds and seeing to his care, not worrying about the cost.

As Nurse Anderson reminds us, touch is very powerful and if our fears are in control, we may wish to shield ourselves from it. What if the black doesn't rub off on us, but the humanity of the outcast does? What then?

And so, we may wish to lock our hearts away where they cannot be broken open. There is a cost to being broken open like that.

Jesus invites Thomas to touch him to make the resurrection real to him, and I believe we are called to follow suit, by making the resurrection real in the lives of those who are wounded in body, mind, and spirit. We respond by allowing our own wounds to be healed and then loving our wounded neighbors with our bodies, minds, and spirits and not being afraid of the cost.

And just a word about the cost. There was a man who lived out his beliefs, not caring what it cost, and it cost him his life. It has been over fifty years now since Martin Luther King, Jr. was shot and killed in Memphis, Tennessee, having gone to that city to help garbage workers who were paid a pittance for the worst work in the city, who were not allowed to let their blackness touch restrooms or eating establishments or places of shelter. These men were not treated as neighbors. They were not even treated as human, so that many of them wore signs that said, "I am a man" in hopes of winning white people to their cause.

1   The Anglican Church in Aotearoa, New Zealand and Polynesia, *A New Zealand Prayer Book* (San Francisco: HarperSanFrancisco, 1989), 599.

Dr. King worked tirelessly for civil rights, and he was often vilified for it. At the time, he was pretty unpopular, even with some Blacks, who feared his message would cause more violence because he spoke out unstintingly against racism, and white society was not ready to open the doors to the humanity of black men and women, as Nurse Anderson experienced. But Dr. King believed that the Gospel compelled him to stand up for dignity and equality. The world was not ready to accept that, and so he paid the price of his life for his work to make the resurrection real in this world. This is a reoccurring story.

So, the work is not finished. Jesus told his disciples that they would need to go out and continue the work after he was gone. This is as true today as it was then. Let us hear the testimony and believe.

3RD SUNDAY *of* EASTER

CASSIDY HALL

"Yes, Lord, you know that I love you."

1ST READING
ACTS 5:27–32, 40B–41

2ND READING
REV. 5:11–14

PSALM
30:2, 4–6, 11–12A, 13B

GOSPEL
JOHN 21:1–19

I'VE BEEN A SKEPTIC ABOUT GOD FOR AS LONG as I can remember. Around the age of eight, I began having reoccurring dreams about death, dreams of floating in a sea of nothingness: alone, lost, stagnant in limitless space and eternal time. Even years before these dreams began, I was already asking questions of the divine.

But, throughout my life, these questions weren't always welcomed. In middle school, I became really interested in spirituality and the possibilities it held. I had friends in various youth groups and from time to time I'd attend those groups with them. At that age, the events were more about feeling a sense of belonging. The gatherings were often deeply entangled with the emotional manipulation of the minds and hormones of young teens.

Once, while I was at an evangelical conference with the local youth group, I continued my skepticism and questioning, but this time was different. During one evening's session, I was moved to participate in an altar call and was immediately flooded with questions about what I had just done. As we gathered in our small groups after the session, my youth leader told me, "Your questions are of the devil." My insides stirred with a surprised, "*Huh?*" But, baffled and confused, I went along with the adult in the room and regretfully shut my mouth.

Over twenty years later, I find myself in seminary and pursuing ordination —and more full of questions about the divine than I've ever been. Only now, I remember to show them off like treasures, reminding others and myself that questions innately connect us to the divine by the very fact that they belong to mystery. Now, I claim my questions *and* doubts with pride. I remember to bask in the questions, because they mean growth, change, and movement. But, perhaps most importantly, I remember that questions take me to the place of infinite possibility, the place where God resides.

It seems to me that faith and doubt are not mutually exclusive. Faith makes room for doubt's entrance as doubt demands faith for its existence. One cannot host doubt unless there is some knowledge of that which is being doubted. Therefore, to doubt is to both have and demonstrate faith.

When I look at John 21, I sometimes wonder if Jesus asked Peter three times not because of his three denials, but because Jesus actually doubted him. Perhaps the humanness of Jesus needed a sense of affirmation and clarity, like the times I need to hear a truth on repeat from a loved one. And, what if Jesus was also instilling his faith in Peter by revealing his doubt? What if doubt belongs to faith more than knowing or even *thinking I know*?

In my experience, humans have ruined my doubts and questions. God, on the other hand, has valued, honored, and even respected them. I often find the more I question and am honest about my doubt, the more God shows up—in the mystery, in the uncertainty, in the *unknowing*. And so I wonder: What if Jesus asking questions is a model for our own questioning? What if Jesus was living and loving the questions?

"Be patient toward all that is unsolved in your heart and...try to love the *questions themselves*," wrote Rainer Maria Rilke to young aspiring poet Franz Xavier Kappus. "Live the questions now. Perhaps you will then gradually, without noticing it, live along some distant day into the answer."[1]

What if Jesus, in his humanness, was openly living and loving the questions amid his uncertainty of what the church might become? What if

---

1   Rainer Maria Rilke, *Letters to a Young Poet*, trans. M. D. Herter Norton (New York: W. W. Norton, 1954), 27.

Jesus, in all his divinity, was modeling a way to hold uncertainty, unknowing, and the infinite possibilities within the unknowing?

For me, doubts and questions are fruits of a life of faith. Doubt reminds us to engage our questions, to search the books, to ask the neighbor, to grow and learn and engage. Doubt belongs to faith in the same way that mystery belongs to God. And my teenage questions were not of the devil, and neither are my thirty-seven-year-old doubts.

I remember the shock and surprise my young teenage self felt when I arrived back home after that trip with my youth group. Being that I was the only "nonbeliever" on that trip, I was a kind of project for people to huddle around and convert. And amid all that misinformation, amid all the lies and good intentions with false pretenses, God was with and within me:

- honoring my unbelief,

- respecting my doubt,

- reminding me to love and live the questions, and

- opening me into the infinite possibility, where God is.

4TH SUNDAY *of* EASTER

ROBERT ELLSBERG

"My own sheep listen to my voice; I know them and they follow me."

1ST READING	2ND READING
ACTS 13:14, 43–52	REV. 7:9, 14B–17
PSALM	**GOSPEL**
100:1-3, 5	JOHN 10:27–30

THE BIBLE HAS A LOT TO SAY ABOUT shepherds. Psalm 23 begins with one of the most beloved verses in Scripture: "The Lord is my shepherd, I shall not want…" You don't have to live in a shepherding culture to appreciate the tenderness and pathos of that line. "Even though I walk through the valley of the shadow of death, I will fear no evil, for you are with me; your rod and your staff, they comfort me." Jesus refers to himself as the Good Shepherd, whose defining mark is his willingness to lay down his life for his flock. The Good Shepherd knows his sheep and they know him.

So much for the Good Shepherd—but what about the Good Sheep?

The reputation of sheep is that they are not the brightest creatures in the field. Sheep don't know much, but at one thing they excel: They recognize and respond at once to their master's voice. This is a very important trait—even today, in the Middle East, where flocks of sheep intermingle while grazing or drinking at an oasis. Apparently, at the sound of their shepherd's voice, a flock of sheep will immediately separate from the rest and follow where they are called.

And perhaps that is the defining characteristic of good sheep: that in all the circumstances in which they find themselves, they recognize the voice of their shepherd and follow where that voice calls them.

But here the difficulty begins. Sheep are programmed from birth to recognize and respond to one voice. It would be simple for us if we could easily distinguish the voice of God from the many other voices that call to us in a thousand different tones, whether from Hollywood, Madison Avenue, or Facebook—sometimes soothing, sometimes threatening or seductive, sometimes even *claiming* the authority of God.

How do we become attuned to the *true* voice? How do we learn to recognize the inflection, the distinctive pitch and rhythm of that one voice that belongs to the Good Shepherd? That is the challenge that confronts us.

In daily life, we find ourselves in many different situations, sharing space with different flocks and with those who follow other shepherds. Can we imagine a situation in which, at the voice of the Good Shepherd, we would all know where we belonged—we would drop what we were doing and immediately fall into line?

One thing is certain—we can't simply take our cue from the rest of the flock.

I have always been challenged by the story of Franz Jägerstätter, an Austrian peasant who was executed in 1942 for refusing to take an oath to Hitler. He lived in a small village and served as the sexton in his local parish. He was married and had several children. By all accounts, he was a very ordinary man with nothing to set him apart from his neighbors. But then the Anschluss came, and Austria was absorbed into Nazi Germany. There were Austrians who opposed the Nazis (remember *The Sound of Music*!), but most went along.

Franz stood apart. As a devout Roman Catholic, he believed that the Nazis were a satanic movement leading his country on the path to hell. So, when he was called up for military service, this posed a crisis of conscience. He did not see how he could take an oath of loyalty to Hitler. So, he went to his local priest and asked for advice. The priest told him he shouldn't worry about such things—he had a higher responsibility to care for his family and to serve his country. But this didn't satisfy him, so he took a train to the next town to consult the local bishop. The bishop told him the same thing: As a Christian, he could serve in good conscience, assured that he was doing his duty; as for the bigger questions, those weren't his responsibility.

So, Franz had consulted the highest moral authorities available to him and all of them had told him to relax and go along with the rest of the flock. But Franz heard a different voice. And so, he got up at dawn, said goodbye to his family, and walked to the recruiting station in the next village where he turned himself in to the authorities.

He was arrested and put on trial, and once again, remarkably, the judge and military prosecutors pleaded with him to change his mind. How could he, an uneducated peasant, presume to know his duty better than the civil and religious authorities? For that matter, how could he be so sure that he was right when *every* one of his fellow Christians saw things differently? Wasn't this the height of arrogance? Wasn't this the sin of pride? They used that kind of argument.

Then they used the hardest argument of all—what about his children? Was he willing to make them orphans? He responded that in wartime many children become orphans, but he could do more good for his children by his example of obedience to God's law and by his prayers in heaven, than he ever could by sacrificing his immortal soul.

There was nothing more to say. On August 6, 1942, Franz Jägerstätter was beheaded. He was the only Catholic layman executed in Austria for refusing to serve in Hitler's army. He was beatified in 2007.

Such a story puts today's gospel text in a different light, because the voice of the Good Shepherd is not simply calling us to stand in line in our Easter bonnets. It may be a voice calling us to join the Shepherd himself in laying down our lives for others.

Perhaps on some level we know that, and so we prefer to stuff our ears with cotton, or turn up the noise around us, and go with the flock—mouthing the same slogans, pursuing the same goals, living by the same values.

Either way, we are sheep. The question is, *what kind of sheep* are we called to be?

Some years ago, there was a short-lived television show called *Joan of Arcadia* about a teenage girl who has conversations with God. The catch is that, in every episode, God appears to her in the guise of a completely different identity: an old man, a little girl, a bus driver, a shop clerk. And each time she is taken by surprise and realizes that the person speaking to her is really God.

It is a bit gimmicky, but the point is that God's voice doesn't come to us booming from heaven, like Morgan Freeman. It might come to us in the comforting words of a nurse at our hospital bedside or a friend who says, "I know how you feel; I am here for you." It might be a homeless person on the side of the road, or a nameless stranger, holding up a corny sign that says, "Honk if you love Peace."

There is no way of knowing exactly how God will speak to us or what God will say. But as Thoreau wrote, "Only that day dawns to which we are awake."[1] The first task is to be awake—to live, like Joan of Arcadia, with confidence in the reality, incredible as it may seem, that God can and does speak to us constantly, whether we recognize his voice or not. Once we open our hearts to that possibility, God will speak to us, and God alone knows where we might be led.

In one of the most mysterious stories in the Bible, the prophet Elijah, hiding from those who would take his life, finds refuge in a cave where he awaits some word from the Lord. "Then the LORD said: Go out and stand on the mountain before the LORD; the LORD will pass by. There was a strong and violent wind rending the mountains and crushing rocks before the LORD—but the LORD was not in the wind." Nor it turns out, was the Lord in a subsequent earthquake, or in the great fire that followed. But after that Elijah heard "a light silent sound." And that was the voice of God.

Blessed Franz Jägerstätter heard the voice of the Good Shepherd. He did not hear it in the voices on the radio, or among his neighbors, or even among the shepherds of his church, but in the silence of his own conscience.

What does that voice sound like? How do we recognize it? One person might say it sounds like justice. To another it sounds like mercy or love. Perhaps to us it sounds like the Truth.

Whatever the form or sound of the Shepherd's voice, it only comes to those who are listening—and the good sheep recognize that voice, and follow.

---

1   Henry David Thoreau, *Walden* (Oxford, UK: Oxford University Press, 1999), 297.

5TH SUNDAY *of* EASTER

ANNIE SELAK

"As I have loved you, so you also should love one another."

1ST READING
ACTS 14:21-27

PSALM
145:8-13

2ND READING
REV. 21:1-5A

GOSPEL
JOHN 13:31-35

TODAY'S READINGS ARE FILLED WITH BIG, grand theological statements. There are so many phrases and lines that I feel I have heard hundreds of times, yet I also feel that I have no idea what they mean. Take for example, this line from the First Reading:

> "It is necessary for us to undergo many hardships to enter the kingdom of God."

I have heard this so many times that it almost sounds trite. We are all supposed to take up our own crosses, right? Almost without exception, this will not be a literal cross leading to a public execution. Rather, it will be a metaphorical cross. By this logic, we start referring to mundane things as "taking up our cross." Maybe a particularly difficult boss is your own cross, or a family member who gets on your very last nerve. We use this language so much that it starts to ring hollow and lose meaning.

I have to be honest that this line also makes me really nervous. Language of enduring hardships in order to gain an eternal reward has a long tradition of being twisted to justify abuse. We must unequivocally state that abuse is never justified. Any attempt to convince people to stay in an abusive relationship or situation because we are all supposed to carry our crosses is distorted theology, and it is dangerous.

What happens if we look at these readings with new eyes, stripping away our preconceived notions as much as possible and instead hearing these words anew?

> **"It is necessary for us to undergo many hardships to enter the kingdom of God."**

We hear these words in the midst of Paul and Barnabas traveling around and supporting the early church. These churches were struggling, attempting to live the Good News in a way that radically challenged the power structures at the time. This was really hard! As anyone who has lived in a community knows, communities are difficult in the best of circumstances. Paul and Barnabas were encouraging these communities to keep going when life became difficult, assuring them that they would experience the reign of God when all was said and done.

Let us also remember that the early church thought the reign of God was imminent. This was not something that would happen several millennia in the future, but something that they thought would happen any day now. In hearing these words from Paul and Barnabas, I imagine that the early church was consoled and encouraged. I often tell my toddler, "This is hard, but you can do hard things." This seems like Paul and Barnabas are giving the early church a similar pep talk. Far from giving trite advice, Paul and Barnabas were putting forth an encouraging vision of the community called church. We don't do hard things just for the sake of doing hard things. Rather, following the call of the Gospel involves hardships because challenging power structures inherently brings about hardships.

This sentiment is deepened in the Second Reading from the Book of Revelation. We hear of "a new heaven and a new earth." Again, this is one of those phrases that sounds like a big, grand theological statement. What does it mean to talk about a new heaven and a new earth? When considered with the description of the early church and the promise of the reign of God, we can begin to get glimpses of what "a new heaven and a new earth" might mean. Following Jesus and the Gospel by gathering as church will transform the world as we know it. In theology, we often say that the reign of God is already-but-not-yet. This means that the reign of God is beyond our reach, and it promises such transformation that we cannot even begin to imagine it. Literally, it is beyond our wildest imaginations. It is not puppies and kittens on clouds, but rather, a promise of justice and love that is so rich and deep and pure that we cannot even fathom it. It is a justice where every tear will be wiped away and "there shall be no more death or mourning, wailing or pain."

Yet, if it was only beyond us, where would be the hope? This is where the "already" part of "already-but-not-yet" comes in. God loves us so much that God reveals Godself to us in ways we can know and understand. God is not far off and distant, but radically close! We can catch glimpses of the reign of God here and now. Think of those moments where you're having an incredible conversation with someone and look at your watch and hours have passed, or moments when it felt like time stood still. Those are moments of experiencing the reign of God in our midst. Yet the promise of a new heaven and a new earth reminds us that our current experiences are only glimpses, not the fullness of the reign that we will know one day.

It is in the context of hearing about enduring burdens, entering the reign of God, and the promise of a new heaven and a new earth, that we come to today's Gospel. We are given a new commandment: to love one another. This sounds simple enough, right? But what does it truly mean to love one another? Again, this is another big, grand theological statement I have heard a thousand times, yet paradoxically, I have no idea what it actually means.

Jesus tells his followers that others will know that they are his disciples if they have love for one another. Being a disciple of Jesus is not something that will be determined by social status, occupation, initiation ritual, clothing, or residence, but rather, by the action of loving one another.

It sounds so simple: love one another. In a polarized world and a polarized church, it is becoming more and more difficult to follow this commandment, as simple as it is. I am good at loving my family and friends. I am even good at loving people I don't know, provided they fit a certain description. To be completely honest, it is much easier for me to love someone who is vulnerable. I am very bad at being in relationship with people who are *just a little bit* different than me but have radically different views. Sometimes, I think I would rather have a test of discipleship that involves memorizing answers or following a strict formula instead of the simple commandment to love one another.

Truly loving one another involves sacrifice. It risks rejection or embarrassment, especially in a culture that prizes perfection. It involves vulnerability. It will almost certainly result in hardship. Yet loving one another is the call of the Gospel. It is not optional, or an added bonus that we can do if we master everything else. Jesus tells us simply that it is the defining feature of discipleship.

As we go forward this week, I encourage us all to take a moment and pause to sit with these big, grand theological statements. What does it truly mean to love one another as Jesus loved us? Who are the people who are difficult for us to love in our daily lives? How can we think about and behold a new heaven and a new earth? The promise of the Incarnation is not just that we have these big, grand theological statements, but that God is with us as we make meaning of these questions in our lives today.

6ᵗᴴ SUNDAY *of* EASTER

MARGARET BLACKIE

"Whoever loves me will keep my word, and my Father will love him."

1ST READING
ACTS 15:1-2, 22-29

PSALM
67:2-3, 5-6, 8

2ND READING
REV. 21:10-14, 22-23

GOSPEL
JOHN 14:23-29

THE READINGS TODAY ALL SPEAK ABOUT NEW possibilities. They require a letting go of what is, and what we think things should look like. We have to let go of how we think things should be in order for the new arising to become real. In the first reading, it is letting go of circumcision as a necessary part of identity. In the second reading, it is letting go of the need for the physical temple. In the Gospel, it is letting go of the physical presence of Jesus.

Let's start with the Gospel. Jesus is trying to reassure his disciples that, even once he is gone, they will not be left alone. It begins with the reassurance of Jesus saying to his disciples, "Whoever loves me will keep my word, and my Father will love him, and we will come to him and make our dwelling with him." The deep reassurance is that the connection between Jesus and the Father and the believer—each of us—will continue, and is as intimate as the relationship in the Trinity. There is a recognition that times may not be easy, that there may be a sense of feeling disconnected.

There may be times of tribulation, but the Holy Spirit is going to be sent to dwell in us. That promise is made to the disciples but, through our faith, it is a promise made to us too. For the disciples though, it meant not clinging to the physical presence of Jesus. It meant being willing to let go of his physical companionship.

In the first reading, we hear about the discussion between Paul and Barnabas and some of the other disciples. Here, the question is around which parts of Jewish law should be retained and which parts can legitimately be set aside. This complexity arises because Christianity begins as a sect of Judaism. As Paul ventures further into his mission to the gentiles, more and more non-Jews are wanting to become followers of Jesus. So, the question emerges: What is necessary? For those who grew up as Jews, what is essential to retain? What is essential to be a companion of Jesus? Ultimately, what is being negotiated is the link between Judaism and Christianity. Is this a sect of Judaism or is it something new? With the benefit of hindsight, we know how that played out. But pause for a moment and consider what it might have been like for the disciples. What would the equivalent be for us today?

It is so clear in this first reading that what is happening is a necessary letting go in order for the new arising to emerge. When something new happens in our lives, when a new opportunity comes along—a new relationship, a new job—each of these events will demand that we have to be willing to let go of something in order to make way for the new. What is happening in that first reading is another letting go of Jewish identity. By this stage, the disciples have already let go of the necessity of sticking to the food laws, and now they are letting go of the requirement for circumcision.

The deep invitation here is to risk holding loosely something that seemed central to the old identity. Jews were distinctive in those times, through circumcision and food laws. There were other laws too, of course, but both of these were significant barriers for those joining the Christian movement. In this reading, they are negotiating letting go of one of those things. Why? So that they can open their doors to embrace new members of the community. The consequence is ultimately the emergence of a distinct religion—what we now call Christianity.

In the second reading, there is also a hint of letting go of an image. John writes about an image of the holy city of Jerusalem coming down out of heaven from God. It is important to remember here that the temple was central to the practice of the Jewish faith, and John is writing in the period after the destruction of the temple. What's crucial here is that John doesn't promise the restoration of the temple. He writes that in this new, restored Jerusalem, there is no temple. The temple is the Lord God Almighty and the Lamb. In other words, when one is in the presence of God, one has no need for the temple. Again, remember the significance of the temple to the Jews of the time. In Catholic terms, this would be like saying there is no tabernacle. The tabernacle is no longer necessary because we are in the presence of God. Again, it's a shattering of what was presumed to be necessary in order for something new, something better to develop.

So then, these three readings are all about a learning to let of something in order for the new arising. In the Gospel, Jesus is saying, "You can dare to let go of me because the Father and I will dwell in you and the Spirit is coming to you." In the Acts of the Apostles, Paul and Barnabas are saying, "Can we dare to think about letting go of one of the elements that we thought was essential in order for the church to grow?" Perhaps that reading from John, in the light of the COVID-19 pandemic, may have greatest resonance for us. Many people around the world have experienced a forced absence from churches. Churches were closed in many parts of the world for long periods of time. In the absence of the ability to physically receive the Eucharist, where did you turn? Where did you discover the unexpected presence of God in your own daily practice?

Finally, I invite you to pause and to consider what you may be invited to hold a little more loosely, or let go of entirely, in order for the new arising to take place.

7ᵀᴴ SUNDAY *of* EASTER

FR. JAN MICHAEL JONCAS

"I in them and you in me."

1ST READING	2ND READING
ACTS 7:55-60	REV. 22:12-14, 16-17, 20
PSALM	**GOSPEL**
97:1-2, 6-7, 9	JOHN 17:20-26

FOR NEARLY FIFTY DAYS, WE HAVE BEEN celebrating the Resurrection of Christ. (Isn't it interesting that the preparatory season of penitence and conversion we call "Lent" is only forty days, while the season of celebration comprises fifty? Does that tell us something about the balance of repentance and joy in the Christian life?)

The first three Sundays of Easter all presented us with narratives about Jesus risen from the dead and manifesting himself alive to his disciples. The fourth Sunday, Good Shepherd Sunday, was the turning point, when we turned our gaze from past experiences of Jesus's presence in the flesh toward the future, when he is present to us in new ways: in his Word, in his sacraments, and in our communal and personal prayer. Guided now by a Jesus no longer present to our senses, we are increasingly led by the Holy Spirit, who makes the Risen Lord available to us in faith, beyond the evidence of our senses. So, on this seventh Sunday of Easter, we look ahead to the culmination of Eastertide: the great feast of Pentecost and the permanent outpouring of the Holy Spirit.

In the Church's wisdom, all three cycles of the Sunday lectionary for the Seventh Sunday of Easter recount parts of Jesus's so-called High

Priestly Prayer, the conclusion of the last will and testament that Jesus imparts to his disciples at the Last Supper in chapters 13 through 17 of John's Gospel. We hear the first two parts of this prayer in years A and B, when Jesus prays directly for his disciples. But, in this year's excerpt from the High Priestly Prayer, Jesus prays "not only for them [the disciples at the table], but also for those who will believe in me through their word." He is praying for us.

For what does Jesus pray, as he looks down the centuries to all who have been given life through hearing and believing the apostles' witness and testimony? He prays for unity among his followers; he prays that his followers might be with him to see his glory; and he prays that they may be completely enfolded by love.

First, he prays that all Christian believers might be one—and the model for that unity is not a monolithic monad with all individuality crushed by groupthink. No, the model for our unity is the dynamic life of the Triune God, where Father, Son, and Holy Spirit do not surrender their individuality of Personhood, but are completely aligned in love to bring about the transformation of the world. Jesus says that the reason we Christian believers must manifest our unity is so "that the world may believe" that Jesus has fulfilled his divine mission of redeeming us from our sinfulness and inviting us, transformed by love, to share in the Holy Spirit's work of transforming all of creation. Unfortunately, over the centuries, Christian believers have shattered the unity for which Jesus prayed, scattering into a variety of denominations. But we can still have great hope that the ecumenical movement, arising especially after the Second World War, is drawing Christian believers ever closer in obedience to the Holy Spirit.

Second, Jesus prays that all Christian believers might be with him to "see [his] glory." We English speakers rather naturally think of "glory" in visual terms, as a kind of radiance that emanates from holy people and things. But the Hebrew term for "glory" (*kabod*) is rooted in the physical reality of "weightiness" or "heaviness," and by extension, as "significance." To give anyone or anything glory is to declare the significance of that object in the scheme of reality. So Jesus is here, praying that his followers would experience his significance as the foundational reality for their world, that experiencing his love would be the single most important thing in their lives.

Finally, Jesus prays that all Christian believers might share in the very love that flows between himself and his Abba-God, the love manifest in their Holy Spirit. This love is not infatuation or sensual attraction, nor is it only the bond of social and familial love, nor is it just the free and freeing love of equals in friendship. This love is *agape*, divine love, love that is poured out on the deserving and the undeserving without counting the cost. In our world, until God's kingdom is fulfilled, *agape* will always be suffering love, the radiant love disclosed by Christ crucified. And we Christian believers have been given the incomparable privilege of sharing in the suffering and transforming love of God for the sake of the world.

Just as Jesus has revealed God the Father's name to us, John the Seer in today's second reading reveals the mystery of Jesus in the names he gives him, each one representing an aspect of his Person: Alpha and Omega, First and Last, Root and Offspring of David, Bright Morning Star. May we believers who thirst for unity of purpose, the vision of Jesus's glory, and the love that passes understanding experience ever more deeply and completely the transformation we received in our baptism's life-giving waters.

ASCENSION *of the* LORD

RICHARD ROHR, OFM

He was lifted up, and a cloud took him from their sight.

1ST READING
ACTS 1:1-11

2ND READING
HEB. 9:24-28; 10:19-23

PSALM
47:2-3, 6-9

GOSPEL
LUKE 24:46-53

ONE OF MY RECENT BOOKS IS CALLED *THE Universal Christ*, where I try to help people understand that Christ and Jesus are not exactly the same—which I know is shocking when you first hear it. For Christ and Jesus became one and the same, which is what the Ascension is all about—when Jesus fully becomes the eternal Christ and returns to his father.

But for thirty-some years, Jesus lived here as a full human being who looked just like us. I do believe his human mind had to struggle with faith just like you and I do. He walked the journey just like you and I do. He had to choose to believe that he was God's beloved son. And, of course, he was, but that was a journey of exploration and understanding, little by little.

So, I know we say we believe in Jesus Christ. We put those two words together, but really, they're two different names. The Christ existed—to use our contemporary language—from the moment of the big bang, the moment God decided to manifest the Godself, to show the Godself in a visible form so our eyes could see material reality. That's the birth of the Christ. That's the first incarnation. That's the Christ that existed from the beginning. And that's very clear in scripture. Jesus only came around 2,000 years ago, which is a mere blip in geological time. And we can't believe that all of history, which we now suspect is 13.6 billion years, was empty of God. If you doubt that, go visit the Grand Canyon. We've been here a lot longer, or the Earth has been here a lot longer than 2,000 years.

So, whenever we have the material world revealing the Spirit of God, we have the Christ, and that Christ was available to every nationality, every race, since the stone age: the Mayans, the Babylonians, the Persians, the Italians, the French, and all those little nations you've never heard of. God could not have left them apart from God. He created them. He created all things, but we somehow settled for a very small notion of God: that God just started being interested a few thousand years ago.

And again, 2,000 or 3,000 years is a blip, a drop in the ocean of time. So, we need a God that is at least as big as the world we now know of. If God is any smaller than that, how can he possibly be God? When I was interviewed by Oprah about my book, this is what she wanted to talk about. She seemed to be excited. She had the book all marked up—and it is worth getting excited about, if I dare say so myself, because what it does is reframes our religion, showing that we're not a tribal religion. We're not a religion for a few white people in America. We're a religion for all human beings—and even beyond human beings: for everything that was ever created, including animals, including plants. We Franciscans called creation the first Bible. The first Bible existed from whenever God decided to create.

The second Bible is a mirror that's 3,000–4,000 years old. We have both. We have the first Bible—creation, but most of us weren't taught to take it very seriously. We just stepped on it. We polluted it. We poured pollutants into it. We spoiled it because it wasn't sacred. It didn't matter. Much of the human race has felt they could torture animals. Now we must have a whole society to prevent cruelty to animals because most Christians don't even see animals as sacred.

We whittled the sacredness of God down to Christians, and then it wasn't even all Christians. It was just Roman Catholics. And then it wasn't even all Roman Catholics; it was just the nice people who come to church on Sunday. It ended up that God didn't love hardly anybody. Let's be honest: God became very impotent and empty in most people's eyes, not a God worthy of the name. And let's again be honest: That's why most of the millennial and younger generation is not here in church. No offense, but most of us are pretty old. Religion isn't interesting to people who've got modern science.

Religion is interesting if the universe is bigger than God, and we were given a universal Christ, a Christ who existed from the beginning. Ephesians says we were chosen in Christ from the beginning. Go home, pick up your Bible. Read the first chapter of Ephesians. It says, two or three times, that we were chosen in Christ from the beginning. The problem was solved. We didn't need a later blood sacrifice to talk God into loving us. God always loved what God created.

But I say this not to be clever, not to be unorthodox, not to sell books, but quite simply to give us a religion that we can be not just proud of, but excited about. We are believers in both Jesus and Christ. We have a religion that is both personal and universal—and isn't it interesting that this is the very name we took? I know that the word *catholic* means *universal*, but we weren't very universal. We were pretty European, pretty identified with empire, with the colonists, with the upper class. So much of the world has lost interest in our message, but we have been given a Christ that no one will lose interest in.

PENTECOST

DAVID A. DAVIS

And suddenly there came from the sky a noise like a strong driving wind.

1ST READING	2ND READING
ACTS 2:1-11	ROM. 8:8-17
PSALM	**GOSPEL**
104:1, 24, 29-31, 34	JOHN 14:15-16, 23B-26

A NOISE LIKE A STRONG DRIVING WIND....

and they devoted themselves to the teaching of the apostles and to the communal life, to the breaking of the bread and to the prayers.
All were amazed and perplexed because they each could hear them speaking in their own language, telling about all that God had done...**and they devoted themselves to the teaching of the apostles and to the communal life, to the breaking of the bread and to the prayers.** When Peter preached about how everyone who calls on the name of the Lord shall be saved and that everyone should know with certainty that God has made this Jesus both Lord and Messiah, the Bible says that they were cut to the heart...and that **they devoted themselves to the teaching of the apostles and to the communal life, to the breaking of the bread and to the prayers.** According to Luke here in Acts, 3,000 people were baptized and added that day, many wonders and signs were done by the apostles, awe came upon everyone...**and they devoted themselves to the**

teaching of the apostles and to the communal life, to the breaking of the bread and to the prayers. All who believed were together, they would sell their possessions and goods and share proceeds according to who was in need. They spent much time together in the temple, broke bread in their homes, ate food with glad and generous hearts, praising God and having the goodwill of all the people...**and they devoted themselves to the teaching of the apostles and to the communal life, to the breaking of the bread and to the prayers.** *Teaching, fellowship, the breaking of bread, and prayer.*

The first lecture I heard on the Holy Spirit as a seminary student was in my introduction to theology class. The professor opened every class with a reading of scripture. I remember one morning, after he opened his Bible, he took a 3x5 notecard and swept the crumbs from his breakfast off the page. Crumbs of toast and maybe some eggs were tossed into the front row. You may hear that and think it sounds kind of gross. Or, you may hear that and think about him reading his Bible at the breakfast table.

At one point during the lecture, the professor stopped, looked up from his notes, stepped in front of the lectern, and shouted, "The Holy Spirit matters!" He let out a laugh and yelled it again: "The Holy Spirit matters, and I mean that in every possible way!" He went on to tell of a fellowship hour conversation with a woman after worship. She was announcing to the professor, who was the guest preacher for the day, her disillusionment with her church and the lack of the Holy Spirit. During that conversation, people from the church kept coming up to her and asking about her health, offering a touch on the arm, mentioning they had been praying for her in the aftermath of some illness. Surrounded by the fellowship of the church, the witness of prayer, the touch of concern, the smell of coffee hour, the professor confessed that he found the woman's take on the Holy Spirit ironic.

Here she was, surrounded by what the preacher in the Book of Hebrews calls "a great cloud of witnesses." A rag tag, run of the mill, feeble flock. A group of people that the cynics of the world often refer to as a "church full of hypocrites." They were broken followers of Jesus just trying to devote themselves to the teaching of the apostles, fellowship with one another, the breaking of bread, and prayer. After he told that story to the class, he again bellowed, "The Holy Spirit matters!" And he took his hands and rubbed his fingers together. He might as well have said, "When it comes to the Holy Spirit, lower your expectations."

In all these years of pastoral ministry, I have long since given up questioning or doubting when someone honors me with the sharing of a profound, inexplicable spiritual experience that has moved them deeply and has great meaning for them. I just listened to another one Friday morning. To share examples of what folks have shared with me seems like sharing something too intimate, too raw, too confidential. But along with those profound, mystical experiences that stretch the boundaries of comprehension, these years of ministry have also brought me to lower my expectations of the Holy Spirit.

I don't mean that in a diminutive way at all. Rather, it is affirming a role of the Holy Spirit that matters, or having the eyes to see and the ears to hear and the heart to believe that God is present and active and moving in the ordinary places of our lives. Or, to put this in church terms, in our teaching and learning of the gospel, our fellowship, our breaking of bread, and our prayer.

The theologian Karl Barth once wrote that the miracle of preaching is not that the preacher finds something to say each week. The miracle is that people come back week after week expecting the preacher to have something say. They come each week expecting to hear and experience a word from the Lord. Every preacher knows the experience of standing at the church door and having someone say, "Pastor, it was like you were speaking directly to me this morning!" The person goes on to reiterate what was heard, what the preacher said, and of course, in her head, the pastor is thinking, "I don't recognize a word of what the person thought I just said in that sermon." The Holy Spirit matters.

I have had a similar thing happen to me, far too many times to count, when I am visiting the hospital. When pastors go to visit someone in the hospital, being able to see family members is just as important, sometimes maybe more important, than seeing the patient. So, it can be a disappointment when those family members aren't there. An example might be when someone is in surgery and the pastor was hoping to sit with a loved one for a while. Or the patient is asleep and there is no one else in the room at the time, so you just have to leave a note.

Often, when that happens, the pastoral visitor goes looking around, just hoping to see a family member. Check the waiting areas, the lobby. Look in the cafeteria or the coffee shop. So many times, I don't find folks in those areas. More often, I turn a corner and they're walking down the hall, or the elevator door opens and there they are. Just last Sunday, after a visit at Capital Health in Trenton, I was leaving through the lobby after a brief visit to see a church member and the spouse was just walking in. No, I don't think God and the Holy Spirit give much of a hoot about you finding a parking spot, but I do believe the Holy Spirit matters.

When I was a freshman in high school back in 1977, I endured an upsetting youth group experience surrounding perceptions of the Holy Spirit. That year, several young adult church members were serving as youth group advisors. In my Presbyterian church in the south hills of Pittsburgh, there was a growing small group that considered itself charismatic and strongly in touch with the Holy Spirit. Two of the youth advisors were part of that small group.

One Sunday evening after fellowship, two of those advisors asked a few of us in the youth group to stay after for prayer. The youth pastor, I am guessing, had no idea this was happening. I know he wasn't around when we went into the sanctuary. The sanctuary was about this size and it was dark except for the lights turned on in the chancel. We circled up in the split chancel, the pulpit on one side, a lectern on the other. We circled up for prayer. The young adults explained to us that they were going to pray over each of us, one at a time, so that we might receive the Holy Spirit's gift of speaking in tongues.

We took turns in the center of the circle with everyone else laying hands on us. The older folks prayed out loud. The one leading the prayer spoke words that made no sense, words that didn't sound like a language. I figured that he was speaking in tongues. I had heard about it, read about it from the Apostle Paul, but had never heard it or anything like it. For what seemed like a long, long time, we were there in that chancel. As far as I could tell, none of the youth group members received the gift of tongues that night. The reaction from the advisors was a mixture of disappointment and, "We'll try again later." Their conclusion was, "The Holy Spirit just didn't come this time." I went home convinced I wasn't good enough and wondering why the Holy Spirit wouldn't come that night.

Decades later—college, graduate school, years of ministry later. Count-less small groups, prayers groups, clergy groups later. Years of ministry, several spiritual directors later. Having told that story many, many times, it was only a few years ago, when someone—I can't remember who—heard that story from me and gave a response I never considered. Instead of lamenting with me over what I have sometimes described as "spiritual abuse," or giving me the proverbial pat on the back about an upsetting memory I can recall in such vivid detail, the person said, "Well, clearly that prayer was answered." The look on my face must have indicated I didn't understand, so there was a follow up. "Well, you've been preaching for what, twenty-five, thirty years? And you're pretty good at it. That sounds like tongues to me." In other words, the Holy Spirit matters.

When I teach over at the seminary or grab coffee with a student who wants to talk about preaching, inevitably the questions turn to the process of sermon preparation, sermon writing, sermon delivery. Amid all the technical questions, a bigger question is in play. "How do you do it every week?" My answer is always the same. I've been doing this a long time, and week after week after week, God has never, ever, ever let me down. Certainly every sermon is not great, but there has always been a word and you always come back. Some of you always come back. I've never had to say, "This morning, we're going to have a hymn sing." A lot of Sundays—a lot—and God is faithful...still. And I have learned that the Holy Spirit matters.

Every time I remember the confidence I have, the certainty I have that God will meet me here, that God is present with us in here, that the Holy Spirit is here—then comes the prayer: my prayer, our prayer, that God will give us that confidence, that certainty, that assurance that God will meet us out there in the world. That God is present with us out there. That the Holy Spirit is out there.

That God will fill our hearts with knowledge and the comfort that the Holy Spirit surely matters.

Ordinary Time

2ND SUNDAY *in* ORDINARY TIME

DEACON JIM KNIPPER

"But you have kept the good wine until now."

1ST READING
ISA. 62:1-5

2ND READING
1 COR. 12:4-11

PSALM
96:1-3, 7-10

GOSPEL
JOHN 2:1-11

SO, HAS EVERYONE PACKED UP THE CHRISTMAS decorations…taken down the lights…put away the crèche, and consumed the last of the Christmas cookies? This Sunday, the beginning of Ordinary Time, always seems a bit of a shock when we walk into this church and all the trees and poinsettias are gone and the sanctuary looks empty. But, in light of the theme of today's gospel, this transformation seems somewhat appropriate.

You see, Jesus became incarnate so that he could show what transformation is needed for us to know how to be human, how to be for others, and how to be in relation to God. I think this is why the Church, every year, begins Ordinary Time with a gospel taken from John. For while the Synoptic Gospels of Matthew, Mark, and Luke provide focus on the Kingdom of God, it is the Gospel of John that focuses on relationships: Christ's relationship with God and our relationship with Christ—a core theme throughout the year and one that is manifested in today's gospel story.

This story gives us the beginning of Christ's public ministry, with the first miracle—or, as John calls it, the first "sign" of Christ's divinity. It is a story that we have heard many times and, seeing that the author is a poet, it is a story overflowing with symbolism and meaning. At the same time, it is a story that we can easily relate to since it takes place at a wedding feast—something most, if not all, of us have attended. And thus, it is a story that you can easily place yourself within—so I ask that we do so, and we look at this story from the role of the servers.

So here we are, at what seems to be a large wedding feast. The town is small, so everyone knows everybody and thus you would expect a large gathering. Keep in mind that, in those times, weddings were celebrated for days, throughout the town—not just for a few hours at the local reception hall. John does not give us insight into whose wedding it is, but you could assume that the couple must be close to Jesus and his mother since, when trouble hits with the wine shortage, Mary is the one who steps in and calls out the problem to her son.

Now remember, you are the servers at this wedding, your job is to keep all the guests happy, and you have no more wine to pour—your decanters are empty; the people are thirsty. And Jesus seemingly responds with little enthusiasm to his mother's request to fix this problem. However, this motherly request actually carries a deeper meaning, for she is telling her son that it is a time for him to be made known, a time for him to begin his ministry, a time for this Epiphany of Jesus as the true Christ—a time to begin his journey, which he knows will end at Calvary.

So, what does Jesus do? He instructs the servers to take the large jars that were used to hold water for the ceremonial purification rites and to refill them with water—and with that...and through the divine grace of God, he transformed the ordinary into the fruitful, abundant, and extra-or-dinary: the finest wine to be served. In short, for that transformation to take place, it was necessary for the wine to run dry, for the jugs to be emptied so that Christ could take the ordinary and transform it into the extraordinary.

And there is no doubt that this transitional time of a new year on our calendars is when many people especially feel the emptiness of their lives. Perhaps it is due to the loss of a spouse, the lack of employment, dealing with family issues, or simply being overwhelmed with global events. You can hear it in the voice of the teenager who is bored with life, or the voice of a parent who has a son or daughter dealing with addictions, or the voice of one who cries out for personal healing and peace.

We have all experienced, at some point in our lives, the feeling that the wine has run out—that hopeless feeling, like the servers who were running around trying to determine how to satisfy those around them. And this is the time in our lives when we need to remember this gospel story. We need to remember the directions from Mary at the wedding. We need to remember her words as she points to her son and says, "Do whatever he tells you." Jesus the Christ—who saw a need in front of him, took common water, and turned it into a gift—is the same person who can open our eyes to see life in the ordinary as a gift and grace.

And for this transformation to take place in our lives, three things are needed.

First, we need to listen to the voice of God in places we may not expect. Remember the story of Elijah, who was told to meet God on the mountain? He looked for God in all the great things, but found him in a whispering sound—a sound similar to the breath that we each take. We need to listen to God not only in the joy and the ordinary, but in the addiction, the discomfort, the failures, the losses...for God indeed speaks to us in all those places. And to use the words of the mystics, we need to then ask: What is this abandonment asking of me? What is this tragedy asking of me? What is this emptiness asking of me? And we need to then listen—and this listening is called prayer.

Thus, the second thing we need to do is to create space and time for this prayer. Like Elijah, we look for loud and spectacular things to fill our empty spaces, and yet we still feel empty. Perhaps this is the year that you may consider taking three or four days to go on a retreat or pilgrimage. Perhaps this is the year that you look to find some time each day to allow quiet space to tell God that you feel empty, you feel confused, you are tired of trying to fill that emptiness with the material world—and then learn to be able to be still, and be open to God. Listen to the words of St. Paul in today's second reading: "There are different workings but the same God who produces all of them in everyone"—everyone! And for God to produce, we must be willing to provide fertile ground for that transformation to take place. It has been said that prayer is not primarily saying words or thinking thoughts; rather, it is a stance, a way of being present.

Lastly, we need to heed the advice of Mary at the wedding feast, when she turns to the servers and utters the last of her words ever recorded in the Bible. She simply says, "Do whatever he tells you." Do whatever he tells you! And through the gospels, he tells us to read scripture; do works of charity, fasting, and prayer; reach out to others in ordinary kindness; and, most of all, to forgive others. This is how the grace of God allows the ordinary to become grace-filled—to become the richness that fills our emptiness...to become the transformation we seek.

We are called to be the servers in this life, and in doing so we often *hear* that there is no more wine; we, at times, *feel* the emptiness of the vessels; and so often we *see* the suffering of others who are in need. Acknowledging all of this, we must listen for the Spirit of God. We must create space for God to provide and work, and we must act to serve the least of our sisters and brothers. For God calls everyone to this banquet table, to receive the abundance of God's grace.

The table is set. The wedding feast has been prepared, and the invitation was given to each and every one of us at our baptism. Thus we all hold the response card in our heart and soul. It is up to each of us to respond. So, how are you going to answer?

MICHAEL LEACH

If one part is honored, all the parts share its joy.

1ST READING
NEH. 8:2–4A, 5–6, 8–10

2ND READING
1 COR. 12:12–30

PSALM
19:8, 9, 10, 15

GOSPEL
LUKE 4:14–21

OUR FAITH HAS SO MANY BEAUTIFUL teachings; it's a wonder that our hearts don't burst with joy. Consider these two:

The Incarnation. The Son of God becomes the Son of Man so we can become the children of God. That is the core of our faith.

The Mystical Body of Christ. Have you heard of the Mystical Body of Christ? It is one of the most beautiful teachings of our faith, yet, surprisingly, one of the least taught. It's an extension of the Incarnation, one that joins all of us to each other and the Lord. Nowhere is it more clearly expressed than in today's reading from St. Paul (1 Corinthians 12:12):

> "As a body is one though it has many parts, and all the parts of the body, though many, are one body, so also Christ."

It brings to mind the old spiritual some of us sang as kids: Just as the backbone is connected to the shoulder bone and the shoulder bone connected to the neck bone and the neck bone connected to the head bone—all parts of one body—in Christ, I am part of you and you are part of me and we are really one, indivisible and interdependent. What could be simpler, and more profound!?

Everyone belongs! We *all* belong, to Christ and to each other. Everyone has a purpose. We are one in Christ Jesus and, despite appearances, connected to each other. We need each other. St. Paul writes: "The eye cannot say to the hand, 'I do not need you,' nor again the head to the feet, 'I do not need you.'" We are many members of one body, and what hurts one, hurts all of us. What honors one, honors all. We depend upon Christ; "in him we live and move and have our being" (Acts 17:28)—the Christ who lives in each of us.

We can trace the biblical DNA of the Mystical Body to Jesus himself, who told us that someday we would understand that "I am in my Father and you are in *me*, and I in *you*" (John 14:20), and went on to teach us how to pray by saying, "*Our* Father...." St. Paul then described it, the saints lived it, and in 1943 Pope Pius XII promulgated the teaching in his encyclical, *Mystici Corporis Christi*. That letter describes the church as a mystical union of all Christians, with Jesus as its head, the word mystical meaning "of a spiritual nature."

The term Mystical Body signifies a spiritual union, an essential oneness, an unbreakable wholeness. In 1965, the Second Vatican Council, in a historic document called *Lumen Gentium*, or *Light of the World*, expanded the idea of Mystical Body to embrace everybody, across all time, because Christ died for all of us. St. Paul writes in 1 Corinthians, chapter 12:

> **"For...we were all baptized by one Spirit into one body, whether Jews or Greeks, slaves or free persons, and we were all given to drink of one Spirit. Now the body is not a single part, but many."**

We are all baptized—whether by water or fire or desire—by one Spirit, and, as Paul reminds us again and again, "Now we are Christ's one body."

Isn't it amazing how science now bolsters spirituality, affirming what the mystics have written about for centuries? We hear about "the butterfly effect," how when a butterfly flaps its wings in India a storm brews in Indiana. Everything is connected. What happens to each of us happens to all of us. When a child in Calcutta goes hungry, a child in California can sense her pain. When a Samaritan helps a wounded man on the side of the road, a hospital goes up 2,000 years later. What blesses one, blesses all, independent of space and time. The Mystical Body of Christ is not a dogma; it is a vibrant spiritual community with Christ as its head.

So, we need each other because we *are* each other. Just as a sunbeam can't separate itself from the sun or from every other sunbeam, we cannot separate ourselves from the Light of the World, or from every other ray that emanates from this Light. Our work on earth is to glow for God and become light to each other: the weak and the strong, the celebrated and the ignored, those on the inside and those on the outs, those in the shadows, and even those who are despised.

"To be connected with the church," writes theologian Ronald Rolheiser,

> is to be associated with scoundrels, warmongers, fakes, child molesters, murderers, adulterers, and hypocrites of every description. It also, at the same time, identifies you with saints and the finest persons of heroic soul within every time, country, race, and gender. To be a member of the church is to carry the mantle of both the worst sin and the finest heroism of soul...because the church always looks exactly as it looked at the original crucifixion, God hung among thieves.[1]

Everyone belongs. Everyone counts. We are all connected. "If one part suffers," writes Paul, "all the parts suffer with it; if one part is honored, all the parts share its joy"! The Mystical Body of Christ not only points to a profound truth of our being, it is also profoundly practical. It is the basis for charity. It is the foundation for forgiveness. It inspires us to see the truth—and be the truth—in our daily lives.

When standing in line at the checkout counter, I remind myself that the individual in front of me is, like me, a member of the one Mystical Body of Christ, and that the injunction to love her as I love myself (Mark 12:31) is literally true because she is part of our one Self. A little miracle

---

1   Ronald Rolheiser, *The Holy Longing: The Search for a Christian Spirituality* (New York: Image, 2014), 128–129.

then happens: I not only love her, I *like* her, and if her credit card is no good or the odd piece of kohlrabi doesn't scan, I don't get mad. By the time it is my turn to chat with the dark-eyed checkout girl from Nicaragua, I am madly in love!

While walking down the street, I smile at a stranger walking his pit bull and choose to see him the same way God sees me. I say hello, and an alchemy of grace happens: The stranger smiles back and says hello, and we are strangers no more. What we give, we get right back. Even dogs know that.

While watching the news—seeing people die, children starve, families struggle—I ask Jesus, the head of the Body connected to all those who seem to be "out there," to see for me. I close my eyes and hear him whisper: "Peace I leave with you; my peace I give to you" (John 14:27). We are all members of one spiritual body. Any member can literally give another member her peace, across space and time, and the peace of both will increase and multiply. We can watch the news, ask God for peace of mind, give that peace to someone else, and suddenly experience a peace that is beyond understanding. This is what it means to be a member of the Mystical Body of Christ!

We all belong. We are one. We love our neighbor as ourself because we are our neighbor, and our neighbor is us. We even love those whom we think are our enemies because in the kingdom of God there are no enemies. There is only Christ and each of us, all of us, inseparable members of one great Body of Love. It is real. It is there. It's *here*.

Today's mission is to look in front of you, then turn to your left, then turn to your right, then look behind you, and see and be what you already are.

Go ahead...do it...and don't forget to say, "I love you."

4ᵗᴴ SUNDAY *in* ORDINARY TIME

PATRICK WENRICK

"Before I formed you in the womb I knew you."

1ST READING
JER. 1:4–5, 17–19

PSALM
71:1–6, 15, 17

2ND READING
1 COR. 12:31–13:13

GOSPEL
LUKE 4:21–30

"MAYBE THE JOURNEY ISN'T SO MUCH ABOUT becoming someone. Maybe it's about getting rid of everything that isn't really you."[1] This quote by Paulo Coelho is significant if read against the background of the Scriptures for this Sunday. In the first reading, we hear about God's call of Jeremiah, one of the major prophets of the Old Testament. Jeremiah was often called the "weeping prophet" because of the difficulties he experienced in life prior to his accepting the call to be a prophet.

I think Jeremiah also had a difficult time accepting the role to be a prophet to Israel. In fact, at one point, he says to God that he is too young and lacks the words to fulfill such a role. Nevertheless, God assures Jeremiah that he will have the words needed to fulfill his mission. He needed to call Israel back to a relationship with the true God and to demand they stop with worshipping false gods.

Being a pastoral counselor for many years, I have counseled many men, women, and young people who, over time, came to believe that they were

---

1   Paulo Coelho (@PauloCoelho), "Maybe the journey," Twitter, June 24, 2018, 5:38 a.m., https://twitter.com/paulocoelho/status/1010864837784690689?lang=en.

unloved. Many came from toxic families, where they took on an identity that was not really them. In an addicted household, the roles or identities are very rigid and defined. There are the enabler, the hero, the scapegoat, the mascot, the lost child, and the person addicted to substance or process addictions. It isn't important to go into detail about these roles, except to say that the roles became like gods to the clients who played them. The role was who they believed they were, despite hearing the Christian message that they were children of a loving God and, because of this, God loved them unconditionally before they were even born. Somehow and in some way, they came to believe in someone they were not meant to be, i.e., a false creation.

It's usually when these identities no longer deliver that people find themselves in therapy. They long to get back to who they were meant to be. The process of getting back in touch with the real self involves exposing some of the negative, unhealthy messages we give ourselves every day. These messages are subtle and very deeply rooted. "I am not good enough" or "I am not smart enough" are a couple examples of the messages that play over and over in our minds. Sometimes we need to erase these messages by changing the tape and recording more positive messages. It sounds simple, but it's very difficult to do. When we change the messaging, what follows is a change in behavior and belief in ourselves.

God had to remind the prophet that he was not only known before he came into this world, but also that he was loved. If we listen to Jesus in today's gospel, we get a glimpse at the messaging that perhaps is going through his mind as he confronts the people that were familiar to him, who knew him as a carpenter's son. The messaging they were giving themselves was, "He's familiar to us. God can't work through him. Look and see whose son he is and where he's from. He can't help us!" When Jesus confronts their lack of faith and exposes their thinking and behavior, they want to kill him—but were unable to do so at this point.

Let's begin to dismantle the false roles and messages we have come to believe define who we are. Let us feed on the identity we have before God. Often, such identities give us the courage to go against the crowd, as Jesus challenged those who made ignorance into gods on a frequent basis in the gospels. Let's believe in the message to Jeremiah: "Before I formed you in the womb I knew you."

5TH SUNDAY *in* ORDINARY TIME

FR. JAMES MARTIN, SJ

"From now on you will be catching [people]."

1ST READING
ISA. 6:1–8

PSALM
138:1–5, 7–8

2ND READING
1 COR. 15:1–11

GOSPEL
LUKE 5:1–11

WHO DOESN'T KNOW TODAY'S INCREDIBLE
Gospel reading? It is among the most moving and vivid of what are known as
the Call Narratives, that is, the stories of Jesus calling his disciples. Here, in
Luke's retelling of Jesus's meeting with Peter, we witness not only a miracle,
but also a powerful display of Peter's humility. Struck by his unworthiness
in the face of the miraculous catch of fish, Peter shrinks from Jesus. In fact,
he asks him to leave: "Depart from me," he says. It's a human reaction to
the divine. As a Jesuit spiritual director once said to me, in the sunshine of
God's love, we see our own shadows. Yet Jesus calls Peter anyway. There
are many of us who hear this story and see ourselves in it.

Yet maybe not all of us can see ourselves in the Gospel so easily. Why
not? For want of a word. The original Greek of Jesus's most famous words
in this Gospel passage may surprise you. In the English translations of the
passage, we read Jesus saying to the repentant Peter, "Do not be afraid;
from now on you will be catching men." The Greek is both more earthy and
more universal: "*Me phobou, apo tou nyn, anthropous ese zogron*," or, literally
translated, "Fear not, from now on it is people you will be taking alive."

The other two Synoptic Gospels, Matthew and Mark, recount this call narrative differently. As you may recall, Jesus strides up to Peter and Andrew on the shores of the Sea of Galilee and simply says, "Come after me, and I will make you fishers of men." They drop their nets and follow him, no miracle required. But, even though the story is different than Luke's version, both Matthew and Mark use the word *anthropon*, that is, "people."

Yet it is hard for some people to hear the passage translated like this, even though it's accurate. A few years ago, when I used this translation in a homily, someone wanted to correct me in the narthex after Mass. "It's fishers of *men*," she said, "not people." By the way, that complaint came from a female parishioner.

Of course, you could argue that Jesus didn't speak in Greek anyway. He spoke Aramaic, as did his disciples. Yet these are the words we have from the Gospel writers and the words that the early church heard. So, we have to grapple with them. You could also argue that we're meant to understand "men" as standing in for "humanity," but that's not the way that it sounds to many people today, especially some women. It sounds like Jesus is asking Peter to go after men, to find male disciples. And this is, of course, what Jesus does when he chooses twelve people as his apostles—all men.

Interestingly, though, the Gospels don't even agree on the names of the twelve apostles, and this, some New Testament scholars say, may indicate that not all the apostles were active leaders in the early church. In other words, if all twelve were well-known leaders in the early church, the Gospel writers would certainly have known their names. Jesus's choosing of them may have been more for symbolic reasons: a kind of gathering in of the twelve tribes of Israel. Still, twelve apostles, all men.

But among his disciples, his larger circle, among those for whom Jesus and Peter went fishing, were many women, Mary Magdalene chief among them. Remember, it is Mary Magdalene, a woman, to whom the Risen Christ first appears on Easter Sunday, at least according to John's Gospel. Then it is Mary Magdalene who announces the Resurrection to the other disciples. In fact, in that time between her encounter with the Risen Christ and the time that she announces the Good News to the disciples, in that hour or two, Mary Magdalene was the church on earth. Because, at that time, only to her had the Paschal Mystery been revealed. Thus, her title: Apostle to the Apostles.

Besides Mary Magdalene, several other women are named in the Gospels: Joanna, wife of Chuza, Herod's steward; another woman named Susanna; and "many others who helped Jesus and the Twelve, out of their sustenance." In the Gospel of John's account of the Crucifixion, besides Mary Magdalene at the Cross were Jesus's mother, his mother's sister, and Mary the wife of Clopas.

You can add to this incomplete list of female disciples the names of Mary and Martha, the sisters of Lazarus, who offered Jesus hospitality at their home in Bethany, and a host of unnamed women. One is the woman who anoints his feet, and about whom Jesus says that whenever the story is told, it will be done "in memory of her." Yet, despite even that, as the theologian Elizabeth Schussler-Fiorenza points out in her book called *In Memory of Her*, we still don't know her name. Despite Jesus specifically asking his disciples to remember her, her name wasn't even included in the Gospels.

Why am I mentioning this? Because it's important that we don't write women out of the Gospels. The Gospels were written by men in a patriarchal age, in part to appeal to people who lived in patriarchal societies, and so a certain writing of women out of the story is a part of their history. But we don't have to write them out of the story, because writing them out of the Gospels means writing them out of the church. And writing them out of the church makes it harder for them to feel part of what is, after all, their church; it makes it harder for all of us to hear their voices; it makes it harder for us to see them as leaders in their own right; it makes it harder for men—including priests, bishops, cardinals, and popes—to be challenged by them; and it makes it more difficult for all of us in the church to continue to fish for them—that is, for women.

Because women, along with men, make up the *anthropous*, the people that Jesus is talking about today: the People of God.

6ᵀᴴ SUNDAY *in* ORDINARY TIME

THE REV. TIM SCHENCK

"Blessed are you...."

1ST READING
JER. 17:5-8

2ND READING
1 COR. 15:12, 16-20

PSALM
1:1-4, 6

GOSPEL
LUKE 6:17, 20-26

"GOD BLESS YOU."

Isn't it odd that the only time we ever bless one another is when we sneeze? I mean, you might get your boss's blessing to proceed on a project at work. And at the end of a church service, the priest or bishop pronounces a blessing upon the congregation.

But the act of blessing one another is a lost art—and that's a shame. It shouldn't take an involuntary bodily function in order for us to pronounce blessings upon one another. And of course, saying "bless you" when someone sneezes is almost as involuntary as the sneeze itself. It's become little more than a Pavlovian response of politeness—we hear a sneeze, we say "bless you." So it's hardly the most sincere form of blessing.

In fact, the reason for saying it at all is rooted in the ancient belief that a sneeze indicated an evil spirit exiting the body. Saying "bless you" was a protective oath to ensure that the spirit didn't return to the sneezer's body, which, to me, sounds more like superstition than genuine blessing.

Scripture is full of stories of blessing. It is Jacob who tricks his blind father Isaac into giving him a blessing instead of his older brother Esau, for whom the blessing was intended. Old man Simeon blesses Mary and Joseph in the Temple when they arrive to present their newborn son. Jesus blesses the disciples as he ascends into heaven.

In Biblical times and beyond, blessing was something that average people did for one another. They blessed each other when leaving for or returning from a journey, or when a difficult or arduous task was at hand. These blessings were offered as signs of good will, along with an acknowledgment of God's active presence in people's lives.

We don't bless one another on a regular basis, and I believe we're poorer for it. And here's a secret: You don't have to be a member of the clergy to bless someone. If we believe that in a blessing we are invoking God's presence upon another soul, anyone can offer a blessing. It's not an act reserved for the professionals, and that's because human beings don't own the power of blessing. We merely borrow it from God. A blessing is a gift we pass on to one another from the God from whom all blessings flow.

And so we come to the Beatitudes. A beatitude is simply a fancy church word for "blessing." Luke's version, which is appointed for this day, opens what's known as the Sermon on the Plain and includes four Beatitudes, as opposed to Matthew's more popular and better-known Sermon on the Mount version, which offers nine.

But, number of clicks aside, there's something wonderfully compelling about the whole notion of the Sermon on the Plain. Jesus, his very presence in the world a sign of God's blessing upon us, comes down from on high onto the flatlands of the plains to be with the people. This movement says much about the role of Jesus in our lives. He isn't remote or inaccessible; he dwells among us. And so, whether or not we acknowledge him or even accept him, Jesus is always in our very midst, on our level, speaking with us and seeking after us. This doesn't make Jesus any less holy or special or divine. But it does say something astonishing about the nature of God. God doesn't reside "up there" or "away," but down here, with us.

I wonder what it would mean to live in a world where we blessed one another on a regular basis—not just in church, but at home and at work and in the coffee shop. What would the world look like if we took the time to recognize that each one of us is uniquely blessed by God, and then openly acknowledged that by blessing one another? What if we blessed our fellow children of God at times other than in response to a mighty sneeze?

The late Dutch theologian Henri Nouwen wrote that, "To bless means to say good things. We have to bless one another constantly. Parents need to bless their children, children their parents, husbands their wives, wives their husbands, friends their friends.... Whether the blessing is given in words or in gestures, in a solemn or an informal way, our lives need to be blessed lives."[1]

The prophet Jeremiah offers his vision of what it means to be blessed by God. He says it is like a tree planted by water, sending out its roots by the stream, which is a wonderful image of abundant blessedness. And it invites the question: What is your own vision of blessedness? For me, it might be soaking up the sun at a spring training game in Florida, watching my beloved Baltimore Orioles beat the New York Yankees. The day is full of the hope of a new season. The reality of the Orioles' lack of starting pitching hasn't sunk in and the losses haven't started piling up. That snapshot is, for me, a fleeting moment of blessedness, and I'm sure you can think of something that relates to your own life, something that reflects your own image of blessedness.

If the whole concept of the Sermon on the Plain tells us something of God, the power of the Beatitudes is that they, too, reveal something about the nature of God. What they are not are directives on how to live our lives, which is often how they're perceived. We're not being asked to be poor or go hungry or weep or be hated. Purposefully doing so won't bring us any closer to God.

That's because the Beatitudes aren't about us, they're about God. They offer us insights into the very heart of God. God cares especially for the poor and downtrodden and oppressed, not because their condition makes them more virtuous, but because God seeks to lift up the lowly, to fill the empty with good things. God's preferential love for the poor is because their condition is contrary to God's will, and so they are especially blessed. This doesn't make others any less loved or blessed; it just highlights the loving compassion and mercy of God and encourages us to bless those in our midst through radical acts of kindness that help bring about God's vision for the world.

So, "God bless you." Not because you just sneezed, but simply because you exist as part of God's wonderful and blessed creation. Consider taking that blessing and sharing it with others, as we seek to draw ever closer to realizing God's kingdom here on earth.

1 Henri Nouwen, *Bread for the Journey: A Daybook of Wisdom and Faith* (San Francisco: HarperOne, 1997), September 7 entry.

7ᵀᴴ SUNDAY *in* ORDINARY TIME

GREG BOYLE, SJ

"But to you who hear I say, love your enemies, do good to those who hate you."

1ST READING
1 SAM. 26:2, 7-9, 12-13, 22-23

2ND READING
1 COR. 15:45-49

PSALM
103:1-4, 8, 10, 12-13

GOSPEL
LUKE 6:27-38

A HOMIE NAMED SERGIO, WHOM I CALL MY "spiritual director," says, "We are called to do Jesus one better. So, Jesus says, 'Love your enemies,' but we should decide just not to have any." That *is* better. I heard someone once suggest that, instead of "Love your neighbor as yourself," since we're not good at loving ourselves, try loving your neighbor as you love your child. Also, way better.

We aren't meant to have enemies and then just keep our distance from them. The gospel invites us to remove distance from each other—at the soonest of soons.

A man named Trayvon, four days out of prison after a twenty-three-year stretch, is in my office, wanting to start our eighteen-month training program at Homeboy Industries. He's never been here before and I'm writing a note for him to show at the next weekly drug testing: "Drug Test any Friday at 10."

While I'm writing, I ask him, "How'd ya hear about Homeboy?"
He says, "Some female told me. Yeah...her kids were fathered by you."
I stop writing. "Say what now?" I ask.

Trayvon snatches his words from the air. "Wait. That's not right...no...
her kids were BAPTIZED by you!!!"

"Well, that's a little bit different," I tell him. And whatever distance
there was separating us as strangers got obliterated—separation as illusion.
We laughed, as the homies say, "from the stomach."

"Forget the drug test," I tell him. "You start tomorrow."

We can harbor enemies and settle for distance from them, but we
need to hold out for the tender heart that brings everyone in and makes
room for all.

I took two homies, Carlos and Robert, to help me give some talks in
Sacramento. We arrive late Sunday evening and it was dark. We board the
shuttle bus to take us to the car rental location. Robert and I sit facing each
other near the back, but Carlos situates himself in the middle of the very
last row. His nickname is Chamuco, a playful take on Satan, since he sports
two very large and pronounced devil's horns tattooed on his forehead.
Folks board the bus, but I watch as many do this evasive foxtrot, spotting
Chamuco and quickly deciding they don't want to sit next to Lucifer.
Finally, two seats remain on either side of Carlos. A couple of reluctant
passengers gingerly place themselves on either side of him.

We make our way to the rental car center, passing through a very dark,
secluded, and wooded area. Suddenly, our electric tram shuts down. We
are silent as the driver turns the key to no avail. "Sorry folks." No one says
a word as we hear the clicking of the ignition key. Then, from the back
of the bus, breaking the silence, comes this: "I saw this in a movie once.
It...does...not...end well." The laughter is unanimous and full throttled.
All are included in the silliness, no one left out. Space is carved for those
who voted one way in a recent presidential election and those who opted
another way. Polarities and division all melt in an instant kinship, and it's
all brought to you...by Chamuco.

It's certainly true that the traumatized will more probably cause
trauma. But it's equally true that the cherished are more likely to find their
way to the joy of cherishing themselves and others. Homeboy Industries
is jam packed with gang members from enemy/rival gangs. We don't coax

folks to "love your enemies." We invite them into a culture of cherishing, where all injuries are healed, and wounds welcomed as trusted friends. Hatred of enemies is no match, when cherishing is the air we breathe.

Puppet once walked to a corner store, some distance from his house. He made his purchase and took a shortcut home. Because of this detour through an alley, he was suddenly surrounded by ten members of a rival gang. Ten against one. They beat him down. When he fell, they would not stop kicking his head. Someone found his lifeless body and took him to White Memorial Hospital, where he was declared, effectively, braindead. After 48 hours, they removed him from life support and I rubbed a cross of oil on his forehead. His head was many times its normal size and it was quite difficult to train your eyes on him. I buried him a week later.

But, in the first 24 hours, while Puppet lay beaten in the hospital, a co-worker, Youngster, calls me. When Puppet and Youngster met six months before, their hatred for each other was quite personal and deep. They were determined never to exchange words with each other: Enemies, kept at a distance.

"Hey," Youngster tells me over the phone, "That's messed up, about what happened to Puppet."

"Yeah, it is," I tell him quietly.

"Is there anything I can do?" he continues earnestly. "Can I give him my blood?"

We both fall silent under the weight of it. In his gentle sobbing, he locates the spirit of cherishing, invited by Jesus to do him one better, and says with great deliberation: "He was not my enemy...he was my friend.... We *worked* together."

Our own deepening Christ-consciousness widens our views and suddenly we have new containers for things. We don't really have enemies. We have injuries that present as hatred but are really pain waiting for our attention and transformation. Jesus is never threatened but heartened when we inhabit a view that's even more expansive. "Doing one better" is what Jesus longs for. His dream come true is a community of beloved belonging, where we cherish our neighbor as we love our child. It is the distance we bridge that no longer permits daylight to separate us.

8ᵀᴴ SUNDAY *in* ORDINARY TIME

WILLIAM J. BAUSCH

"The good person out of the store of goodness in his heart produces good."

1ST READING
SIR. 27:5-8

2ND READING
1 COR. 15:54-58

PSALM
92:2-3, 13-16

GOSPEL
LUKE 6:39-45

AN ELECTION OR TWO AGO, *USA TODAY* RAN
a series of articles on what Americans are worried about. After all the
comments about employment, jobs, the economy, the terrible wars, and
violence, the persistent and basic concern was about moral values, about
how the country is basically soul sick: so rich in things but poor in people;
so near to self, so distant from community; so strong on "me" yet so
fragile on "us." The impression is that, as a nation, we cling to shadow
over substance, personality over character. We are awash in celebrities,
smothered in advertising. Responsibility for our actions, respect for others,
fairness, and integrity are values that were missing. In short, people felt
the moral center is not holding.

Unfortunately, these sentiments haven't changed over time, and I could
launch into all kinds of long sociological and theological explanations that would
put you to sleep. Instead, in search of an answer, I am going to tell you a half-
dozen stories about real people. People's lives are always the best homilies.

A woman once wrote that when she was ten, she found a brown wallet. There wasn't any money in it, but she was savvy enough to know that when she returned it, she would get a reward. She could hardly wait. All day, she called the number found in the brown wallet, but there was no answer. Finally, her dad drove her to the owner's address. It was a modest military housing unit with a torn screen door. As she rang the bell, her dad took three $20 bills and tucked them into the wallet. She remarked that it turned out that her reward was getting to see one of life's true heroes in action. She still remembers and tries to live according to that memory.

When Michael Keaton, whose real name is Michael Douglas, won the Golden Globe award as best actor for the film *Birdman*, he delivered a memorable speech that focused on his family:

> My name's Michael John Douglas. I'm from Forest Grove, Pennsylvania. I'm the son—seventh child—of George and Leona Douglas. And I don't ever remember a time when my father didn't work two jobs. When my mother wasn't saying the rosary or going to Mass or trying to take care of seven kids in a rundown farmhouse, she was volunteering at the Ohio Valley Hospital where I was born in the hallway.... In the household in which I was raised, the themes were pretty simple: work hard, don't quit, be appreciative, be thankful, be grateful, be respectful.... My best friend is kind, intelligent, funny, talented, considerate, thoughtful.... He also happens to be my son, Sean. I love you with all my heart, buddy. This [holding up his award] is for all those people.[1]

Do parents ever realize the great privilege, the awesome responsibility they have? Love of God, respect for others, forgiveness, and what really matters are lifelong messages they are forging every day. Faith, hope, and love begin with them, as with no other.

For example, there are growing daughters like eleven-year-old Rosalie Elliot, a spelling champion from South Carolina who was asked at the

---

1   As quoted in Kirsten Acuna, "Michael Keaton Gave an Incredibly Personal Acceptance Speech about His Tough Childhood," *Yahoo News*, January 11, 2015, https://www.yahoo.com/news/michael-keaton-gave-incredibly-personal-052500866.html.

thirty-ninth National Spelling Bee in 1966 to spell "avowal." However, her soft southern accent made it difficult for the judges to determine if she had used an "a" or an "e" as the next to last letter of the word. The judges deliberated, listened to recording playbacks, but still couldn't determine which letter had been pronounced.

Finally, the chief judge put the question to the only person who knew the answer. He asked Rosalie, "Was the letter an 'a' or an 'e'"? Rosalie knew by then the correct spelling of the word but, without hesitation, she replied that she had misspelled the word and used an "e." As she walked from the stage, the entire audience stood and applauded her. She did not win the contest, but she had definitely emerged a winner that day.[2]

No mystery where she learned that.

Then there's an incident that happened a dozen years ago when, on Christmas Eve, a stressed-out Christine Basney was raising four children, studying in college, and working in a small Michigan country store when Richard Heath walked in. Heath bought a scratch-off lottery ticket and won $100. He asked for the winnings in two $50 bills, then he gave one to Basney and one to another coworker as holiday gifts.

Fast forward ten years later. Basney, a registered nurse, walked into a patient's room to introduce herself. She was surprised to see it was Heath. They both recognized one another. "As soon as I saw him, my eyes welled up with tears," she said. "I told him that Christmas 2002 had been the roughest one ever for me and that $50 went a long way. I was deeply honored to be caring for him. I never forgot how kind total strangers can be"—and here's the spiritual zinger: "and I have tried my hardest to be as kind as the lottery man."

That's how love works: It isn't taught. It's caught.

A few years ago, an unemployed mother of three, Jessica Robles, attempted to steal $300 worth of groceries from a supermarket in Miami. She was caught. It just so happened that police officer Vicki Thomas arrived at the scene and asked Robles her reason for shoplifting. She responded that she did it to feed her three kids. Instead of taking her to jail, the cop

---

2 "Honesty of Young Speaker Brings Her Standing Ovation," *The Victoria Advocate*, June 9, 1966, https://news.google.com/newspapers?nid=861&-dat=19660609&id=YLZdAAAAIBAJ&sjid=710NAAAAIBAJ&pg=5681,1076528&hl=en.

gave her a notice to appear in court on a misdemeanor charge. But then Officer Thomas used $100 of her own money to buy groceries for the Robles family. She delivered them herself and witnessed the joy on the kids' faces that they actually had something to eat. When the story spread around, another $700 was donated for the Robles family and soon a local business owner hired Robles for a job.[3]

Just as greed and selfishness spread from one to one, so do kindness and generosity.

Finally, there's George Shuba of the old Brooklyn Dodgers baseball team. When he died at age 89 in 2014, he rated a long obituary in the *New York Times*. Why? Because way back in 1946, when a baseball player named Jackie Robinson—the first black player in the history of major league baseball—made his debut with the minor league Montreal Royals, he hit a homer. When he ran the bases, George Shuba did what so many others were unwilling to do: greet him at home plate with a warm handshake.[4] That was witness.

If our country has lost its soul, it's because too many lives have not been enfolded early on with the moral embracers we call parents, family, friends, neighbors, community, and public icons. But where it happens, we have fathers with compassion, actors with gratitude, kids with integrity, strangers with heart, officers with pity, and ball players with courage.

As a result, hopefully kids will grow up to be politicians who put the common good before vested interests, CEOs who put people before profit, legislators who put justice before party, and media moguls who put human dignity before exploitation.

The moral to all these stories is that restoring our national soul begins with us, one by one. Not the government, not education, not even the Church can match that. They can only support us, one by one. One by one, need I say, is you and I, and we are here beseeching God's Spirit to grow in us.

3   Aaron Tabor, "Police Officer Bought This Struggling Mother $100 Worth of Groceries Instead of Arresting Her for Stealing," *Jesus Daily*, https://www.jesusdaily.com/police-officer-bought-this-struggling-mother-100-worth-of-groceries-instead-of-arresting-her-for-stealing/.

4   Associated Press, "George Shuba: 1924–2014," *Legacy.com*, https://www.legacy.com/us/obituaries/cantonrep/name/george-shuba-obituary?pid=172630960.

9ᵀᴴ SUNDAY *in* ORDINARY TIME

BRIAN McLAREN

"*I am not worthy to have you enter under my roof.*"

1ST READING
1 KGS. 8:41-43

2ND READING
GAL. 1:1-2, 6-10

PSALM
117:1-2

GOSPEL
LUKE 7:1-10

HAVE YOU EVER BEEN SO FRUSTRATED, SO ticked off, so downright furious, that you could barely speak—or, maybe worse, that you couldn't control yourself to stop speaking? Paul appears to have felt a little bit of both when he wrote his brief but intense letter to the Galatians. Read the whole letter and you'll see: He packs this short letter with really strong language, some of it bordering on profanity!

What had him so riled up? The Galatians had heard the gospel, the good news of Jesus, the best news that anyone could ever hear—and before long, they were twisting the message, watering it down, reshaping it to fit within their preconceptions and prejudices. What especially bothered him was this: In the gospel, we learn that God loves all people, no exceptions. From a gospel-centered viewpoint, there is no longer us or them, clean or unclean, insiders or outsiders, first class or second class. Everyone is beloved, each is equal in value, and all are one.

But the Galatians were rebuilding old walls to shut some out. They were making distinctions between men and women, Jew and Gentile, slave or free. They were favoring some and disfavoring others. They were letting issues of gender, politics, nationality, religion, and economic status divide them. That, to Paul, was absolutely intolerable!

Imagine if Paul looked at Christian communities today. Many of us who call ourselves Christian are still at it, making distinctions that defy and deny the gospel. We're buying into divisions based on gender, politics, nationality, religion, and economic status. We're seeing one another through our lenses of judgment, not through the compassionate eyes of Christ. We're culture warriors more prone to reject or attack or cancel enemies than understand and love them. And here's how preachers today know that is true: The surest way to get church members angry is to tell them they're supposed to love as family the people they currently see as enemies or inferiors or "the other."

Think back over American history. Most early Christian colonists saw the Native Peoples as savages to kill or drive from their lands, not brothers and sisters to know and respect. The vast majority of their Christian children and grandchildren saw kidnapped African slaves as subhuman property to exploit, not children of God, equally beloved, to cherish and honor. As waves of immigrants came from Ireland, Germany, Italy, and elsewhere, Protestants were encouraged to look down on Catholics, and vice versa. The only time when Protestants and Catholics were unified was in their prejudice against Jews, Muslims, Asians, and others who seemed different. Any preacher who told them the truth—that God loved all humans equally and saw beauty and dignity in all peoples—would almost certainly be vilified and squeezed out to find another congregation.

So, what happened? Most preachers just stopped preaching this very truth that Paul thought was so important. Most preachers told the people what they wanted to hear, and avoided upsetting their apple carts of prejudice, bigotry, and ignorance. And so American bigotry went on, unchallenged—baptized, as it were, by Christian complicity. That history challenges all preachers like me to do some deep soul searching. Do we have the courage to name the prejudices here and now, in our congregations? Or do we tickle people's ears and give nice, comforting but unchallenging sermons that never upset anyone because all they do is tell people what they want to hear?

Just as Paul's letter to the Galatians raises a very personal question for me as a preacher, it also raises a personal question for each of you who are listening today. If God had a message for you—a message that addressed some of your deepest prejudices—would you get mad, or would your heart be open enough to listen and maybe even change?

In today's gospel lesson, Jesus models the freedom from prejudice that should inspire—and challenge—each one of us. A Gentile centurion has a slave who is very ill. He loves this slave and wants to help him. He even wonders if Jesus might help. But he is afraid that Jesus will be prejudiced against him because the centurion is of another religion and works for a government that is oppressing Jesus and his people. So, he enlists some of Jesus's fellow Jews to come on his behalf and ask for help. Jesus agrees to go to the centurion's home, and before Jesus arrives, the centurion sends a message: "Look. I know it's considered improper for Jews to enter the home of Gentiles. I don't want to put you in a difficult situation. But I believe you can heal my slave from a distance if you just speak the word."

Jesus could have just quietly healed the sick fellow and left without upsetting any apple carts. But notice what he says: "This fellow is of another religion. He is a military officer in an oppressive enemy regime. But notice his amazing faith! I have never seen this kind of faith among people of my own nation and religion!"

Do you see what Jesus is doing? There's a technical theological term for it: He is *blowing their minds*. He is challenging their prejudices. He is forcing them to see something that had always been true, even though few dared to see it: God loves everyone, no exceptions. Everyone: Gentiles as well as Jews. Women as well as men. Gay people, transgendered people, immigrants, citizens, refugees, Ivy League graduates, blue collar workers, the lady in the donut shop, gun owners, anti-gun activists, socialists, capitalists, rich guys, poor guys, and even you! Even me!

There's something else about that centurion that you should notice. He was a man of power and privilege. His title meant he had a hundred men under him. But notice that he deeply valued one of his slaves who got sick. He believed that enslaved lives mattered. Not many Romans would have felt that way.

And here's the question: Do you have enough faith to believe that God's love is that big, expansive, and inclusive? Do you have extraordinary faith like that centurion, or do you just have the normal prejudiced faith of too many religious people?

So here we are, at this moment of history. You and I have to look in the mirror. What kind of preacher am I? Am I one who will challenge you to greater faith, faith that blows up your prejudices and invites you to love? And what kind of congregation are you? Are you a congregation that is willing to follow the example of that Roman centurion, and to see every single human as a beloved child of God with great value?

Or, to put it differently: If Paul were writing a letter to us as he did to the Galatians, would he be ticked off at us, or would he see us as people who really, truly understand the gospel and seek to let it shape us, deeply, from the heart? You have to think about that. So do I.

10ᵀᴴ SUNDAY *in* ORDINARY TIME

MARGARET BLACKIE

"Young man, I tell you, arise!"

1ST READING
1 KGS. 17:7–24

2ND READING
GAL. 1:11–19

PSALM
30:2, 4–6, 11–12A, 13B

GOSPEL
LUKE: 7:11–17

IN TODAY'S READINGS, WE HAVE THE juxtaposition of the first reading and the gospel. In both, we have the miracle of a son brought back to life. In both cases, the mother is a widow. In both cases, it seems that this was the only son—and in the ancient world, that would mean destitution for the mother.

In the first reading, we find the widow turning to an approach we so often use ourselves in times of distress. We want to find a cause. The mother's immediate presumption is that somehow bringing Elijah into her house has caused this death. The mother is seeking understanding. She is looking for something to explain how this happened. Elijah echoes her in his first question to God. He says, "LORD, my God, will you afflict even the widow with whom I am staying by killing her son?" Importantly, though, having asked the question, he moves on to pray for healing. Elijah is willing to ask the question of God. The widow has raised a fear in him, which he takes to God. But he doesn't get stuck there.

The mother's response is so instinctual. She is looking for an answer, looking for something to make sense of her experience. She may even be looking for somebody to blame. We too fall for the same temptation, seeking answers and attributing causation when at best there may simply be correlation. Just because events are linked in time doesn't mean that one causes the other. Elijah's visit coincided with the son's death, but it is highly unlikely that the two were causally linked. It is important to ask such questions, but, more often than not, there are no real answers. Our pursuit of meaning or understanding can paralyze us, or it can mean the souring of a relationship. If Elijah hadn't moved on to seek healing, this death could have brought about a double tragedy—the breakdown of the relationship between the widow and Elijah. It is so easy, in the haze of grief, to compound our suffering.

The scene in the gospel is very different. Jesus doesn't need any of the dialogue. He understands the consequences of this death for this woman. And, simply moved by compassion, Jesus brings the son back to life. One wonders what the woman and her son would have spoken of that evening.

There is clearly a link in the gospel to the great prophets Elijah and Elisha, who both raised sons from death. Whether Luke is intending to make this connection is less obvious. There is also a connection to the claims written in Isaiah of the dead being raised, etc. Luke was himself a gentile and was writing for a gentile audience, so it is not likely that many of his readers would make the mental connection. It is interesting nonetheless, that this story only appears in Luke's Gospel.

It is useful to remember that Luke has a particular focus on the poor, the marginalized, and the outsider. Jesus's response to the widow of Nain is quintessentially the Gospel of Luke. This woman, with the death of her son, has lost her identity, her security, and her beloved child. Jesus doesn't wait to inquire about what she desires. He simply acts.

He is so moved by her plight that he touches the coffin. In Jewish law, this would make him unclean. As with the story of the good Samaritan, which is also only found in Luke's Gospel, we find a clear message that when compassion and purity laws are at odds with one another, we are to err on the side of compassion.

11ᵀᴴ SUNDAY *in* ORDINARY TIME

THE REV. MARK BOZZUTI-JONES

"Her many sins have been forgiven; hence, she has shown great love."

1ST READING
2 SAM. 12:7–10, 13

PSALM
32:1–2, 5, 7, 11

2ND READING
GAL. 2:16, 19–21

GOSPEL
LUKE 7:36–8:3

IF WE ONLY HAD THE PLEASURE AND THE honor and the grace (to show great love) to invite Jesus to eat with us.

Would you invite Jesus into your house to eat with you? Would you invite Jesus into your heart, into your mind, into your soul, and into your life? Would this be a serious invitation? Would you invite Jesus to come eat with you, to come be with you, to come live within you and to take his place at the head of your table and the head of your life?

Today, this day, right now. This is the moment and the encounter of salvation. God the Creator has always invited you to live in God and live for God. Your creation, your existence, you and all your desires are God's invitation to break bread, and there is no denying that we always see God in the breaking of the bread.

To eat with someone is to share our heart.

To eat with someone is to break the words of our heart.

To eat with someone is to start the meditation of our hearts: press the wheat, crush the grapes, press the heart to give love.

Would you invite God to eat with you? Remember Abraham and remember Sarah.

Jesus said to him, "Simon, I have something to say to you."

"Tell me, teacher," he replied.

"Two people were in debt to a certain creditor; one owed five hundred days' wages and the other owed fifty. Since they were unable to repay the debt, he forgave it for both. Which of them will love him more?"

Simon said in reply, "The one, I suppose, whose larger debt was forgiven."

He said to him, "You have judged rightly."

When invited in, Jesus takes his place at the table and in the penitent heart.

When invited, Jesus will wash your feet.

"Do you see this woman?"

In every heart, there lives a woman who learns, a woman who knows where to find God, a woman who is unafraid, a woman who will make her way, and a woman who will demonstrate and show that she knows what love is.

Knows what forgiveness is.

Knows what courage is.

Brings an alabaster jar of ointment.

Knows what resurrection is.

A woman like this, who loves likes this, shows up unbidden.

Sophia lives in every heart and shows up all the time to eat....

Invite your heart to look at God.

See the sinner, see the sinner, see the sinner.

Jesus said to him, "Simon, I have something to say to you."

"Tell me, teacher," he replied.

"Two people were in debt to a certain creditor; one owed five hundred days' wages and the other owed fifty. Since they were unable to repay the debt, he forgave it for both. Which of them will love him more?"

Simon said in reply, "The one, I suppose, whose larger debt was forgiven."

He said to him, "You have judged rightly."

One who learns where God and Mercy eat, stands behind the throne of Mercy, washing those feet.

A loving heart knows that if Jesus is eating in the lion's den, the belly of the whale, the fiery furnace, a locked jail, the valley of the shadow of death, or the Pharisee's house—

A loving heart knows it can beat and not be afraid.

In the presence of Jesus the Merciful and Beneficent, there is a wideness in God's mercy and no shaming and no blaming.

Would you invite Jesus into your house to eat with you? Would you invite Jesus into your heart, into your mind, into your soul, and into your life? Would this be a serious invitation? Would you invite Jesus to come eat with you, to come be with you, to come live within you and to take his place at the head of your table and the head of your life?

Out there, where the named meets the unnamed, the unknown is known and loved by God.

"She stood behind him at his feet, weeping, and began to bathe his feet with her tears and to dry them with her hair. Then she continued kissing his feet and anointing them with the ointment."

In encounters with God, in encounters like these, it is never what the eyes see, but always the heart.

What a privilege and what a joy divine to anoint the feet of Jesus.

Jesus said to him, "Simon, I have something to say to you."

"Tell me, teacher," he replied.

"Two people were in debt to a certain creditor; one owed five hundred days' wages and the other owed fifty. Since they were unable to repay the debt, he forgave it for both. Which of them will love him more?"

Simon said in reply, "The one, I suppose, whose larger debt was forgiven."

He said to him, "You have judged rightly."

Would you invite Jesus into your house to eat with you? Would you invite Jesus into your heart, into your mind, into your soul, and into your life? Would this be a serious invitation? Would you invite Jesus to come eat with you, to come be with you, to come live within you and to take his place at the head of your table and the head of your life?

Of course, God knows our heart and name.

Of course, God knows that each of us has at least seven demons—God knows.

Of course, God knows who you are and whose you are.

God knows thoughts, words, deeds, and all that is left undone and comes and comes and comes again to call sinners to repentance.

Jesus said to him, "Simon, I have something to say to you."

"Tell me, teacher," he replied.

"Two people were in debt to a certain creditor; one owed five hundred days' wages and the other owed fifty. Since they were unable to repay the debt, he forgave it for both. Which of them will love him more?"

Simon said in reply, "The one, I suppose, whose larger debt was forgiven."

He said to him, "You have judged rightly."

In the beginning, there was really one commandment: Show great love. Show great love to God. Show great love to your neighbor. Show great love to your enemy. Show great love to the world.

Those many sins that we all have, will fall away when we see God's love and forgiveness and seek this love and forgiveness.

Would you invite Jesus into your house to eat with you? Would you invite Jesus into your heart, into your mind, into your soul, and into your life? Would this be a serious invitation? Would you invite Jesus to come eat with you, to come be with you, to come live within you and to take his place at the head of your table and the head of your life?

"Do you see this woman? When I entered your house, you did not give me water for my feet, but she has bathed them with her tears and wiped them with her hair. You did not give me a kiss, but she has not ceased kissing my feet since the time I entered. You did not anoint my head with oil, but she anointed my feet with ointment. So I tell you, her many sins have been forgiven; hence she has shown great love. But the one to whom little is forgiven, loves little."

Your sins are forgiven. Go say this and show this to others.

Your faith has saved you. Go in peace.

Go and show great love. Amen.

12TH SUNDAY *in* ORDINARY TIME

FR. JAN MICHAEL JONCAS

"Who do the crowds say that I am?"

1ST READING
ZECH. 12:10–11; 13:1

PSALM
63:2–6, 8–9

2ND READING
GAL. 3:26–29

GOSPEL
LUKE 9:18–24

I STILL VIVIDLY REMEMBER MY CONFUSION about Jesus's name in early grade school. From toddlerhood, I had heard that his name was "Jesus Christ," so I naturally assumed that "Jesus" was his given name and "Christ" was his family name. I even imagined that the mailbox outside his home at Nazareth read, "Mr. and Mrs. Joseph Christ." (Of course, I'm not even going to mention my wonder at what Jesus's middle name was, since I had heard my father on more than one occasion offer the pious ejaculation "Jesus H. Christ" when he was exasperated. Was Jesus's middle name "Herbert"? "Henry"? "Howie"?)

My confusion was cleared up by Sr. Apollonia, my second-grade teacher, who explained that Jesus's name was "Jesus," but that "Christ" was his title. She also made it clear that this title meant "the Anointed One," a translation of the Hebrew term "Messiah," which was his Jewish title. (Looking back, that was a lot of information for a second grader to take in, but that was the blessing of a Catholic education in the old days.)

This experience always comes to mind when I read the Gospel story of Peter's confession of Jesus as "the Christ of God." After much prayer,

Jesus quizzes his disciples on what descriptive titles his co-religionists had for him, much as we hear people today refer to a jazz saxophonist as "the new John Coltrane" or a contemporary painter as "the new Pablo Picasso." His disciples reply that some folks call him "the new John the Baptist," identifying him with John's role as a contemporary prophet calling people to repentance. Other people call him "the new Elijah," locating Jesus's meaning and ministry in heralding the coming Anointed One, while yet others lump him in with the succession of prophets who had spoken God's direct message to God's people.

Up to this point, Jesus's inquiry evokes an impartial survey of public opinion. But his new question turns the tables: Jesus asks them, "But who do you say that I am?" Peter, with his typical pattern of speaking and acting rather impulsively, declares on behalf of the group: "You are the Messiah, the Anointed One, the Christ of God." In other words, Jesus cannot really be compared to past religious heroes; in his life and ministry, something radically new has entered human history.

Unlike Matthew's version of the story, where Jesus immediately commends Peter for his insight; or Mark's version, where Jesus has to correct Peter's presumption since he doesn't understand what the Messiah's role is; here in Luke's version, Peter's confession provokes Jesus to describe in grim detail the suffering and death of the "Son of Man" as the new revelation of God's activity in history. Jesus then calls each of his disciples to take up his own cross, joining him in his redemptive passion. Only in Luke do we get the detail that taking up one's cross is not something done once-for-all; disciples are called to take up their cross "daily."

Jesus's challenge to his disciples echoes down the centuries to us. We are not called to embrace pointless suffering with some kind of masochistic passion. God does not call us, any more than he called Jesus, to undergo a sadistic form of child abuse to satisfy God's offended honor. Rather, we are called each day to live by the values of God's reign, which will inevitably bring us into conflict with the world as we know it.

For example, refusing to divide our brothers and sisters into the "undeserving" vs. the "deserving" poor will influence our political choices, our conversations with neighbors, and our own giving patterns. We may have to bear the cross of being called "naïve do-gooders" or "un-American socialists"; we may be "chumped" by folks who take advantage of our generosity. But how else will we embody the values of the Messiah, who tells us elsewhere in Luke's Gospel: "Give to everyone who asks of you, and from the one who takes what is yours do not demand it back. Do to others as you would have them do to you" (Luke 6:30–31)?

So, what is the good news in coming to confess Jesus as the Anointed One of God and taking up our crosses daily at his command? Jesus invites us to join him in embodying the divine will for the world, God's reign of compassion, mercy, justice, and peace. And even if we might frequently stumble on the path Jesus has mapped out, God has such a high opinion of us that God gives us the grace not to live according to "worldly wisdom," God's grace incorporates every tiny act of love we do into the divine vision of the future, and God delivers us from our ultimate fear: going into death-as-oblivion, having lived a meaningless life. As Jesus says at the conclusion of today's Gospel passage: "Whoever wishes to save his life"—a life lived according to the standards of this passing world—"will lose it, but whoever loses [this world's] life" because of Jesus's vision and values "will save it." May this eucharist give us the nourishment we need to follow Jesus's path and may the Holy Spirit strengthen our discipleship.

13ᵀᴴ SUNDAY *in* ORDINARY TIME

LUKE HANSEN

For freedom Christ set us free; so stand firm and do not submit again to the yoke of slavery.

1ST READING
1 KGS. 19:16B, 19–21

PSALM
16:1–2A, 5, 7–11

2ND READING
GAL. 5:1, 13–18

GOSPEL
LUKE 9:51–62

GOD WANTS US TO BE FREE! WE ARE MEANT for freedom! It's important to take a moment to receive this Good News.

Is there something that's oppressive in your life right now? What's holding you back from living into your truest self and who God has called you to be? Is it our economic system and the financial pressures we face daily? Is it a toxic situation at work? Is it a broken relationship that's in need of healing? Have we created unnecessary obligations that actually weigh us down and keep us from living God's call?

St. Paul is frustrated that some people in Galatia are emphasizing the need for converts to Christ to also adhere to parts of the Mosaic Law, specifically the law of circumcision. Paul says these "false brothers" are preaching an alternative gospel that is attempting to enslave (Gal. 2:4). Instead, Paul preaches that we have freedom in Christ (2:4) and that we are no longer slaves, but adopted children of God (4:5, 7). We hear today: "For freedom Christ set us free; so stand firm and do not submit again to the yoke of slavery" (5:1).

What's the freedom that St. Paul is writing about?

It's not *freedom from* responsibility and accountability and sacrificial love for others. It's not *freedom for* fulfilling our every desire and doing whatever we want, regardless of others. It's not an opportunity or license to follow the "desire of the flesh" (Gal. 5:16).

St. Paul is very clear about what this freedom is for. It's to love more freely and generously. It's to "serve one another through love" (5:13). He writes, "For the whole law is fulfilled in one statement, namely, 'You shall love your neighbor as yourself'" (5:14). That's the test of every obligation and every act: Does it reflect the love of Christ?

In the Gospel today, Jesus shows us something important about the freedom to love.

We are at a turning point in Luke's Gospel. Up until now, Jesus has been engaged in healing and teaching ministries in Galilee, but now we are told, "He resolutely determined to journey to Jerusalem" (Luke 9:51). The New American Bible, Revised Edition, notes that "he resolutely determined" literally means "he set his face" toward Jerusalem. We know what will happen when Jesus arrives there.

Luke then provides a detail about Jesus's journey from Galilee to Jerusalem that should not be overlooked, since it reveals something about Jesus's freedom and mission.

Luke narrates, "On the way they entered a Samaritan village" (Luke 9:52). John's Gospel is even more explicit, saying that during the journey, Jesus "had to" pass through Samaria (John 4:4).

In fact, Jesus didn't "have to" pass through Samaria. Due to the historical conflicts and deep-seated animosity between Jews and Samaritans, it was normal for Jews to bypass Samaria by taking an alternative route on the other side of the Jordan River. However, seeing it as part of his mission, Jesus deliberately chose to enter this foreign territory.

In Luke's Gospel, Jesus's messengers do not find welcome in a Samaritan village. In response, James and John ask Jesus if they could "call down fire from heaven to consume them." Jesus turns and rebukes them (9:54–55).

In John's Gospel, Jesus not only talks to a Samaritan, but to a Samaritan woman (4:7). Details in the story indicate that this woman was especially marginalized and socially stigmatized. Later, when the disciples see Jesus talking to a woman, they are "amazed" (4:27).

Jesus demonstrates the freedom to cross boundaries and to break various kinds of conventions and laws, but he doesn't do so to simply be rebellious and a "rule-breaker." He does so for the sake of love. For Jesus, no one is excluded from the plan of salvation and the love of God—not even Samaritans. Not even a person who has had "five husbands," as we hear in the encounter between Jesus and the woman at the well (John 4:18).

Jesus crossed boundaries and broke rules in order to heal, to reconcile, and to help build the beloved community. Jesus invites us to that same freedom and to respond with urgency to the sacred mission to which he calls us.

In today's Gospel, when Jesus encounters people along the road who are ready to follow him, he emphasizes the radical nature of Christian discipleship. Even the obligation to bury one's parents cannot get in the way of freely proclaiming and living the kingdom of God. That's true freedom in Christ.

Is there something standing in your way today? What's holding you back from the freedom Jesus desires for you? "For freedom Christ set us free; so stand firm." Let's ask Jesus for the grace to respond generously to his call.

14ᵀᴴ SUNDAY *in* ORDINARY TIME

JOHN WHITNEY, SJ

"The harvest is abundant but the laborers are few."

1ST READING
ISA. 66:10–14

PSALM
66:1–7, 16, 20

2ND READING
GAL. 6:14–18

GOSPEL
LUKE 10:1–12, 17–20

ON JUNE 18, 1994, AFTER ELEVEN YEARS of study and Jesuit formation, I was ordained a Roman Catholic priest at St. Joseph Church in Seattle. It was shortly after that, thanks to a very kind— and very determined—Sister of St. Joseph of Carondelet, that I began to learn what it means truly to be sent out as a disciple of Jesus Christ.

I was working at Seattle University in the Office of Campus Ministry, just a month after my ordination, when a call from a "Sr. Ann" was directed my way. Recently moved from Los Angeles, Sr. Ann had received permission to have a weekly Mass at the King County Youth Detention Center, where young people are kept while awaiting trial—and while it is decided whether they will be tried as juveniles or as adults. She said she was looking for a priest to help out, and thought Seattle University was a good option, since we were only a few blocks away. Already involved in student retreats and sacramental preparation, teaching two sections of philosophy, and organizing campus liturgies, I tried to say that I was too busy, but Sr. Ann was not taking my no for an answer, asking me at last to come *"just one time."* And so it began, and every Tuesday night for the next four years, I would head down the street into a community and a world that I knew nothing about—not exactly a "lamb among wolves," but still something of a fish out of water.

Yet, for all my worries of having little to give to this community, I found each week that just being present was an opportunity for God to work in all of us. Few of the young people who came to Mass were Catholic. Most just wanted some time away from their rooms—or to see members of the opposite sex—and occasionally there would be some issue or conflict. I learned to watch for gang signs or the simmering tensions between rivals. Yet, I also saw how Sr. Ann, who treated each young person with dignity and respect, always received respect from even the toughest of kids. Though neither she nor they would say it this way, she bore, like Paul, "the marks of Jesus" on her, and those who had, themselves, been so scarred by the world, could sense her compassion and strength. I came to realize that her calling me into this community was part of the reason I was received and trusted.

It was on one of these Tuesday evenings that a young men asked me to pray with him after Mass. This wasn't unusual, since it was a way for the young people to stay out of lockup a little longer. But this time, as we sat there together at a library table, there was no small talk. Instead, he started to tell me about his crime. At first, it was like listening to a hundred stories you've heard on the news: He was, he said, "burned in a drug deal" and sought to get even by driving past with his friends and shooting up the place. And in this drive-by, two other young people—who had nothing to do with the incident—died in the gunfire.

But if the story seemed familiar, sitting there and looking at this little boy was nothing like watching the news. In this child, who should have been shooting hoops instead of shooting guns, violence was not a statistic, nor a sociological problem—it was instead something alto-gether different: a force of the enemy that we had let into our home. A dark power that indicted me as an American and humbled me as a person of faith. How had this young boy come to believe that shooting indiscriminately into a crowd was the answer to his feelings of anger and frustration? How had he landed there, alone on the street, with no one to guide him or care for him except his equally unguided peers? And what of his victims, those dead whose lives were snuffed out before they had the chance to blossom?

"The harvest is abundant but the laborers are few." Where were the laborers who should have been in this field? Where were those people of faith who could have helped?

I couldn't answer these questions for myself that night, and years later I still can't. Sitting beside him in that library, I struggled to pray. I felt inadequate to the moment. But, at the same time, prayer seemed essential, and so I took his hands and told him what I could of God's mercy and grace, knowing that only the Spirit of God could bring the healing and hope needed. Only the cross of Christ could bring redemption.

These days, how often we hear bishops—especially in the United States—who profess that our Church must become smaller and more "pure," who teach that we must drive from the altar all who do not adhere with sufficient fealty to the doctrines of the faith. Like those, in the days of St. Paul, who longed to have all converts receive physical circumcision—to become Jews before they could become Christians, these self-professed traditionalists seek a circumcision of conscience from all believers and conceive of a faith not so much grounded on the living Jesus as on the lifeless ideology of subjugation and merit.

In this vision, human society is often seen as an enemy, and the "unique grace and privileged position" provided by faith means that we may act with *charity* toward the world, but must never conceive of ourselves as in *solidarity* with it. Rather than going out, as pilgrims, into "every town and place" where Jesus might visit, we must shake the dust of the world from our feet and wait in our fortress Church for the world to come humbly to us.

But waiting and watching in the purity of our doctrine is not the call of the gospel. For the message of Christ is not simply about *faith*, but about *faithfulness*; not only about the Spirit of *abstract truth*, but also about the Spirit of *truth in action*—about a Word that takes flesh and abides among the tents and tensions of this world. We may speak of our faith—as Paul so often spoke—as a transformative gift; but if we do not live and act as a people transformed, we have not yet known Jesus Christ. If we do not go out, like the seventy-two, and risk growing weary in the work of the kingdom, we can never really know that our names are "written in heaven."

Today, the violence that marks our city, our state, and our nation—violence brought home to me on that evening in detention, and replayed again in Orlando and Newtown, on the streets of Chicago and on the steps of the Capitol—is a sign that we still live as people with only half a message. For, to be a disciple of Christ means more than sitting in the right Church; it means offering a cup of water to those who are thirsty. To be a disciple of Christ means more than gathering at the right table; it means making room at that table for all who are hungry or lost or afraid, all who long for mercy and have nowhere else to go. To be a disciple of Christ means more than *possessing* the Spirit of God as some abstract doctrinal truth; it means that the Spirit of God *lives* in me—and in us—as courage and compassion, as a prayer for which I have no words and as a mission that I have never imagined. It means carrying, with a mother's love, those who have been forgotten—the violent and the violated, the hopeless and the poor—and giving to them the comfort of God, not because they have earned it but because they are beloved.

Today, every Christian is appointed by Jesus to go out as a disciple into the world and to proclaim with boldness the coming of the kingdom. We are ignited by the Spirit—whispering to us like a voice in our hearts or summoning us like the phone call from a persistent nun. We are commanded to leave the security of our pews and our churches, the safety of our offices and rectories, the fortress of our ideological certitude and our dogmatic assumptions, and to seek out all who are lost, and to stand in solidarity with all who dwell at the edge of despair. We are sent into the harvest, guided only by the cross and the message: "The kingdom of God is at hand for you."

And if we are faithful to this appointment, if we live what we have been given to believe, then, in the merciful fullness of God, the innocent will be raised up, and the violence that surrounds our children and ourselves will come to an end. Then the gospel will indeed be proclaimed, not just in words but also in deeds, not just in this community but for all God's people.

15ᵀᴴ SUNDAY *in* ORDINARY TIME

RORY COONEY

"And who is my neighbor?"

1ST READING
DEUT. 30:10–14

2ND READING
COL. 1:15–20

PSALM
69:14, 17, 30–31, 33–34, 36–37

GOSPEL
LUKE 10:25–37

IN THE SECOND HALF OF THE GOSPEL TODAY,
we hear the beloved parable of the Good Samaritan. It's such a good story that we feel we know it by heart, but there are some details that might have escaped our notice, and we might have interpreted some things like twenty-first-century Americans, unable to hear the story with the edge it once had, as Jesus told it.

A lawyer engages Jesus the rabbi on a clarification of Torah. Jesus asks him, "Well, what do you think?" The lawyer replies, and Jesus affirms him: "Right answer. Do that and live." Only the lawyer wants more; he's testing Jesus. There's probably dissent in the community about a word or two, so he asks Jesus, "And who is my neighbor?"

Jesus finds all of us—Jewish lawyer, tax collector, bishop, senator, church musician, whomever—and exposes our fascination with our comfort, our habits, and our biases. The lawyer probably should have quit while he was ahead, but then we might not have this great parable to wonder about. Jesus is not going to leave him, or us, or anyone, ever, comfortable with the world as it is, because it has not yet surrendered to God's rule. Conversion is hard—it's hard like dying—but we are called to change.

Built into this parable about "some guy" (*anthrōpos tis*) who gets beaten up on the way to Jericho is a triad of characters who encounter his half-dead, beaten body on the side of the road between Jerusalem and Jericho. Jesus sets up the parable with an axiomatic trio: "priest, Levite, Israelite." This grouping is part of Jewish lore and jargon, the way "Three guys walk into a bar: a minister, a rabbi, and a priest" functions in many jokes.

Some homilists and teachers over the years have alleged that the priest and Levite were too preoccupied with the requirements of their liturgical duties to help the injured man. But Jewish law and rabbinic tradition put the care of the sick and burial of the dead above the purity laws of Torah, even for the high priest. Furthermore, the priest and the Levite were traveling *in the same direction* as the victim—that is, *down* to Jericho, away from Jerusalem and their ritual duties. So, the priest and Levite in the story fail in their calling to be *good Jews*. Once Jesus's listeners hear that the priest and the Levite have passed by the unfortunate traveler, they are able to identify with the hero. They are ready for the punchline, which should start with, "...but the Israelite...." Instead, it's an enemy, a hated Samaritan. The parable has gone off the rails.

We all want to be the hero, but now the hearers, ourselves included, have to reidentify or disengage from the story. Dr. Bernard Brandon Scott, professor of New Testament at the University of Tulsa, tells us that there are three choices. First, the hearer can say, "That will never happen." That's the disengage option: The story is fiction. The opportunity for change is lost. Second, the hearer can identify with the Samaritan. But this is impossible for most of us: to live in the skin of an enemy. The only other option is to identify with the victim. Here, there is hope, a glimmer of possibility for change. If we are willing to take a chance that our enemy might in fact want what is good for us, it may be possible for us to change our mind about our enemy. If that can be, then the world might be different. "The way things have always been" might become "the way things could be," might become "the reign of God."

So, the answer to "Who is my neighbor?" seems to be, "Anyone. Everyone. Maybe even my enemy." How is this even possible? We humans identify ourselves against others. Borders, fences, political parties, team colors, religious affiliation and non-affiliation, brands of computers and cell phones—there's no apparent end to the ways we differentiate ourselves from each other. In the most serious of times, principally between nations and blocs of nations, political parties, economic ideologies, and religious faiths, differences degenerate into name-calling, demonization of the other, attacks on property, and, ultimately and unavoidably, physical violence. Where do we turn for help in times like these?

Well, we turn to religious and civil authorities, who are no less vulnerable to the same biases and prejudice as the rest of us. We have seen, up close and in detail, the kinds of violence that can happen on a large scale: the Nazi holocaust, the Cambodian genocide in the 1970s, the Balkan wars of the 1990s, and the ongoing violence in the Middle East, particularly between Israel and Palestine. We've seen the consequences of racial hatred and the refusal of the white majority in America to accept responsibility and make restitution to the black minority for the action and effects of slavery every time we see, for instance, voter suppression laws enacted, or institutionalized violence against black people by law officers.

The law says that loving the neighbor and loving God are the same thing. The first letter of John goes so far as to say that anyone who says they love God and does not love their neighbor is a liar (1 John 4:20). But who is my neighbor? Jesus doesn't really answer that question. Instead, he tells a story about any of us, "some guy" or "this woman," who needs a neighbor, and discovers that a stranger who *acts* like a neighbor is just the person we need, even though we thought they were our enemy.

It seems impossible, but we've been lied to by our culture—all of us, in every culture, from birth. We have been taught who is like us, and who isn't. We've picked up our parents', our neighbors', our culture's marks of good and bad, right and wrong, friend and enemy, beloved of God and God's despised, and all of it is wrong. Like the fish swallowing the bait "hook, line, and sinker," we will die from our mistake. How can we escape the hell of fear and hatred of the different "other"?

Deuteronomy tells us that it's not only *possible* to live by God's law, but also "something very near to you, in your mouth and in your heart." You only have to carry it out. We are, after all, made by love, made for love, and the great lesson of life is to learn how to love fearlessly. Rather than absorbing more lies from our culture about who is good and who is bad, who's a friend and who's an enemy—judgments all based on the things we crave for ourselves that we're willing to pay any price to obtain, including injury, exploitation, and even war—Jesus tells us to imitate God, "for [God] makes his sun rise on the bad and the good, and causes rain to fall on the just and the unjust" (Mt. 5:45).

Finally, the great hymn from Colossians that is today's New Testament reading reminds us that by imitating Jesus, we are acting like God, out of the creative love that sustains the universe in all its parts, because Jesus Christ "is the image of the invisible God." As Pope Francis wrote in the first paragraph of *Misericordiae Vultus*, announcing the 2015 year of mercy, "Jesus Christ is the face of the Father's mercy.... Jesus of Nazareth, by his words, his actions, and his entire person reveals the mercy of God."

What is the alternative for us to being neighbor to our enemies? Scott suggests we consider Shakespeare's tragedy, *Romeo & Juliet*. The two lovers, from families engaged in a blood feud, dare to cross the line and fall in love, and secretly marry. The hatred between the families, as we all have come to know, brings calamity on both houses, irreversible loss and shocking desolation. Another image might be the scene from the movie *Gandhi*, when a Hindu man comes before the Mahatma, who is weakened by a hunger strike. "I'm going to hell! I killed a child! I smashed his head against a wall...because they killed my son. The Muslims killed my son!" This is no unseen or mythical hell of the afterlife, but hell on earth. Hatred is hell on earth. But that isn't the end of the story. After a pause, Gandhi tells him, "I know a way out of hell. Find a child, a child whose mother and father have been killed and raise him as your own. Only be sure that he is a Muslim and that you raise him as one."[1]

Among its attributes, the church of Jesus Christ is "catholic," or "universal." There is no "us and them" in "universal." Everyone is in. With Christ's, our eyes are on the victim and the needs of the victim, "some guy" on the side of the road. There is no other task than to serve the needs of the victim, because that is where God is. That is the place Jesus occupies for us, and where we know he will be found. To be a neighbor, we advocate for, nurture, empower, and restore the victim. That is the alternative to hell. Christ, the innocent victim, is the image of the invisible God.

---

1   *Gandhi*, directed by David Attenborough (Culver City, CA: Columbia, 1982), https://www.imdb.com/title/tt0083987/characters/nm0001426.

16TH SUNDAY *in* ORDINARY TIME

WILLIAM J. BAUSCH

"Mary has chosen the better part and it will not be taken from her."

1ST READING	2ND READING
GEN. 18:1-10	COL. 1:24-28
PSALM	**GOSPEL**
15:2-5	LUKE 10:38-42

THIS MARTHA-MARY STORY IS A FAMILIAR ONE. You may be surprised to find that it has two levels, one obvious and one hidden. Let's take the obvious one first, the one you're used to hearing.

We start off by observing that, in many ways, the surface Martha-Mary story has got to be one of the most annoying episodes in the gospels. It's annoying because it always seems to leave you between a rock and a hard place. If you're too much like active Martha, then you're all over the place and ignoring your host. If you're too much like passive Mary, then you're lazy and ignoring the necessities. Martha may be Martha Stewart, but you hate her for it. Mary may have chosen the better part, but dust balls are collecting underneath the beds.

I tell you, I've been to Martha's house. She's someone I haven't seen in a while, and I want to do some catch-up time. She has welcomed me with great enthusiasm. She has put out the best china and linens and served great desserts, and every time I look down, my coffee cup is miraculously refilled. She pops up and down to check the stove, the refrigerator, the microwave, and talks while moving about, until I've had it and finally exclaim, "For cryin' out loud, will you just sit down and talk with me?!" After all, I did come to be with her, not her dishes.

I have also been to Mary's house. The moment I arrived, she grabbed me by the arm and ushered me to the couch. We sit and talk, and talk and sit, sit and talk, and the hours go by and go by, and I'm getting hungry and beginning to feel faint. I have to cough before a glass of water is offered. The room grows cold and the window is open, but she doesn't get up to close it or turn up the heat. Well, I guess we had a good visit, but I leave cold, hungry, and uncomfortable.

In popular misconceptions, Martha and Mary come off like that: the Oscar Madison and Felix Unger of the first century. They're both wrong, of course, if they go to extremes, but, even so, it's Martha who usually gets the bum rap here: too busy with practical things. Why can't she be more like Mary? Why can't we?

But we have to stop making a false opposition between the activism of Martha and the quietude of Mary—action and contemplation—as if one were better than the other.

Jesus's remark that Mary had chosen the better part is not to dismiss the necessary business of Martha, but is meant to underscore balance, as if Jesus were saying to the Marthas of the world, "Stop what you're doing and reclaim your center." That is, "What are you doing all this for? Have you lost a sense of life's purpose? What motivates you? How does your life, your work, fit into the larger picture?"

Which is to say, if, like Martha, we are all action and no refection, we will soon dry up spiritually. Our lives will become empty routine, devoid of meaning and purpose. We all need to sit at the feet of Jesus now and then to discover *why* we're doing *what* we're doing. Remember, we're not here just to make money, but also to make a life—a life committed to faith, hope, and love.

If, on the other hand, like Mary, we're all reflection and no action, all talk and no walk, then what Jesus asked us to do goes undone: feed the hungry, give drink to the thirsty, and so on—and the world suffers. If we're all Martha, the center evaporates and burnout sets in. If we're all Mary, charity and service go undone. These two pioneering women,

Martha and Mary, aren't opposites, and we should not separate them. They are the yin and yang of a balanced spiritual life.

Now, with that being said and prayed over, let's move on and turn to a hidden and quite subversive part of this gospel that we miss, but that the ones who first heard the story didn't, and it surely gave them something to think about.

Let's go back to Mary. Take another look at what she is doing, where she is. The gospel says Martha "had a sister Mary who sat beside the Lord at his feet listening to him speak." Why is that sentence not at all shocking to us, but scandalous to those who first heard it?

Here's why. Give the customs of the time, where male and female roles were strictly demarcated, with women confined to the kitchen and the men to the parlor, Mary crossed boundaries!

She boldly came in where Jesus was and did what only men were allowed to do: She sat at the feet of Jesus. This, you must know, was the customary sign that someone wished to be a master's student, his disciple, something only open to men. There is, after all, that verse in the Talmud that states, "The words of the Torah should be burned rather than entrusted to women."[1] Mary ignored all this, presented herself as a disciple, and thereby assumed equality with men. Jesus not only allowed it, but also praised it—and so, once more, he turned the world upside down.

Now, note, lest you get your partisan antenna up, that this has nothing to do with an early kind of feminism. No, it fits squarely into Jesus's concept of universal worth and universal love. Jesus was being consistent here. He was constantly inclusive, much to the horror of his critics, as he touched untouchable lepers, healed the Roman oppressor's servant, cured a foreign woman's daughter, and broke bread with outcasts and sinners.

This happened once before, and here we have to reference another well-known gospel story concerning Martha. She appears in John's gospel, where she and her sister Mary are grieving over the death of their brother Lazarus.

Do you recall that it is forceful Martha who speaks up and dares to scold Jesus? She says, "Lord, if you had been here, my brother would not have died." But, more than that, it is Martha who, on this occasion, winds up making a stunning profession of faith every bit equal to that of

---

1 Jerusalem Talmud Sotah 3:4, as quoted in Rachel Keren, "Torah Study," *Jewish Women's Archive*, December 31, 1999, https://jwa.org/encyclopedia/article/torah-study.

St. Peter—who, at the village of Caesarea Philippi, in answer to Jesus's question, "Who do people say I am?" responded, "You are the Messiah, the Son of the Living God."

Well, here, near her brother's burial place at the village of Bethany, Martha says the same thing to Jesus. After Martha's complaint, Jesus had said to her, "Whoever believes in me, even if he dies, will live." And then he asked her, "Do you believe this?" And Martha responded, "Yes, Lord. I have come to believe that you are the Messiah, the Son of God, the one who is coming into the world" (John 11:20–27).

So there she is, proclaiming the same words, the same faith, as Peter, thereby becoming his female counterpart and a co-founder of the faith!

You can see why the first hearers of the Martha-Mary stories scratched their heads. Was Jesus saying that in his community of disciples, people are equal before God; that the oppression and the exclusion of others, so common in his time (and alas, as we are so painfully aware today, in our time), was not his way; that all—men and women, Jews and Gentiles, slaves and free—are called equally to sit at his feet, become his disciples, and treat each other equally? Apparently so, even though it took a long time for this to sink in.

His latecomer apostle St. Paul would write this, a few decades down the road: "There is neither Jew nor Greek, there is neither slave nor free person, there is not male and female; for you are all one in Christ Jesus" (Galatians 3:28).

I think that in giving our attention to the first part of the Martha-Mary tension, we tend to miss this subversive teaching of the gospel. But maybe the gospel gives us a clue on how to correct that. Perhaps, like Mary, we have to sit with it a while to get its import. Perhaps like Martha, once we get the message, we will act on it.

17ᵀᴴ SUNDAY *in* ORDINARY TIME

MICHELLE FRANCL-DONNAY

"Knock and the door will be opened to you."

1ST READING
GEN. 18:20-32

PSALM
138:1-3, 6-8

2ND READING
COL. 2:12-14

GOSPEL
LUKE 11:1-13

ABRAHAM IS BOLD. THE FIRST READING TELLS us he stood before God, and then took a step nearer. Abraham gets bolder still, daring to bargain with the almighty God for the lives of the just souls living in Sodom. Getting what he wants, he boldly asks for more, daring to go back again and again. Six times he pleads for mercy, not for himself, but for people he may not even know. And six times, God acquiesces. Even if there are so few righteous souls in Sodom that Abraham could count them on the fingers of his two hands, God says, "I will relent."

How bold are we in prayer? We can worry that we do not have the standing to beg God for anything, let alone anything for ourselves. We are not Abraham—or Jesus. We can think that our prayer should be eloquent and selfless, concerned with the big problems facing us and the world; that we should come before God tidy and recollected; that we ought to wait until we are in a church, or at least have a moment of peace and quiet. But as we hear in this gospel passage, Jesus asked none of these things of his disciples, nor does he ask them of us. Jesus doesn't demand poetic elegance; he gives us the words to say. He doesn't say, "Pray only for the big thing." He says,

"Pray for the simple things, the everyday needs. Pray for bread and mercy and patience. Pray for just enough to get through today."

In Luke's Gospel, Jesus urges us again and again to be persistent in prayer. Knock until the door is opened. Keep looking until you find what you seek. In the story Jesus tells of the late-arriving friend, the word translated as "persistance"—*anaideia* in the Greek text—could also be rendered as "shamelessness." There is nothing we can say that God will not listen to, no matter how insignificant it seems, and no limit placed on the frequency of our requests. Just as we cannot ask too much of God, we cannot approach God too often.

I am reminded of the work of Hubert Duprat, a French artist who uses caddisfly larvae to create small, jeweled sculptures. Caddisflies build their carapaces out of whatever is to hand, whether it's the gold and pearls Duprat offers them or the sticks and bits from the shells of dead snails they find in their natural habitat, turning all these things into shelters. Perhaps I need to take a few lessons from the caddisfly larvae and be willing to gather into my prayer whatever is at hand, precious or not. The weeds growing through the stones on the back patio, the construction that impedes my drive to work, the hurricane that threatens the homes and lives of thousands—all are worth bringing to God in prayer. And, just perhaps, in that gathering I might realize just how precious all these things are to the God who promises that not a sparrow falls from the sky unseen, to the God who loves me as a daughter.

Finally, Jesus does not prescribe where we should pray. He just says pray, pray to the Father who will always hear us no matter where we are. So yes, we can pray fervently for the light to change while sitting in the car with a howlingly hungry baby in the back seat. We can raise our eyes to the glittering stars on a clear night and pray in awe to the creator of the universe as we drag the garbage to the curb. We can pray when we are calm and recollected and when we cannot even scrape together the words to express the depths of our distress.

In the Our Father, we dare to pray, not just as Jesus did, but dare to pray *with* Jesus, as his brothers and sisters. We pray to *our* Father, for *our* daily bread. We pray this prayer as the Body of Christ, wounded and thirsting, but certain we are heard, certain we are held in the very heart of the Triune God.

Can we be as bold as Abraham? Can we be as bold as Jesus tells us to be? We can and should, for, as Jesuit theologian Karl Rahner reminded us, these prayers are a "pledge of [our] faith in the light of God in the darkness of the world, for [our] hope for life in this constant dying, for [our]...love that loves without reward."[1] So, dare to beg God for what you desire. Dare to be persistent. Dare to be shameless. Dare to pray for the improbable and the impossible. Dare to pray for the insignificant and the inconsequential. Pray boldly, as long as you have breath, for our God always bends down to listen.

---

1   Karl Rahner, *The Need and the Blessing of Prayer*, trans. Bruce W. Gillette (Collegeville, MN: Liturgical Press, 1997).

JOHN CHAFFEE

"Take care to guard against all greed."

1ST READING
ECCL. 1:2; 2:21-23

2ND READING
COL. 3:1-5, 9-11

PSALM
90:3-6, 12-14, 17

GOSPEL
LUKE 12:13-21

OF COURSE, MANY PEOPLE KNOW THE LINE from Ecclesiastes, sometimes translated as, "Meaningless! Meaningless! Everything is meaningless!" It sounds as though it comes from a soliloquy of Shakespeare, but it comes from an ancient and obscure writer that the book of Ecclesiastes names as Qohelet. The Hebrew word for "meaningless" is *hevel.* This ancient word can also mean "smoke, vapor, vanity, nonsense." The Jerusalem Study Bible translates it as "utter futility." *Hevel* shows up thirty-eight times in the book of Ecclesiastes.

This means that Qohelet keeps coming back to this final statement on meaninglessness. Like any good writer of wisdom literature, Qohelet is having a discussion with the world around him. He goes through all the various injustices that he sees, as well as the seeming futility of hoarding up riches, only to die too young to enjoy them properly. Of course, Ecclesiastes comes around in its final chapter with a surprising answer, but this refrain of Qohelet on the "utter futility" of the things of life is deeply profound.

On some level, from the first moment we read, "Meaningless! Meaningless! Everything is meaningless!" we already know it is true in one way or another. Think back to times at the beach, how the sandcastles you built were washed away in the tide. Or how about the chalk art you drew on the street that was washed away by the next rain (or the poorly placed sprinkler)? Looking at the experiences of our own lives, we might echo the author of Ecclesiastes: "Everything is meaningless."

And that brings us to the Gospel reading for today.

It all starts with a family feud: "Tell my brother to share the inheritance with me." In that culture, the first-born son received the majority of the father's inheritance. It is likely that this is being said by the younger brother of the family, who is looking for more inheritance for himself. There is no obvious statement by the brother about what his intentions or motivations were, but how Jesus replies might help us answer that question.

In response, Jesus exhibits what counselors and therapists today would call "good boundaries." He does the rabbi thing and replies to a question with a question: "Friend, who appointed me as your judge and arbitrator?" Then he proceeds to cut to the heart of the matter: "Take care to guard against all greed, for...life does not consist of possessions."

What Jesus then does next is absolutely brilliant. He tells a parable. More than that, it is a parable that leads us to wonder just how familiar Jesus was with the book of Ecclesiastes! Why? Because the Parable of the Rich Fool almost reads as if it were a parable straight from Qohelet!

The Rich Fool in the parable is presented with a problem. He has had a "bountiful harvest," and in his deliberations, responds to his abundance with a hoarding heart. Rather than share his bounty, he decides to build larger barns. Then, similar to the book of Job, God shows up and sets the record straight.

In the Scriptures, to be called "wise" is an incredible compliment, which means to be called a "fool" is not a happy event. The Rich Fool was planning on storing up his abundance for years and decides to take life easy: "Rest, eat, drink, be merry," *alone*. There is no mention in the parable of the Rich Fool's community or concern for others. Throughout the entire parable, the Rich Fool only ever talks to himself. Greed has the hideous ability to isolate us from one another, does it not? It can distort as well as distract. In addition to all of this, there is no mention of the Rich Fool thanking or praising God for his surplus, and clearly no inquiry to God as to what he should do with his surplus.

But what does it mean to be rich toward God? In context, richness with God is closely linked with loving one's neighbor. The final line of the parable cues us in on this reality. "Thus will it be for the one who stores up treasure for himself but is not rich in what matters to God." What if the opposite of storing things up for oneself is sharing that abundance with those in need? Is that what it means to be rich in what matters to God? The meaningless life is one that is spent in vain, solitary pursuits, one that seeks to store up goods for oneself, yet not to give even so much as a glance to others. The life that is rich in what matters to God is one that is rich toward others.

It is through this parable that Jesus invites someone in the thrall of their addiction to addiction to value something completely other. Christ calls each of us, through this parable, to utterly change our value systems and to devote our lives to that which cannot be taken from us. Christ is always calling us beyond our own survival and good life into pursuing the survival and good life for others as well. To shift from a me-oriented life to an us-oriented life is a holy transformation.

So, let's tie it all together. If we combine the insights of Ecclesiastes and the Parable of the Rich Fool, what do we get?

All our activities that are done in pursuit of selfish greed, hoarding, etc. are...

meaningless,

smoke,

vapor,

vanity,

nonsense,

utter futility,

hevel.

The Good News is that we do not need to spend our best time, energy, and resources just on ourselves. The Good News is that Jesus came to liberate us from our own selfish cycles of self-destruction. The Good News is that our lives are enriched, not impoverished, by sharing our lives with others. The Good News invites all of us up out of our own selfish meaninglessness and into shared lives with meaning.

And so, may we all be rich in compassion, generosity, and love. May we not hoard these riches for ourselves in larger and larger barns, but be rich in what matters to God by being rich toward others. Amen.

19ᵀᴴ SUNDAY *in* ORDINARY TIME

TIMOTHY SHRIVER

> *"Do not be afraid any longer, little flock, for your Father is pleased to give you the kingdom."*

1ST READING
WIS. 18:6-9

PSALM
33:1, 12, 18-22

2ND READING
HEB. 11:1-2, 8-19

GOSPEL
LUKE 12:32-48

ACCORDING TO ONE ACCOUNT, THE GREAT American poet Emily Dickinson believed that the whole Bible was captured in these three words: "Consider the lilies." Dickinson was ever brief and a master of the craft of packing meaning into tight phrases. But in these three words, "consider the lilies," she met her match. She didn't need more.

And yet I've never seen these words hanging in a home or carved into church doors. And I've never heard them quoted by political leaders or songwriters. The ten commandments are everywhere, telling us mostly what we shouldn't do. Admonitions to believe in Jesus's divinity are everywhere, telling us what we're supposed to believe ("I am the way.").

Teachings around forgiveness, service, and love abound. They're all good, and true, and beautiful in their own way.

But what about those lilies that are more beautiful than Solomon? Or the birds of the air that neither sow nor reap? What about this stunning teaching that we are held, cared for, beautiful, and precious, just as we are? What happened to the sacrament of the lilies?

I think we tend to avoid those lilies because they demand something so complete and intense that we can't imagine really *considering* them. After all, can we really trust that we're as beautiful as the lilies? Who among us trusts that they will be fed like the birds of the air? Really? Sitting in the pews, tired from a full week's work, trying to support children or parents or spouses or friends, knowing there are bills to pay and people to impress, it might seem foolish to trust God with our responsibilities. God may be many places, but in the work to pay for clothes and food doesn't seem to be one of them.

So, we may think, "Nice idea, those lilies, but not realistic." And that's the moment when we dismiss what might be one of the most powerful lessons of the gospel.

The great contemplative Thomas Merton, writing in the middle of the twentieth century, saw what so many of us so often miss. Merton's wildly successful autobiography, *The Seven Storey Mountain*, introduced the inner life of the gospel and the mysteries of Benedictine spirituality to millions of readers, both secular and religious. He wrote prolifically of his journey to get "to the heart of things." At the heart of things, Merton wrote in his *Asian Journal*, "the deepest level of communication is not communication, but communion. It is wordless. It is beyond words, and it is beyond speech, and it is beyond concept."[1]

The deepest level. That's where we need to go to consider the lilies. I think Jesus's teaching is offering us a precious key to unlock how we can learn to see from "the heart of things" and still make it in the world. I don't think he's telling us to quit our jobs or dress unattractively. But I do think he's revealing to us reality at its most subtle but powerful level—the reality at the heart of it all. "Consider" is a key word: Literally, it means to be with (*con*) the stars or heavenly bodies (*siderus*). I think Jesus is inviting us to draw our attention deeply into the wholeness of those lilies—to see

---

1   *The Asian Journal of Thomas Merton* (New York: New Directions, 1975), 308.

them as manifestations of the reality that is beyond words or concepts, but hiding in plain sight. It's as though we operate most of the time in distraction and anxiety and fear. Stay with any lily long enough to notice, to study, to dissolve, to drop into a level of consciousness where the beauty infuses everything and where we get a glimpse into the heart of God. It's all there—life, color bursting on the petals, the beauty of the thin stem, the reach toward the sun, the short life, the eternal cycle.

But lest you think this is all abstract, let's try it now by considering a fellow human being! Imagine you're at a Special Olympics race and you happen to catch the eye of one of the athletes—let's say a twelve-year-old with Down Syndrome. What goes through your mind (be honest!)? "She's sad"? "He's overweight"? "She can't speak"? "He won't go to college"? "Her mother must be a saint to manage all that"? "His father must be so disappointed"?

Now, see if you can put up a stop sign to all that thinking and just consider her. For even a split second, look deeply, as if considering a heavenly body. Close your eyes now, if you're comfortable, and consider that child. Let your heart soften to the beauty of the life in front of your eyes. Let your eye release itself from labels and judgment and fear. Just let them go. Do you notice the smile? The eyes of the child looking at you? The reflection of the hand of God? Try to notice the energies of love between this child and his parents, her friends. Consider. Can you sense that not even Solomon in all his glory is as beautiful? Can you see the precious lily in front of your eyes?

We spend so much time in the rat race, trying to look good, trying to compete, trying to prove we're right. But, as Anna Quindlen reminds us, "If you win the rat race, you're still a rat."[2] But beneath the distractions is a view of priceless value. It's not, as Merton wrote, "that we discover a new unity. We discover an older unity. My dear brothers [and sisters], we are already one. But we imagine that we are not. And what we have to recover is our original unity. What we have to be is what we are."[3]

What we are is just like the birds of the air, just like the lilies of the field: beautiful, cared for, precious. All of us are evidence of our original unity.

I'm with Emily Dickinson. "Consider the lilies" is enough for me.

---

2 Anna Quindlen, *A Short Guide to a Happy Life* (New York: Random House, 2000), 7.

3 Merton, *Asian Journal.*

20TH SUNDAY *in* ORDINARY TIME

"Do you think that I have come to establish peace on the earth?"

1ST READING
JER. 38:4-6, 8-10

PSALM
40:2-4, 18

2ND READING
HEB. 12:1-4

GOSPEL
LUKE 12:49-53

IT IS EASY TO READ TODAY'S GOSPEL FROM our contemporary perspective. Many of us have experienced the dysfunctionality of modern family life. As divorce has been so rampant in our culture, most of us have been touched by the pain of failed marriages, either that of our parents, or our own. Many of us also know the pain of family discord and the seemingly irreparably broken relationships between parents and siblings. These types of familial pains are not limited to us moderns; people have experienced some forms of broken familial relationships throughout time. However, this is not really what Jesus was addressing.

We read in Luke 8:21, "My mother and my brothers are those who hear the word of God and act on it." This declaration by Jesus takes on a particularly scandalous meaning when read within his own cultural reality. Familial relationships in first-century Palestine were a bit different than they are today. When I lecture on this, I tell my students that my public identity has little to do with my family. I am not known as Kyle ben

Jack (Kyle, son of Jack). I am just Kyle, or Father Kyle. While I love my father, my life as an adult in modern America is not one in which I spend energy trying to bring greater honor to my father or my family—though, of course, I don't want to do anything that would embarrass them. In Jesus's social world, bringing honor to one's father and family was a duty. Avoiding shaming one's family was a duty as well.

One of the titles Christians have attributed to Jesus is *Prince of Peace.* Many contemporary Christians have come to believe that Jesus revealed, in his words and actions, a God of nonviolence. For those who embrace this vision of God, the words of Jesus in today's gospel—when he says, "Do you think that I have come to establish peace on the earth? No, I tell you, but rather division. From now on a household of five will be divided, three against two and two against three"—are jarring, even a bit unpalatable. Is Jesus attributing violence to God and to himself? To see that he isn't, it is important to read this text in light of the whole of Luke's gospel.

The central theme of Jesus's ministry was to proclaim the kingdom of God. He attempted to bring people to understand that one's sole loyalty and commitment was to this kingdom. As idolatry was, and is, considered the greatest of sins in Judaism, this call to commit oneself completely to God and his will would not have been so revolutionary to the Jews of his day. But Jesus understood this loyalty in a radical and revolutionary way. Loyalty to God's kingdom meant that even long established, culturally defined social relationships were to be dispensed with in light of this allegiance.

One such culturally entrenched structure was the family. In Luke 8:21, Jesus is proclaiming among his followers a whole new familial relationship. While the Jews of his time would have defined family as members of one's religious and ethnic group, Jesus is claiming that one's true family consists of those who do the will of his Father—that is, those who may or may not be of one's biological, religious, or ethnic kin. This could potentially include non-Jews! This would have been considered ludicrous by many Jews who heard it. If one took Jesus seriously in his time, it is not hard to see how divisions and conflicts would arise in one's family. A change in social and cultural practice tends to have destabilizing consequences, and Jesus was perceptive enough to know that his teachings would bring about such conflict.

While Jesus's teachings about this new form of familial relationship may seem rather commonplace for us who live in a multicultural, multiethnic society and church, there is something more radical in Jesus's teaching, a radicality that many Christians miss, or simply ignore. Jesus states that one is a member of his family if they hear the word of God *and* do it! This is where the rubber hits the road. Luke's gospel records a sermon, the sermon on the plain, that can also be found, in a slightly different form, in the gospel of Mathew. This sermon captures the essence of Jesus's message of the kingdom. I recall, when taking a course on the gospel of Mathew in my doctoral program, that the professor gave us a list of quotes by various theologians over the centuries who tried to demonstrate that Jesus's sermon was either hyperbole or else a utopian idealism that could only be fulfilled in heaven. But, in fact, Jesus was not a utopian dreamer, an idealist spouting spiritual abstractions. He was calling for a radical transformation of human society, a metanoia, a transformation that St. Paul called a "new person."

If one reads either version of the sermon, one will recognize that the kingdom of God is radically different than the kingdoms of the world. Human history is replete with social divisions, social violence, oppressive domination of the strong over the weak, rich over the poor, men over women, and so many other divisions. Psychologists studying infant behavior have observed that from the earliest moments of an individual's life, there is a compunction to divide up into tribes. Tribalism seems to be a congenital defect of the human species. We feel good when we have a sense of belonging. In fact, we tend to bristle when we believe our group is being maligned, or attacked, or belittled. It is hard to overcome this natural tendency to form exclusive groups. Jesus faced this reality in his own day. His teachings, as shown by that on the family, went against a deeply entrenched cultural belief. He knew that his teachings would not only be rejected by many, but would create conflict and divisions in both families and society. Thus, he knew his words were not going to bring peace, at least not the kind of peace promised in the kingdom of God.

The peace that the world offers is very different from that offered by Jesus. The peace of the world is founded on human conflict. Such conflict is typically ameliorated by force, bringing about a form of peace that uses sanctioned violence, such as the police and military, to maintain social order and harmony. The peace of the kingdom of God is founded on nonviolence and a profound concern for those marginalized by structures of oppression. These all-too-human structures need the purifying fire of God's love. This is the fire of the Holy Spirit, who descended on the disciples and called them to ministries of reconciliation, peace, and healing. This is the word of God that we are called to do, making us truly mothers, brothers, and sisters of the Lord.

We too are called to be this fire that burns away hate and division and gives light to God's nonviolent love. This call starts with our own transformation, allowing the purify love of God to burn the dross that keeps us from being instruments of God's peace, God's reconciliation, God's nonviolent love. Those of us who reject the God of violence, who reject a tribal god of division and vengeance, may find ourselves rejected by those who believe that God is the God of the few, the chosen. But we must hold fast, hear the word of God, and do it by loving even those who reject us.

JOHN WHITNEY, SJ

"Will only a few people be saved?"

1ST READING
ISA. 66:18-21

2ND READING
HEB. 12:5-7, 11-13

PSALM
117:1-2

GOSPEL
LUKE 13:22-30

RECENTLY, I FOUND MYSELF SITTING OUTSIDE
my neighborhood coffee shop on a warm summer morning, reading the
news and bemoaning the truly disordered condition of the world. Sensing
my heart sinking deeper and deeper into despair, I repeat to myself the
litany of human-caused sorrows that seem to vary but never end.

I recall stories of enraged women and men, driven by dogmatic ideologies and denial, who condemn the "fake news" of the pandemic and
"moral compromise" of vaccines, even as their own sisters and brothers
fill hospitals and wear down an already fragile health community. Or of the
southern border, where people who are blessed by peace and power hasten
to return the most fragile among us to dangerous and violent homelands
on the questionable premise that mercy or even justice endangers our
freedom and may limit our prosperity. I think of Afghanistan, where the
Taliban, newly empowered after a misbegotten war, crushes the hopes of
women who have never had a voice, never known one day in which they
were not just objects in the plans of violent, ambitious men. Which leads
me back to thoughts of my own city and nation, where each day a dozen

veterans, forgotten by their government, take their lives in despair of ever truly returning home.

And as the litany of sorrow rolls on, I think of the leaders of the Church that I have so long served, who, un-humbled by revelations of abuse against children and indigenous peoples, continue to build barriers instead of bridges, acting as guard dogs around the table of mercy that Jesus's own blood and body has prepared for us.

With so many issues, vast and seemingly insoluble, rattling around in my brain, I feel my righteous anger rising, and I wonder if the whole world isn't going to hell. In a visceral way, I begin to understand the question of today's gospel: "Lord, will only a few people be saved?"—because it sure as heck seems that a whole lot of us won't be, and indeed, shouldn't be.

And just as I'm composing my list of who shouldn't be saved, a small dog scurries beneath the table, his pointed ears shifting—one up, one down, both up, both down—as he sniffs purses and book bags, apparently convinced we are holding out on him. Looking up, his brown eyes are full of expectation and joy; his tongue, slightly out, is panting. He knows nothing but this moment. For him, there is no global climate crisis nor Q-Anon conspiracy, no epidemic of lies nor sexual abuse crisis; there are no MAGA people or socialists, just hands that rub his ears or that he gets to lick for salt or crumbs left from the morning coffeecake. He is pure and present, fulfilling the end for which he was created: praising God by his joy at being the dog he is.

And suddenly, in that little face with its hopeful, hungry eyes, I realize that my righteousness is not what I imagined: it's not God's fury, but a dangerous temptation.

Caught up in the evil of the world, I too often become the very thing that leads me to despair: drawing circles and building walls—telling God to make sure *those people* are excluded, so that I can, in my own mind, guarantee my own inclusion. Here I am, on this beautiful day, long on hurt and outrage, but alarmingly short on the liberating virtue of humility, so present in this little dog. And in my outrage, the doorway narrows, not by God's work, but by my own.

So often, the question, "Lord, will only a few people be saved?" reflects not the love of God, nor even fear for my own soul, but my desire to exclude those "others" whom I find so annoying, to count myself among those who *merit* the kingdom that God offers. Yet, if that is *my* question, it is not Jesus's. It is I, or perhaps we—the self-righteous, the outraged—who want salvation to be narrow, so that only we can enter.

Yet, rather than affirm our narrowness, Jesus's reply is filled with ambiguity and challenge. "Strive to enter through the narrow door," he says, while never saying that this narrow door is the only way in. We must, he suggests, *strive* to enter by the narrow door—strive to live the difficult call of the gospels—for our own good, but that doesn't mean that the narrow door is the only entrance God can use.

What Jesus proclaims today is that we must stop trying to figure out who is excluded, stop comparing ourselves to others, as though their failures were a guarantee of our salvation. Like the little dog, we must be humble enough to love the people who come into our path, and to heal the suffering that we encounter, without judgment or self-righteousness. For in striving to close the gate, in laboring to bar the door, we may find ourselves on the outside, because there is no merit that can win us salvation—except the love of Christ for the world. There is no magic formula nor privilege that will let us in—not professing Jesus Christ as our personal Lord and Savior, not the fact that "we ate and drank in your company and you taught in our streets"—but only the grace of the God who enters this world of struggle and rage, of murder and foolishness, and loves it to the end; who gives his life into the hands of sinners and invites us to follow.

Thus, the true question of salvation is not: "Will only a few people be saved?" The question of salvation is: "Am I living as one loved and called to love?" Are we living, as a community and as individuals consecrated to life, open to this moment—to the little dog before us, and the beggar up the street, to the widow and the orphan, to our anti-vaxxer brother and our pro-choice grandma, to the wondrous variety and miraculous diversity of God's incarnation? Are we seeking to "strengthen [our] drooping hands and [our] weak knees" and welcome "all your kin from all the nations"? Are we laboring, not to build walls of judgment that will hold out the unworthy, but to set a table at which all may recline in the kingdom and mercy of God?

This is our mission and our salvation: to break open the doors of our hearts; to lay waste to the narrowness of our minds; to make room in our lives, in our parish, in our Church, for all those of whom God speaks when Isaiah proclaims, they "have never heard of my fame, or seen my glory; and they shall proclaim my glory among the nations."

22ND SUNDAY *in* ORDINARY TIME

THE REV. DR. MARGARET BULLITT-JONAS

"*Everyone who exalts [themselves] will be humbled, and the one who humbles [themselves] will be exalted.*"

1ST READING
SIR. 3:17–18, 20, 28–29

2ND READING
HEB. 12:18–19, 22–24A

PSALM
68:4–7, 10–11

GOSPEL
LUKE 14:1, 7–14

ONE OF MY LATE-SUMMER JOYS IS SPENDING A week of vacation at a family camp beside a lake in New Hampshire. Our little group relaxes by swimming, hiking, playing cards, and canoeing, and three times a day we gather for meals in the dining hall. The camp's dining-room tables are assigned according to an intricate system of ranking that is based on how many years each family has been coming to camp. The most coveted spots are the tables by the windows, where diners enjoy a breeze on a hot summer day, a direct view of the lake and woods, and perhaps the envy of other guests.

By contrast, the tables by the dessert tray are the least desirable, for there you are subjected to the hubbub of kids crowding your table as they pick up their ice cream. In between are the middling tables, deemed more or less desirable according to their relative serenity and lakeshore views. Week by week, as different families arrive and leave, the head waiter must sit down and figure out in advance who will sit where. As the years go by, the office manager must keep track of each family's progress away from the dessert tray. The goal, presumably, is to work your way upward until you, too, have earned the place of honor: a seat by the window.

Assigning tables ahead of time is one way of handling the human tendency to scramble for the best seats in the house. Everyone wants to be special. Everyone longs to be recognized as a person of worth. In our desperate fear that there isn't enough love to go around, we jostle against each another as we vie for a place in the sun. "Look at me! Value me! Admire me!" human beings implicitly cry out to each other. "Notice that I'm worth something! Notice that I'm *here!*" The urgent need to be recognized and valued turns into a search for power, and off we go, driven to make an anxious beeline for the places of honor, to guard whatever rank and position we have managed to attain, and to look down from our small eminence on the unfortunates who are stuck in the seats below, the people who presumably lack our talent, brains, or connections, or who simply haven't been coming to camp as long as we have.

But then, along comes Jesus, turning everything topsy-turvy, as he always does, interrupting our self-seeking and our insatiable appetite to be top dog. As Jesus suggests in today's parable, when we clamber over other people to grab the seat of honor for ourselves, someone more distinguished will eventually come along, and the host will send us down to the lowest table.

Competing for recognition and status is a fool's errand. Ironically, it leaves us even more vulnerable and insecure: There will always be someone more famous, wealthy, athletic, or beautiful than we are. If we insist on choosing the place of honor, watch out. "All who exalt themselves will be humbled," Jesus tells us, and he's right: When we proudly hold ourselves above other people, claiming to be superior for one reason or another, God will find a way to burst the bubble and send our pride packing.

Jesus suggests a more excellent way: When you are invited to a wedding banquet, choose the lowest place. Jesus is not telling us to cower abjectly in a corner, filled with shame and self-loathing. On the contrary, he is inviting us to experience true humility, which means being rooted and grounded in the love of God. Isn't it interesting that the word "humility" is closely related to the word "humus"? In the rich, loamy soil of humility we connect with the ground of our being, and we experience how fully and graciously God loves us despite all our faults and weaknesses. A humble person is someone who is secure in the love of God. When we know in all humility that our deepest identity is given to us by God—when we understand that love and power spring not from social status and recognition, but from the God who calls us "friend"—then we are set free from the endless, futile quest to promote ourselves, justify ourselves, and prove our worth. We can stop wasting our time in the pursuit of power or prestige. We can rest in the knowledge that we are loved to the core.

Humble people are people who feel their connection with all other people and with the rest of God's creation. Humble people are not doormats, but people whose self-worth comes from within—from the God who says, "You are my beloved."

Humility erases separation and isolation and generates hospitality; when you throw a party, says Jesus, open your doors wide and invite "the poor, the crippled, the lame, the blind" (Luke 14:13). Humility leads us to solidarity with those who have no social capital and with everyone who has been marginalized and oppressed.

Pride tells me to claim the head table, but God, in God's mercy, sends me back to the lowest table to learn humility.

Pride tells me to separate myself from the lowly and the outcast. Humility reveals my union with them.

Pride tells me that there is a shortage of love in the world and that (luckily for me) I am one of the fortunate few who is worthy of love. Humility tells me that God's love is boundless, and that I manifest that love when I stand with those who have been subordinated.

Pride tells me that I must forever earn, deserve, and hoard whatever recognition I can get. Humility tells me that at every moment, all of God's love is entirely mine and yours and ours, freely given and undeserved.

There is a revolutionary power to true humility. Humble people understand that God invites everyone to the feast, not just those of a particular race, gender, or class. A Spirit-filled energy of justice and love can propel humble people to challenge social arrangements that are organized around seizing resources and rank and holding on tight. A Spirit-filled energy can likewise propel humble people to challenge the lie that a particular species—Homo sapiens—has the right to claim the place of honor and to ignore the needs, hungers, and intrinsic value of the other species with whom we share our planet.

The surprise, of course, is that there is nothing grim, gloomy, or self-hating about true humility. Do you think that the people in Jesus's parable who chose to sit at the lowest table spent the meal picking at their food, hanging their heads in shame and self-hatred, and secretly wishing they could move up to a higher table? I don't think so. As I imagine it, there would be a lot of laughter and singing going on down there. If we slipped into one of the open chairs, we would discover that the hunger in our hearts for status and recognition had finally been satisfied. We would know that we were held in the embrace of God, that we exist within a vast circle of love that has no top or bottom. "Friend, move up to a higher position," the Host would say to us, but there would be no "higher"; the first would be last and the last would be first. Indeed, the terms "first," "last," "higher," and "lower" would no longer have any meaning. We would be gathered into the circle of love that brings everyone to the feast.

23RD SUNDAY *in* ORDINARY TIME

LUKE HANSEN

For who knows God's counsel?

1ST READING	2ND READING
WIS. 9:13–18	PHLM. 9–10, 12–17
PSALM	GOSPEL
90:3–6, 12–14, 17	LUKE 14:25–33

JUST A FEW MONTHS INTO HIS PAPACY, IN A wide-ranging interview that reintroduced Pope Francis to the world in an even more personal way, the pope was asked about the challenge of *seeking and finding God in all things*, the famous maxim of St. Ignatius Loyola.

His response may have been consoling to some but challenging for others.

"When we desire to encounter God, we would like to verify him immediately by an empirical method," the pope said. "But you cannot meet God this way. God is found in the gentle breeze perceived by Elijah."

Francis continued, "If a person says that he met God with total certainty and is not touched by a margin of uncertainty, then this is not good. For me, this is an important key. If one has the answers to all the questions—that is the proof that God is not with him. It means that he is a false prophet using religion for himself. The great leaders of the people of God, like Moses, have always left room for doubt. You must leave room for the Lord, not for our certainties."[1]

---

1   Antonio Spadaro, "Interview with Pope Francis," *Libreria Editrice Vaticana*, September 21, 2013, https://www.vatican.va/content/francesco/en/speeches/2013/september/documents/papa-francesco_20130921_intervista-spadaro.html.

I have to admit that I was surprised by these comments, coming from a pope. Isn't he supposed to help us to feel more certain about God, not less? Yet it seems that Pope Francis is inviting us into a deeper mystery at the heart of faith.

The writer Anne Lamott gets it. In her bestselling *Plan B: Further Thoughts on Faith*, she writes, "The opposite of faith is not doubt, but certainty."[2]

This is the wisdom of today's reading from the Book of Wisdom, where we hear a version of Solomon's prayer to God for the gift of wisdom, "That she may be with me and work with me, that I may know what is pleasing to you" (9:10).

"For who knows God's counsel, or who can conceive what the Lord intends? For the deliberations of mortals are timid, and uncertain our plans," Solomon prays. "Scarcely can we guess the things on earth, and only with difficulty grasp what is at hand" (9:13–14, 16).

The way to know God and God's counsel is through the gift of Wisdom.

We hear echoes of this message in the Book of Job. When Job challenges God, God reminds Job that he was not there when God created the universe.

Job's response: "I have spoken but did not understand; things too marvelous for me, which I did not know" (Job 42:3).

In short, we are not God. We live in that mystery.

It's why the theologian Karl Rahner preferred to call God "an always-ever-greater Mystery."

We make big decisions in our lives based on what we think God wants for us, only to realize later that God is inviting us down a different path. Even though we may have had the best of intentions, maybe we were short-sighted and didn't really know ourselves.

It's good to take a moment to reflect on our lives and notice how we have changed and how God has been a part of this growth and maturation.

As we continue our journey, can we have a healthy skepticism toward our certainties and instead place our trust in God's spirit, holy Wisdom, to reveal and lead us to the next step? And can we be open to being surprised by God?

Maybe this challenge and invitation is not only for individual believers but for our faith community as well. Even the Church needs to stand

---

2   Anne Lamott, *Plan B: Further Thoughts on Faith* (New York: Riverhead, 2005), 256–257.

with humility toward its history and some of its teachings and practices. What are some of the ways that we as a Church have felt certain, only later to realize that our perspective has shifted and our understanding has changed?

In today's reading from the Letter to Philemon, St. Paul writes about Onesimus, a slave who had converted to Christ and is being returned to his "master." Paul does refer to Onesimus as a "brother" and "beloved" (1:16), but he does not condemn the ownership of human beings as an intolerable violence against human dignity.

Concerning slavery, the teaching of the Church has evolved, thank goodness, just as it has changed on other questions like usury, religious freedom, and capital punishment. Remembering this history should help us to walk forward with humility. Where else do we not yet have the complete picture, the full truth?

I think especially of the question of women's leadership in the Church. For centuries, women were regarded as naturally inferior to men and naturally subject to men in the social order. In our time, there's a new appreciation for the equality of women.

Today, rather than approaching the question of women's leadership with certainty about what women can or can't do, based on a previous view of God's will for eternity, maybe we can approach the question with humility and an openness to change. Where is holy Wisdom leading us today?

In *The Joy of the Gospel*, Pope Francis shares this conviction: "Whenever we make the effort to return to the source and to recover the original freshness of the Gospel, new avenues arise, new paths of creativity open up, with different forms of expression, more eloquent signs and words with new meaning for today's world."[3]

What are these new paths in our lives and in our Church? We don't know. Come, holy Wisdom. Guide us in *your* ways.

---

3   Pope Francis, *Evangelii Gaudium: The Joy of the Gospel* (Dublin: Veritas, 2013), 14.

24ᵀᴴ SUNDAY *in* ORDINARY TIME

DEACON JIM KNIPPER

"Everything I have is yours."

1ST READING	2ND READING
EXOD. 32:7–11, 13–14	1 TIM. 1:12–17
PSALM	**GOSPEL**
51:3–4, 12–13, 17, 19	LUKE 15:1–32

GOOD MORNING, AS WE GATHER ON THIS twenty-fourth Sunday in Ordinary Time, a Sunday that has been designated by the American Catholic Bishops as Catechetical Sunday—a time to pause as a community to celebrate and applaud those who minister by teaching our faith. It is a time that we recognize and give thanks to those teachers and volunteers who work within our parishes, and a time to remind our catechists—and all of us—that we are called by God to love one another, as God has loved us, by what we say and do. And today's Gospel gives us insight into what that love looks like.

Without a doubt, this story of the Prodigal Son is by far my favorite Gospel passage, for it is one of the greatest stories ever told. Judged by the Pharisees and Scribes for not being as "holy" as them, Jesus tells this parable to focus his disciples on the divine law of love and compassion versus Mosaic laws of cleanliness.

Now, many people think that the word "prodigal" means one who runs away, or one who comes back. Rather, the word refers to someone who recklessly squanders what they have. For, in this story, we have a young son who sees what he has and what he has coming to him and takes it all:

runs off with it and squanders his wealth until, broken and hungry, he comes back home to his father, looking for forgiveness.

Then there is the older brother, who also has all the wealth and love of his father but doesn't see it and thus cannot appreciate it. He is angered by his father's forgiveness and acceptance of his brother who has returned.

And lastly, we have the father, who loves his two sons without judgment or conditions. And he gives his love and forgiveness away to his sons in a way that could be considered blessedly reckless and prodigal in nature. Through his words and his deeds, he defines for us a "character of being" that is Christ-like.

But I am afraid that many of us live our lives like the brothers. Perhaps we are like the self-absorbed younger brother who wants nothing to do with family or friends and is just focused on self-gratification. Or maybe we are more like the resentful, dutiful, righteous older brother, who refuses to come to the banquet because he feels that, unlike his brother, he is the one who has done all the right things, has followed all the rules and regulations, and is not being properly recognized.

But, through Luke's story, we are called to be like the prodigal father, who shows his love by seeking, caring, coaxing, waiting, watching, welcoming, and honoring those in his life. Through his actions, he recklessly gives abundant love for others.

This care for others brings me back to this celebration of Catechetical Sunday and why the Church sets aside one Sunday a year to remind all of us about the importance of catechizing. The word "catechize" means to teach by word of mouth *in order to promote a change or transformation in another.* So, while we live in this highly visual world of video, email, and text messages, catechism in the early church, and still today, requires this verbal storytelling and careful listening—it is one reason why we proclaim the readings at mass—so that the words will be heard...so that the words will teach...so that the words will transform.

So, we are very grateful to those who give of their talents to support our schools and religious education programs which transform our children. But let us keep in mind that the reason Catholic education is so important is that our teachers do more than just teach the faith. They institute, nurture, and cultivate personal change in our children. They provide our children a foundational, Christ-centered character.

But that work must begin and be supported at home. So, this is also a time to remind all parents of our responsibility as the primary teachers of our children's spiritual education. It is a promise we made in our wedding vows—that we will accept children lovingly from God and raise them well in the Catholic faith.

It is the call that is embedded in the final blessing that we, as parents, received at the baptism of our children—that we are to be the first and best teachers of our children. And it is a mission that does not end at our child's Confirmation, but rather lasts a lifetime, by what we say and do.

But if Catholic education is to thrive, it requires the whole *ecclesia*, the whole church—i.e., all its members, without exception—to use our gifts, our talents, and our financial resources to come together for a common cause, for we are all called to catechize. When St. Paul was describing the gifts God had given the church, he listed teaching as one of the most important. And the last mandate of Jesus, to all his followers, was to go and teach! Thus, we often hear our pope call for us to go out from our churches into the streets to be Christ to others—even if it makes people feel uncomfortable. For by virtue of our baptism, we are all sent forth to teach, all charged to catechize, all tasked with teaching others, all called to use the talents that God has given us. And, in doing so, we transform ourselves, we transform our children, and we transform each other.

And that is why we gather here each weekend for a Eucharistic celebration: so that we can be nourished and so we can nourish others. It was the Jesuit theologian Robert Taft who said that the purpose of Eucharist is not only to change bread and wine, but to change you and me, for through Eucharist it is we who are to become Christ for others.

You see, Luke tells us this story of the Prodigal Son (or, as I call it, the Prodigal Father) so that we will be reminded of what it means to be like Christ: the Christ who is reckless and prodigal with his love, the Christ who can't wait for us to return home, the Christ who is filled with compassion, the Christ who pleads with us to come to his party—to come to this table—and the Christ who wants us to be teachers of his way of life.

So, as you know, this Gospel story is unfinished. We are left with the brother standing outside in the yard, listening to the din of the party going on inside, wondering if he will accept his father's invitation to come to the table. Thus, the story is left for us to finish, but so is our own personal story. Will we stand outside, claiming to be right, and counting and measuring those who aren't, or will we go inside and belly up to the table next to those who have done it differently and not perfectly—keeping in mind that we are all one, united by the love that God pours upon all of us, in such a reckless and prodigal way?

25ᵀᴴ SUNDAY *in* ORDINARY TIME

RICHARD ROHR, OFM

"You cannot serve God and mammon."

1ST READING
AMOS 8:4-7

2ND READING
1 TIM. 2:1-8

PSALM
113:1-2, 4-8

GOSPEL
LUKE 16:1-13

LET ME START OUT BY SAYING THAT THIS Gospel consists of a number of passages about money that have been thrown together. For I think Luke knows, just as Jesus knew, that most of us, myself included, have a confused, guilt-ridden, obsessive attitude about money. There's hardly anybody who can think in a clearheaded way about it. So, to break this Gospel open, let's begin with the end, where the Gospel writer creates a clear dualism between God and what he calls mammon—a word that we do not use anymore. Mammon was the God of wealth and money, superficiality and success. And we are told that, "You finally have got to make a choice."

Now, most of Jesus's teaching is what we call non-dual. You've heard me talk about this in the past, where he'll say, "Let the weeds and the wheat grow together." Another passage would be, "My Father's sun shines on the good and the bad." But there's one area where he is absolutely dualistic, where "either or" is how it must be said, and it's anything having to do with the poor and anything having to do with money.

He's absolute because he knows what we're going to do. Most of us will serve this God, Mammon. It's even called "mammon illness," and maybe we all have a different kind of mammon illness. It's basically searching for short-term practical gains—and we have to say it: Money does serve to solve our short-term problems. And so, we're all eagerly hoarding it, collecting it, multiplying it, saving it, and after a while we're preoccupied with it because it serves short-term needs.

Now, what I hear Jesus saying in this whole gospel is what would be a long-term answer, which is to seek relationship over money. I think I learned this most strongly over the years when I was able to preach in Asia and Africa, the Philippines, and poor countries where they don't have insurance, or a 401(k) like we do. Do you know what their insurance policy is? Their family. They stick together much more strongly than we do. We really don't need one another and often don't even care about one another. In most poor countries, you have to love and honor your parents. They're all you've got. And the parents have to love and respect the children, because the children are going to take care of them in their old age. All the bonding of these relationships is your 401(k). So, once you know that the real security system is how you relate and how you love, these are the eternal dwellings that last forever.

Now, what's mammon illness? Mammon illness is attained when you think all of life is about counting, weighing, measuring, and deserving. We all think that way! And then we go to places that have sales so we don't have to give so much and can get the same thing. My mother spent much of her years cutting coupons to save 10 cents. And that was good, I guess, but she was still counting, weighing, measuring. It's very hard to get rid of that addiction. Often, we start doing it as soon as another person approaches us. What can she give me? What can I get out of him? How can I get this for cheaper? That's mammon illness.

To enter into the kingdom of God, you have to stop counting. You have to stop weighing, you have to stop measuring, you have to stop deserving, and you have to just let forgiveness and love flow through you. That's a high-level conversion. I admit, I don't think any of us start there, but we learn it from the way God loves us.

The bottom line is that the love of God can't be doled out by any process whatsoever. You can't earn it, you can't lose it, and as long as you stay in this world of earning, losing, weighing, and measuring, not only will you cut yourself short, but you'll expect the same of everybody else. You'll start counting why she isn't very good or why he doesn't come to Mass every Sunday. We get stuck on counting who is not Catholic, who is gay, who is different from us in some way. It never stops, it never stops, it never stops. It's the only game in town anymore: Who's worthy?

But once you dive into the ocean of infinite love, infinite forgiveness, the game is over. And first, you must let that infinite love flow into you and through you toward others.

It makes us so much happier to stop counting, but I have to admit, I'm still a child of my mother, internally cutting coupons. How can I get a better deal? How can I get a better bargain? How can I save money? It's no good. It creates a worldview that we call a worldview of scarcity. Because once you start counting, there's never enough, never enough. The kingdom of God is a worldview of abundance, and it's God who has to lift us up and take us from a worldview of scarcity, which is all about measuring and weighing, into a world of abundance, which is infinity.

So, let God get you there.

26TH SUNDAY *in* ORDINARY TIME

JOHN J. FISHER

"Father Abraham, have pity on me."

1ST READING
AMOS 6:1A, 4–7

2ND READING
1 TIM. 6:11–16

PSALM
146:6C–10

GOSPEL
LUKE 16:19–31

THROUGHOUT MY LIFE, I HAVE MADE GREAT use of mnemonic devices. So, when I first heard of Aquinas's four "substitutes" for God—namely, power, pleasure, prestige, and money—I used my Latin to change money to *pecunia* and forever referred to them as the Four Ps. Not that I needed the memory tool, as they often plague my spiritual life.

Soon after, I was sitting at a lecture given by a former law professor at Notre Dame, David T. Link. After losing his wife and getting ordained, he was asked by his Bishop to minister in prison. He remarked that he was serving those put in prison by students he taught. Now, he was teaching and serving the least, the lost, the lonely, and the last. I said to myself, "the Four Ls, the antidote to the Four Ps." To be legitimately Christlike, to forget about self and serve others, to be other-centered and singularly focused on Christ, we too need to encounter the least, the lost, the lonely, and the last, for in them we find Christ profoundly present.

The rich man and Lazarus are representative of both groups, the Four Ps and the Four Ls, the haves and the have nots, the rich and the poor. We can easily visualize this Gospel scene and deeply sense the longing of

Lazarus, who would gladly have "eaten his fill of the scraps that fell from the rich man's table." The rich man did not heed the third "woe" we hear from Amos today about those "complacent" and "secure," who "lounge upon their couches," eating freely, excessively absorbed with self, without any regard to the need of another.

This "turning on self" in his life of power, pleasure, prestige, and *pecunia* prohibits the rich man from longing for that which can truly sustain and satisfy. Amos could have warned him of the fate that awaited him of being "the first to go into exile, and the carousing of those who lounged shall cease." Luke vividly describes the rich man's torment, brought on by his selfishness, and his desire for Lazarus to "dip the tip of his finger in water and cool [his] tongue." Finally, the rich man has a longing, a care, a need, but it's too late. In his misery and eternal suffering, he finally recognizes Lazarus, no longer sitting at his doorpost, but now in heaven, served and cared for by the angels. In his desperate situation, in need and in pain, the rich man now wants to relate to Lazarus. So severe is his torment that it seems he becomes other-centered for once, asking Abraham to warn his brothers, so they don't suffer his loss. They must be too far gone, as Abraham responds that if they are not listening to Moses and the prophets (like Amos, who challenged hypocrisy and injustice), they are not going to listen to him, someone raised from the dead.

We have another—more important than Moses, the prophets, and Abraham: the first raised from the dead, Jesus Christ. Luke's Gospel is peppered with stories of Jesus seeking the least, the lost, the lonely, and the last. One of Luke's consistent themes is Jesus's concern for the lowly, the downtrodden, the poor, the outcast, the sinner, the afflicted, and those who depend on God for mercy, compassion, acceptance, and an answer to their longing. Mary sings this in her Magnificat, noting the Lord looks with favor on the lowliness of his servants, lifts them up, and fills the hungry with good things while sending the poor away empty. In Luke's Sermon on the Plain, Jesus blesses the poor, the hungry, those weeping, hated, excluded, and insulted—that is, the least, the lost, the lonely, and the last—promising them a rich reward awaits them in heaven.

Complacency, self-absorption, excess, and the like often prevent us from recognizing another in need, another who is our sister and brother. Mother Teresa often noted that the problem with humanity is that we frequently forget that we belong to one another. So, those hurting continue being ignored, kept on the periphery, never invited into that "circle of kinship" that Fr. Greg Boyle, SJ exhorts us to seek. If we remember those times we felt least, lost, lonely, and last, and how God's compassion, especially through another, brought us into love, acceptance, and kinship, then we will be empowered to do likewise.

There are millions of people in Lazarus's situation today, starving for their next morsel. Millions more die and/or suffer from infirmities caused by hunger. As Jesus asked Philip how they could feed the five thousand, he asks us, too, to address the hunger and thirst of our world and church. If we focus on what God has given us rather than what we do not possess, then put these gifts in God's hands, mini miracles can occur daily, and we will see abundance with much left over.

Not at our doorpost, but at the gate entrance of our parish parking lot, sits a trash can that our homeless search through for "scraps" left by other homeless. When we see this, we can stop them and offer a sandwich instead. And then, we can examine how to better serve the least, the lost, the lonely, and the last, our sisters and brothers who belong to us and the circle of kinship.

In the spirituality of St. Francis de Sales, "the most extreme type of poverty was separation from God. Francis de Sales had a regard for the frailness of the human condition and believed that the difficulties of this life would be replaced by reward in the next."[1] Thus, we could assume that the rich man was wallowing in a spiritual poverty that caused him to ignore the needs of others or even fail to recognize their personhood. It cannot be so with us. We can draw inspiration from the "cofounder" of Salesian Spirituality, St. Jane de Chantal, who, before entering religious life, served the poor well at her husband's baronial estate. Long lines awaited her where, from her kitchen window, she dispersed food, medicine, and other goods to the poor in the area. When some of her assistants complained that people were getting right back in line for more, she reminded them of the many times a day we return to God for mercy and forgiveness. I am reminded of this often when the homeless and addicted return to our doors at what always seem to be the most inopportune moments, with their act

---

1   "Francis de Sales," *Vincentian Encyclopedia*, July 11, 2014, https://famvin.org/wiki/ Francis_de_Sales#Salesian_poverty.

still not together, in need of more, of acceptance and recognition. They remind me of myself. They are Christ and they are me and you!

We cannot ignore those hungry for food, recognition, a voice, acceptance, understanding, and forgiveness, for they are Christ waiting for us to serve him. Let us do so and one day we may hear, "I was hungry and you gave me food, I was thirsty and you gave me drink."

27TH SUNDAY *in* ORDINARY TIME

27TH SUNDAY *in* ORDINARY TIME

BRIAN McLAREN

"Increase our faith!"

1ST READING
HAB. 1:2-3, 2:2-4

PSALM
95:1-2, 6-9

2ND READING
2 TIM. 1:6-8, 13-14

GOSPEL
LUKE 17:5-10

"GIVE US MORE FAITH!" THE DISCIPLES ask Jesus.

But Jesus says no. He refuses!

Can you believe that? Why would Jesus ever refuse a request for more faith?

This is a question of vital importance, isn't it? What's going on here?

Whenever you're perplexed by something in Scripture, I've found that it makes sense to look more closely, to examine even the small details of the text to see what you're missing. When we give the story a closer look, here's what we see: When the disciples ask for increased faith, Jesus points to a nearby mulberry tree. "If you have faith the size of a mustard seed," Jesus responds, "you would say to this mulberry tree, 'Be uprooted and planted in the sea.'" Perhaps he's saying something like this: "Guys, you're asking the wrong question! It's not that you don't have enough faith. The problem is that you aren't using the faith you already have!"

I think we can see ourselves in the disciples. When things aren't going right for us, we think the problem is that we lack something. We need more of something. But maybe that's not our problem. Maybe our problem is that we already have what we need. We're just not using it.

If that's what Jesus means, it makes sense of the strangely harsh parable Jesus tells next, about slaves who should do their full day's work before they get their dinner break. In other words, if you're just doing your job, don't expect a standing ovation and a huge trophy. Before you ask for more faith, before you ask for dinner, be sure you're using what you already have. Be sure you're doing what's already in your power to do.

And what is it that is in our power to do? If we look at what happens right before this interchange, we find the answer: We're asked to forgive those we have a grudge against. And that, I think, helps us make sense of Jesus's strange and fascinating refusal of the disciples' request.

When the disciples say, "Give us more faith," they're saying, "We can't forgive others, especially those who keep failing us. To do that, we need more faith." And Jesus responds, "If you had even a tiny bit of faith, you could do amazing things, unbelievable things. So stop asking for more faith, and start doing what you can already do with the faith you have!"

What does that mean for you today, right now? Is there someone you need to forgive? Then just do it. Do it now. Do it because it's right. Do it because you can. Stop making excuses.

Let's get specific. Is there some group of people you are prejudiced against? Some group of people you assume the worst about—Democrats? Republicans? Russians? Venezuelans? Socialists? Capitalists? Texans? New Yorkers? Or maybe your prejudice is racial, or class-oriented, or related to sexual orientation? What if you heard Jesus say, "Enough. No more excuses. Get over it and let go of your grudge. Choose compassion instead of critique. Choose mercy instead of judgment. The problem isn't those other guys. The problem is you. The problem isn't that you can't. It's that you won't. So now's the time."

Maybe it's your carelessness about the environment, about this precious earth and its beautiful creatures. Maybe you see God's creation as little more than an oil well or coal mine or lumberyard for you to plunder for wealth, or maybe you see it as a toilet bowl in which you can pour all your trash and waste. And maybe Jesus is looking at you when he says, "No more excuses. It's time. You can change. You don't need more faith. You just need to exercise the little faith you already have."

The prophet Habakkuk knew that faith isn't simply a matter of lofty spiritual feelings. It's a down-to-earth matter of survival. When he says,

"The just one who is righteous because of faith shall live," he's saying, "The righteous will *survive* by their faith." Like us, Habakkuk lived in a violent time. He lived in a time of environmental instability too, a time when a drought or a flood could mean that the fig trees, the vineyards, the olive groves, the wheat fields, and the pastures of sheep and cattle could fail, leading to economic collapse. (He underscores this danger at the end of his prophecy.) In a violent time, in a time of ecological and economic instability, you'll fall apart unless you have faith—even faith like a grain of mustard seed.

But that faith isn't an escape from your duties. It's what motivates you to do what you can, to do what you must, to do what's yours today.

Let's be honest. Some of us come to church to feel pious and warm and fuzzy, and in the process, we're avoiding taking action that we need to take. There's a difference between talking about faith and feeling all faith-y and actually having a little kernel of faith that makes a difference in how we live.

Faith is a matter of survival, my friends. The way to get more faith isn't simply to ask for it. The way to get more faith is to use the little we already have by putting it into action.

Otherwise, we're just playing a religious game and wasting both Jesus's time and our own.

28TH SUNDAY *in* ORDINARY TIME

THE REV. PENNY A. NASH

"Has none but this foreigner returned to give thanks to God?"

1ST READING	2ND READING
2 KGS. 5:14–17	2 TIM. 2:8–13
PSALM	**GOSPEL**
98:1–4	LUKE 17:11–19

I HAVE A FRIEND, A FELLOW CLERGY PERSON, with whom I have had many conversations about prayers used in public worship. We worked together for several years and both of us, at one point or another, were in charge of creating bulletins for various worship services. We had a bunch of resources for prayers, and it was our custom to cycle through several of each kind during the church year. While each of us had our favorites, he also had a particular pet peeve about the selection of prayers to be used by the congregation after receiving communion. Out of the four or five prayers on the "approved list," two of them did not include some version of "thank you." They said nice things about God and encouraged us to go out into the world to serve, but they didn't explicitly say, "Thank you." When it came time for one of those prayers to be used, I knew that he would grouse as he always groused: "I don't like using this prayer. Where is the 'thank you'? What are we teaching our people who have just received the Body and Blood of our Lord Jesus Christ?"

As a child, when it was my time to say grace before a meal at our family table, I said the only one I knew in a sing song voice: "God is great, God is good. Let us thank him for our food. By his hands we all are fed. Thank you Lord for daily bread. Aaaah-men." Two thank yous, my mother taught me early on. You can't say it enough. Perhaps my friend's mother taught him similarly.

Even if I don't always do it, I want to practice gratitude. I have read all about how much better my life will be if I cultivate that practice. And I experience it sometimes, that feeling of well-being after expressing sincere gratitude to either a friend or a stranger, a family member or a co-worker. "Thank you," I say, "I really mean it," and I do.

I certainly experienced it when I received my COVID-19 vaccination. I thanked the National Guard guys directing us for parking as we drove into the facility. I thanked the check-in lady and the guy who asked us all the questions about our symptoms, or lack thereof, before entering. I thanked the nurse who gave me the shot. I thanked the person at the door on the way out. I couldn't say "thank you" enough because my heart was bursting with joy and relief combined with a great letting go of months and months of fear and dread. I cried while I said "thank you" to pretty much everyone I came near throughout the whole vaccination event.

But it wasn't until that night, in my bedtime prayers, as I was thinking over my day, that I realized, or decided, I should also say, "Thank you" to God for giving human beings the skill to create the vaccine and the will to make it available to everyone.

In our postmodern age, we are more likely to put our trust in human skill and institutions than to acknowledge that God is at the heart of all our gifts and graces. We are uncomfortable with, even vehemently opposed to, those who eschew medical intervention and wait instead for miraculous healing from God without human intermediaries. At the same time, we wonder why it seems that God gives us these terrible burdens to bear—incurable diseases, for example. We wonder if prayer is effective anymore—is our "Have mercy on me, Lord, and heal me" even heard by God? And what if God does hear but does not heal? What then? These are heavy questions, and I can understand why people ask them, even if I have no answers.

But what I do know is this: It is a radical thing now to give glory to God for things that are provided by humans. Even when the ten lepers in

Luke's story were healed by Jesus, only one of them, a foreigner, stopped to say thanks to him. Like city children who do not know where their food comes from, but simply accept that it has appeared on the table, we are conditioned to simply accept the mercies and grace and blessings with which we are showered. And it is only perhaps when we are in dire distress that we can see beyond our feelings of entitlement. We feel good that we have what we have, but we may have forgotten to say thanks.

The good news is that God desires to heal us no matter what. We are God's beloved, the apple of God's eye, and God loves to show us mercy even if we are forgetful of or inattentive to that mercy. But Jesus reminds us that, even so, even when we have to squint to see God's hand at work in our busy lives, it is good to give God thanks and praise.

It is good to say thank you—and maybe even say it twice!

29TH SUNDAY *in* ORDINARY TIME

L. PATRICK CARROLL

"When the Son of Man comes, will he find faith on earth?"

1ST READING
EXOD. 17:8-13

PSALM
121:1-8

2ND READING
2 TIM. 3:14—4:2

GOSPEL
LUKE 18:1-8

THE IMAGE OF MOSES IN TODAY'S FIRST reading fascinates me. It offers a primitive, even ugly image of God, but the story of Moses is great! Picture him with his arms up as the battle goes on. When he keeps them up, the good guys win. When he lowers his arms, they start to lose. He needs to get props, people, use anything or anyone he can to help keep those arms up.

Can we keep our arms up when things get difficult?

This question meshes with the gospel words: "When the Son of Man comes, will he find faith on earth?"

Can we hang in there, believe, hope, struggle, be faithful in the face of suffering, hardship, apparent failure? Can we plead to the ear of an apparently deaf God? Can we show faith as persistent as a nagging widow seeking her due?

The focus in the scriptures today is not so much on the God who answers our prayers, but on our keeping praying, believing that our prayers will indeed be answered.

Let me look with some care at the Gospel.

One morning, I was about half asleep when I heard a slightly crazy neighbor, Daphne, out looking for her dogs—at about 6:30 a.m. Her screeching voice woke me. I thought of the judge in this parable. I too would have done anything I could to stop the screaming. This story of the widow asking for help is taken by Luke from a similar story in the Wisdom of Ben Sirach, a passage in which a widow prays persistently, and God answers her prayer.

Luke's Jesus changes this story in two significant ways. First, the widow is screaming. She won't stop screaming. She is a "nag," not just faithful. She leans dangerously close to obnoxious.

Secondly, God is strangely imaged as a very negative character, a rascal of a judge. This judge has no respect for God or anyone. He has no shame. The implication is that he does his job by taking bribes, helping whoever most crosses his palm. He makes no pretext of fairness, of justice. He is in this just for the money (and thus very difficult for us to grasp in our era, because it's so unlike any judge, or lawyer, these days!).

The widow does indeed have a case, but she is a woman in a man's world. As a woman, she cannot even get into the courtroom. She has no money. She certainly has no man in her life, or he would be interceding for her. She has no power. She cannot bribe the judge. She cannot get a hearing.

So, she stands outside the courtroom and screams her head off; she keeps yelling, hour after hour, day after day. I love the image, and I hear Daphne out in the street below my window.

Many translations of verse 5 have the judge choosing to render a decision "so that she may not wear me out by continually coming." "Wear me out," I am told, is, in the original language, a boxing term, which explains why it is rendered in the New American Bible as "strike me." It literally means she "has opened a cut under my eye." "Made my eye open" is obviously a pun we miss in translation!

Read from one vantage point, the story is about hanging in there in our prayer, because if this corrupt, unscrupulous judge will respond, how much more will God. But the deeper point of the story is more subtle. The subtext is that it may well seem that God is not listening, hearing, or responding. Can we keep on asking, even then?

To grasp this parable, it is important to hear the final line. "When the Son of Man comes, will he find faith on earth?"

Some have read this as Jesus saying something about the end time, the so-called second coming. I prefer the reading that suggests the centrality of the title *Son of Man*. The *Son of Man* is precisely a Messiah who will—who does—suffer. When the messianic presence you have waited and hoped for turns out to be a suffering messiah—taking on himself the vulnerability, fragility, and pain of the entire history of humanity—will your faith persist? Jesus asks whether, when he scandalizes the religious folks and the civil authorities by being arrested, crucified, and killed, when he is "lifted up," will faith still persist?

Jesus is saying, "Will you keep believing in me when I come precisely as *Son of Man*? Will you keep your arms up then?"

This was a question for the disciples who, in fact, *fled when it occurred*. It is a question still.

I read this parable as a challenge to persistent faith, to keeping our arms up, to continuing to shout about justice and peace when it doesn't seem to happen—when things even get worse.

I remember my dear friend Fr. Bill Bichsel—who spent his life fighting for nuclear disarmament, for justice on many levels, who lived with former felons—saying once, with a huge smile, that everything he had ever worked for always got worse...but he kept praying, kept struggling.

Can I keep my faith active when so much poverty abounds in our land, when so many are not cared for, when children still suffer, mass killings continue, our earthly home is being destroyed, and all these concerns are barely mentioned in a national election? Can I keep trusting, praying, and hoping when my life seems to fall apart into little pieces, and I can give no concrete reason for my hope?

When Jesus comes as the Son of Man, overwhelmed in suffering, can I keep praying, keep my arms up, keep believing in the face of the cross because I trust that God is faithful, God will answer, will be more benign than that unjust judge?

Some days more than others, this seems like the right question to bring to Eucharist, where we are caught up into the death and resurrection of Jesus as we celebrate the fidelity of God—no matter what.

30TH SUNDAY *in* ORDINARY TIME

THE REV. TIM SCHENCK

"God, be merciful to me a sinner!"

1ST READING
SIR. 35:12-14, 16-18

2ND READING
2 TIM. 4:6-8, 16-18

PSALM
34:2-3, 17-19, 23

GOSPEL
LUKE 18:9-14

IT WAS A THURSDAY MORNING AT 6:30 A.M.
It was dark and cold and pouring rain. Two clergymen were slogging through a six-mile run at a local state park. As my running partner and I were discussing the upcoming gospel for Sunday morning, we were simultaneously feeling quite pleased with ourselves for our virtuous dedication. We weren't like those *other* runners who wimped out. The ones who looked out the window, turned off the alarm, rolled over, and stayed in bed.

And it occurred to both of us that we didn't actually need to *talk* about the parable of the Pharisee and the Tax Collector from Luke's gospel because we were *enacting* it. We were being self-righteous and regarding others with contempt—precisely what Jesus warns us against—because, while we were *half*-joking, our comments mirrored that Pharisee whose prayer begins, "God, I thank you that I am not like the rest of humanity."

I love this passage because of its absurdity, but it also resonates because of its reality. I don't think anyone actually prays like this—thanking God because they are better than others—but we all certainly act like this at times. We are all vulnerable to pride and self-righteousness, mostly because it makes us feel good! It lifts us up and sets us up as better than others—which in itself is laughable, but it's also deeply embedded in the human condition. Sometimes it comes so naturally and subtly that we don't even realize we're doing it. So, it's not really a matter of *whether* we adopt the attitude of the Pharisee in this story, but of *how* we do so.

You may not actually kneel down in a pew and thank God that you're not like that strange-looking guy sitting two rows in front of you. But when you gaze deeply into your own heart, perhaps part of you gives thanks that you're not like those other people in that lower tax bracket. Or like those other people who live on the "other side of the tracks." Or like those other people who don't have a college education. Or don't have a job. Or don't have legal immigration status. The list goes on and on. And so, when you thank God for the blessings of this life, are you really thanking God that you aren't like those other people who are not similarly blessed?

This is a hard question, especially in light of the example Jesus holds up as the one who is more righteous. This tax collector, this outsider, this sinner is precisely the type of person we're likely to be thankful that we're *not*. He is the epitome of that "rest of humanity." And so, highlighting his virtue is shocking—and it certainly would have been to Jesus's original hearers. But his approach to God—his abject humility—is precisely how we need to enter into authentic relationship with the divine.

Why? Because this tax collector trusts in God without condition. He recognizes that all that he has and all that he is comes from the Lord. The Pharisee, on the other hand, trusts exclusively in himself. Even though he does all the right things in his outward relationship with God—he prays regularly and tithes his income—he has in fact supplanted God with himself. And that's what Jesus is warning against: trusting in the power of our selves rather than the power of God.

Self-justification is an interesting thing. I may not be the best parent, but at least I feed her regularly. I may not pledge to the church prayerfully and intentionally, but at least I put something in the collection plate when I show up on Sunday. I may not clothe the naked, but at least I brought in a bag of clothes I no longer wanted for the clothing drive. I may not be Mother Teresa, but at least I send a check to the food pantry every year.

We all do a lot of good things: bringing in clothes for the needy, sending money to charity, pledging to the church. These are all good and holy things, just as it is good and holy that the Pharisee fasts twice a week and gives a tenth of his income to the Temple. But we could all do more. Jesus doesn't condemn us for not going further, but he extends to us the invitation. The well of good works that flows from faith is deep. God loves us and rejoices in who we are, but we are also continually challenged to go deeper as disciples of Jesus Christ.

Ironically, it is the Pharisee's outward religiosity that proves a barrier to God's grace. When he goes to the Temple, he stands by himself to pray. Wanting to maintain his purity before God and remain undefiled by that "rest of humanity," those sinners, he stands apart. He isolates himself from the mass of sinful people. The tax collector, on the other hand, stands "off at a distance," beating his breast, and "would not even raise his eyes to heaven." And so, the posture of these two mirrors their individual prayers: "God, I thank you that I am not like the rest of humanity" versus "God, be merciful to me a sinner!" One is a prayer rooted in self-righteousness; the other is a prayer rooted in God's mercy. One is a prayer of self-exaltation; the other is a prayer of humility. And Jesus makes it quite clear which approach brings a person closer to God.

I find it interesting that much of the liturgical language of humility has fallen out of favor over the years. It's seen as overly penitential, even as groveling. The emphasis has rightly shifted to the joyfulness of God's presence among us rather than the utter depraved sinfulness of humanity. But if we never use the language of humility before God, we tend to forget our place in the world. Our self-righteousness can take over and we slowly but surely put ourselves on the same plane with God rather than taking our place as humble servants of the living God.

We are worthy as long as we recognize our place in relationship to God: Without God, we are utterly hopeless. And this is easy to forget in this age of self-affirmation, self-reliance, self-indulgence, and self-justification. Amazingly enough, we are worthy as long as we remember our complete unworthiness.

These days, I tend to be the runner who looks out the window and then goes back to sleep if it's raining. But I remain confident that God still loves me, even when I fall short—in exercise, or prayer, or faithfulness. That's the good news of this parable, and I bid you to revel in God's loving mercy.

31ˢᵀ SUNDAY *in* ORDINARY TIME

RICHARD ROHR, OFM

"Zacchaeus, come down quickly, for today I must stay at your house."

1ST READING
WIS. 11:22–12:2

2ND READING
2 THESS. 1:11–2:2

PSALM
145:1-2, 8-11, 13B-14

GOSPEL
LUKE 19:1-10

TODAY'S FIRST READING IS ONE OF MY favorites in the whole Bible, and it's hidden away in the Book of Wisdom. I've used it often, even given it to people who hate themselves—and that's a lot of people. Either by reason of abuse, gender, race, or whatever, it seems like we find endless reasons to believe that we are unworthy.

But listen to this. "Before [the Lord] the whole universe is like a grain from a balance, or a drop of morning dew come down upon the earth"—and nations think they're so powerful. The Bible says nations are just a grain of sand. They're all going to pass away.

"But you have mercy on all, because you can do all things; and you overlook sins for the sake of repentance. For you love all things that are and loathe nothing that you have made; for you would not fashion what you hate. How could a thing remain, unless you willed it; or be preserved, had it not been called forth by you?" It seems to be a universal assertion, no exceptions. If it exists, God chose it to exist, even so-called "bad people."

"You spare all things, because all things are yours, O Ruler and Lover of souls, for your imperishable spirit is in all things!" It doesn't say in some things. It says in *all* things. Don't try to make any exceptions: "The black people don't have it. The gay people don't have it. The poor people don't have it. The handicapped people don't have it." We *all* have the imperishable Spirit of God. You may not, you must not, make an exception.

"You rebuke [us] little by little, warn [us], and remind [us] of the sins [we] are committing, that [we] may abandon [our] wickedness and believe in you, Lord." So, the little trials of our life are not punishments. They're trials to wake us up.

So, with that as the message, let's read a little of the Gospel. This is a favorite for many people. It's called the Gospel for Short People like me. The short guy, his name is Zacchaeus. Now, the stage is set with someone who is unworthy, that we should not like, that we would mistrust. He was a chief tax collector. That means he's an oppressor of the Jewish people, and a non-Jew. And he was a wealthy man. Can you make any connection there? Of course. How did he get wealthy? By overtaxing people.

He ran ahead and climbed a sycamore tree in order to see Jesus. When he reached the place, Jesus looked up and said, "Zacchaeus, come down quickly, for today I must stay at your house." He came down quickly. When he came climbing down the tree, he was earnest—sincere, it seems. He received Jesus with joy.

Now, when the people saw this, they began to grumble. We have Jesus, clearly by his own invitation, eating at the house of a so-called sinner. Can you make any parallels to today? We're going to have a meal in a few minutes. I don't think Jesus would be in the least interested in who of you is worthy, and who of you is a sinner, and who of you is not a sinner. You all are, and I am, too. Just get over it.

Then he stands his ground and apparently we see he was a very good man, more generous than I am: "Half of my possessions, Lord, I shall give to the poor, and if I have extorted anything from anyone I shall repay it four times over." Does anybody here do that?

So, first of all, he looks like a bad guy. By the end of the story, he's a good guy. We know he's a Gentile, like us. That means he's not a Jew, he's an outsider, and Jesus invites himself for dinner and says, "Today salvation has come to this house because this man too is a descendant of Abraham."

Now, it's very clear who the descendants of Abraham are—the Jews. He's just included an outsider in the group. Then, here's his closing line, to show what he's all about: "I didn't come for the nice guys. I didn't come to the perfect people." You know why? Because there aren't any. The human one came to "save what was lost."

So, it seems to me we'd be much more alive, awake, and aware if we admitted that we were lost, and we don't get it; that we haven't been right; that we've made mistakes. That leaves the soul wide open to receive mercy and grace. That's exactly what the first reading said—that this is what God is about. He shows equal favor to all things, and all our making of distinctions—deciding some are up and some are down, some are good and some are bad—are by our own selfish criteria.

Let's just rest inside of an infinite love that even we cannot comprehend and cannot receive. (When we've received it totally, then perhaps we're in a position to tell other people who has it and who doesn't.) You'll see that even the worst of people still have one part of their life where they're loving—at least, that's been my experience. And the best of people still have one part of their life where they're quite selfish, like me.

We're all in this together, brothers and sisters, and the kingdom will descend when we can stop seeking superiority, stop seeking status because it doesn't mean anything to God. All the nations, the whole universe is as a drop on the scales of eternity. So, if the nations and the universe are a drop of sand on the scales of time, what are you and what am I? To live inside of that natural humility is to live free, to live without any reason for comparison, competition, or judgment. Such a world is a world in which love can happen.

32ND SUNDAY *in* ORDINARY TIME

ANNA KEATING

"They can no longer die, for they are like angels; and they are the children of God."

1ST READING
2 MACC. 7:1-2, 9-14

2ND READING
2 THESS. 2:16—3:5

PSALM
17:1, 5-6, 8, 15

GOSPEL
LUKE 20:27-38

WHEN I WAS PREGNANT WITH MY FIRST CHILD, I signed up for a Lamaze class. Once a week for six weeks, my husband and I sat in the waiting room of our OBGYN's office with other expectant couples. We learned breathing exercises, studied the stages of labor, and took notes on when to go to the hospital and what to bring.

I loved and trusted my teacher. She was a nurse who had herself given birth to five children using the techniques she was now teaching us. "This is doable," I thought. "She is proof."

In our last session we learned about caring for newborns. Then the teacher asked if we had any questions.

I raised my hand. I asked, "How do you get your baby to sleep on a schedule?"

I am a person who likes routines.

The teacher just smiled and said, "Newborns don't really have a schedule. At the beginning, they eat and sleep on demand, 24 hours a day. Sometimes they 'cluster feed' and want to nurse more frequently, other times you get lucky, and they sleep for a long stretch. At the beginning, you just follow their cues, follow their lead."

I remember being annoyed. There's no schedule? There's no routine? You just *follow their lead*? How was that possibly going to work? How would I be able to plan my day? Surely there was some kind of trick to getting them on a schedule.

Sure enough, a few weeks later our son Clement was born—with health issues, which means he wasn't one of those babies that sleep trains themselves by four months. There was no schedule, not for a long, long time. My plans went out the window as my husband and I fed and cared for our sick baby, on demand, all through the night, even when we were exhausted. We got up, and changed him, and comforted him, and burped him, and took him to his doctor's appointments, and *followed his cues*. And, in the process, we bonded and were transformed into totally different people, into parents: the kind of people who could die to themselves and put aside their to-do list, for love.

Looking back on it now, as a mother of three, I laugh at my own question about getting a newborn on a schedule. And I realize that my Lamaze instructor did give me an answer. She told me, as kindly as possible, that I was asking the wrong question, by telling me that my life, after my son's birth, wasn't going to look exactly like my life before his birth. What she was saying to me, and what I couldn't yet hear, was that in the process of loving him, I was going to be transformed.

So, I sympathize and identify with the Sadducees in today's Gospel. They are questioning Jesus about the resurrection, which they don't believe. How many times have I, like them, not believed?

Like me, the Sadducees were born into relative privilege and comfort. They came from the upper echelon of Judean society, and it's often harder for privileged people to believe in miracles, because miracles, like babies, are incredibly disruptive to routines. They unsettle the social order. They disrupt. And when things are going pretty well for you, you tend to like to keep your world as it is.

The Sadducees didn't believe in the resurrection. They couldn't imagine it, any more than I could imagine taking care of a baby all through the night and then doing it again and again and again. So, they question Jesus. How could it be possible? What would the resurrection even look like? Wouldn't it be awkward? If a woman has had seven husbands on earth, which one will she be married to after the resurrection? The question itself is telling, because it's so tied up in respectability, in social norms. These men were the guardians of the Temple. They were educated in right and wrong. Surely heaven couldn't include a woman with seven husbands?! What would people think?

And Jesus answers them, as kindly as possible, by suggesting that they are asking the wrong question. He teaches them: You can't picture the resurrection. You can't picture a future in which the dead are alive again and all the wrongs have been put to right. It won't be exactly like this world, except without death. In the resurrection, you will be equal to the angels. There will be no marrying or giving in marriage. You and your legalism will be transformed. To paraphrase Flannery O'Connor, even your supposed virtues will be burned away.

The resurrection is not about creating an exact copy of this world in another location. What matters is not who will be married to whom. What matters is not the seating arrangement. What matters is that it is the will of the Father that no one should be lost. What matters is that we were baptized into Christ's death and resurrection. We went down into the waters of baptism with Him, and we rose with Him. We are part of His mystical body. Every time we receive Jesus in the Eucharist, we are reminded that we are joining ourselves to Him. He has bound us to His side. And nothing, not even death, can separate us from the love of God. We are one body in Christ. We don't have to understand it fully. We can't understand it fully. We can only ask for the grace to live as if it were true.

Because what are the fruits of faith in the resurrection? Saints. Heroes. People with such a secure bond, people so rooted in God's promises, that they are able to do and withstand impossible things with great courage and generosity and love. In the first reading, the Jews are being tortured and murdered "rather than transgress the laws of [their] ancestors." What sustains them? Faith in a God of justice, who will raise them from the dead. They believe, in spite of everything, that evil and hatred will not have the final word—that Love will.

We too believe in the beatific vision, that someday we will behold His face. All of us have known pain, and all of us will know loss. All of us will know the cross. Jesus is giving us strength, hope, and encouragement, that there is a yet another room, in this house called life, a room we have yet to discover.

This is the faith that has strengthened the saints, our spiritual ancestors, and so I lean on them when my own faith is lagging, just as I might lean on the person next to me today in the pew. Just as I might silently ask them to say the creed on my behalf, when, like Mary and Joseph searching for three days, I seem to have lost Jesus.

Just as it comforted me, as a first-time mom, to look at my Lamaze instructor, a woman who had walked this path five times. "If she could do this," I thought, "if she could be so transformed and live, so could I." It comforts me to know the stories of those who have gone before me in faith.

When the people we love die, we are rightly grieved because we don't want to lose them. And Jesus is telling us to take heart, that an eternal relationship in and with God is possible, and that just because we haven't yet been transformed into the kind of people who can fully live it or understand it, doesn't mean it isn't real. Our limited vision does not diminish or determine the eternal vision of God.

33RD SUNDAY *in* ORDINARY TIME

DEACON JIM KNIPPER

"Not a hair on your head will be destroyed."

1ST READING	2ND READING
MAL. 3:19–20A	2 THESS. 3:7–12
PSALM	**GOSPEL**
98:5–9	LUKE 21:5–19

AS WE BEGIN TO WIND DOWN THIS LITURGICAL
year on this last Sunday of Ordinary Time, we celebrate the Rite of Acceptance, where those previously known as "inquirers" become catechumens and candidates. At this liturgy, we will officially welcome and recognize the catechumens' decision to begin the process of becoming a member of the Roman Catholic Church through Baptism and welcome the candidates into the process of full communion with the Church. This first public ritual of their journey is important for all of us, in as much as the word *catechumen* means to re-echo—a reminder for all of us to be re-echoing our faith with these men and women.

But, after listening to today's readings that deal with end times and this type of apocalyptic literature that makes us squirm a bit in our seats—what is it that we are to be taking into our own lives and thus resounding into the hearts and souls of our catechumens? Perhaps a second look at the time this apocalyptic literature was written, as well as how the destruction of the Temple comes into play, may just help give us some direction and insight.

Around the time that this Gospel was written, not long after Jesus died, the Roman armies came down and ravaged the whole of Israel. Taking over Jerusalem, they starved the people and destroyed the Temple, which had been rebuilt some 500 years earlier. Over a million people died in that devastating outrage, leaving only one wall standing, which still stands today—what is known as the Wailing Wall. This devastation is the social context in which Jesus first followers lived, taught, and died...and Matthew, Mark, and Luke all wrote apocalyptic theology to express the fear of it all.

In our own lifetimes, we have seen the destruction of great buildings, the horror of the holocaust, continued nuclear testing, global warming, rising ocean levels, and species becoming extinct—no doubt plenty of fodder for the street-corner prophets warning that the end is near. When will this all happen? No one knows, but frankly, it is the wrong question, and we can't be wasting time worrying about it—because timing is not the point. Rather, our focus needs to be on the Christ who dwells within each of us, no matter what we have done or what we have failed to do. And one of the more insightful explanations of this indwelling comes from theologian N.T. Wright, who begins where our Gospel begins today, and that is with the Temple.

Wright's explanation of the indwelling actually goes back to the first stone temple of the Jewish people, which was built around 950 BC. And the Old Testament tells us that on the day of the dedication of "Solomon's Temple," the *Shekinah*, or glory of YHWH, in the form of fire and cloud from heaven, descended and filled the Temple, just as it had once filled the Tent of Meeting. For the Jewish people, this became the assurance of the abiding and localized divine presence of YHWH and made Solomon's Temple both the center and centering place of the whole Jewish world.

So, imagine the crisis of faith that had to have taken place in 587 BC, when the Babylonians destroyed the Temple and took the Jews into exile. After all, the Temple was where God lived! More than a century later, the people were convinced that they had to go back to Jerusalem and rebuild the Temple so God could be with them again. But N.T. Wright points out that there is no account of the fire and glory of God ever descending on this rebuilt "Second" Temple, which is the only temple Jesus would have ever known and loved.

The absence of visible *Shekinah* glory must have been a bit of an embarrassment and a great source of anxiety for the Jewish people. Wright states it could explain the growth of the hypocritical belief in Jesus's time that if ritual, liturgical, and moral laws were obeyed more perfectly, then the Glory of God would return to the Temple. This is the common pattern in moralistic religion: that our impurity supposedly keeps God away. Despite how hard they tried, and all the altar sacrifices they made, the fire never descended, and they surely must have wondered, "Are we really God's favorite and chosen people?" But then again, isn't this issue of worthiness still a popular question for many people today?

With this background, the events of Pentecost carry so much more meaning. For, on that day, the fire from heaven descended, not in a tent or a stone temple, but on *people*! The Spirit filled *all* peoples—not just Jews! After his conversion, it was Paul who understood this and spent much of his life drawing out the significant consequences. For, in that moment, Christianity began to see itself as universal rather than a tribal religion, which is why they very soon called themselves "catholic"—literally "universal." No wonder St. Paul loved to say, "You are the Temple!"

So, you see, my sisters and brothers, apocalyptic literature is not written as a prophecy about future events. Rather, it is about imminent reality—the here and now. But the reality has nothing to do with how much we can earn God's love in order to be the chosen ones. Rather, it has to do with recognizing and living through the inner presence of Christ, for the supreme idea of Paul is that the new temple of God is you and me—and not the temples and walls of our lives that we like to construct and adorn with jewels.

But that doesn't mean that our lives will always be perfect or without issues. On the contrary, we all have our impurities, we all carry our certain crosses...where life, at times, seems filled with angst, and anxiety, where we find ourselves in that liminal space where there is no going back and yet no clear sense of going forward...and where this end-time literature may seem to resonate the most.

But with God there are no ends—only beginnings, for the deaths which we face every day eventually lead to resurrections! The presence of God is made known and visible not by earning it, but by being instruments of mercy and consolation: when we choose to love, when we choose to forgive, when we choose to reach out to others. When, through our brokenness, the Light of Christ is allowed to shine through our cracks. For when you and I stand in that place, we become quite usable by God—where very real healing, and forgiveness, and answered prayers take place. And once we see it...and live it...and are free to re-echo this and love others through it, then, whenever and wherever we face our final days, we will witness a final victory over death and a new life with the risen Lord.

Feast Days

TRINITY SUNDAY

SHIRIN McARTHUR

The love of God has been poured out into our hearts through the holy Spirit that has been given to us.

1ST READING
PROV. 8:22-31

2ND READING
ROM. 5:1-5

PSALM
8:4-9

GOSPEL
JOHN 16:12-15

LET US PRAY: HOLY GOD, IN THE TRINITY YOU model divine relationship for us. Bless our reflections on the nature of your nature, and your call for us to live in loving relationship with you, each other, and all the world. In Jesus's name, Amen.

My husband, Henry, and I have three wedding anniversaries—and thus three chances to forget(!). There have been years when two of those anniversaries have fallen on the same day, but all three have never again occurred at the same time. Have I confused you? Here are the three anniversaries: May 29, the Sunday of Memorial Day weekend, and today: Trinity Sunday.

Henry and I were married on Trinity Sunday. We call this our *liturgical* anniversary. Although we didn't schedule our wedding with this in mind, it has enriched our understanding of our marriage. It's also a great way to talk about our relationship with God. On our wedding day, we were celebrating and deepening our commitment to our relationship and receiving God's blessing upon it. On the same day, the church calendar was also celebrating a relationship.

In fact, Trinity Sunday is the only church feast that celebrates a relationship. There are feasts celebrating events in the life of Jesus, like Christmas and Easter. There are feasts that celebrate the holy men and women who, throughout the past two millennia, have influenced the lives of the faithful. But this is the only feast that celebrates a *relationship*—the particular relationship between the three persons of the Trinity.

I love the lectionary, even when it challenges me. Historically, for many people, Trinity Sunday has been a challenging feast to preach about. Church leaders and scholars have written a lot over the centuries, attempting to explain how God can be "three in one and one in three." Attempting to explain separate facets of a single coexistence, using lots of big, fancy, theological terms—frankly, it makes the mind glaze over after a while.

For me, it's really about Matthew 7:16: "You will know them by their fruits." The fruits of the Creator are this marvelous creation in which we live, and move, and have our being. One of the most beautiful fruits of the love of this Creator for creation is the gift of Christ, who lived on earth as Jesus to reveal that love when we got seriously off-track in our relationships, with God and with each other. Then Christ and God, together, gave us yet another gift—the Holy Spirit—so that we might each hold within us a spark of that divine Trinity. If we are willing and open, that Spirit will, as Jesus says today's gospel, guide us to all truth.

Over the quarter century of our marriage, the Holy Spirit has guided Henry and I to, and through, many truths, many experiences, and also a number of afflictions. We've survived broken bones, surgeries, and a variety of other illnesses. We've lived through a child being wrongfully arrested and a grandchild's battle with cancer. We've said a lot of goodbyes, living in ten different homes during our first twenty-five years of marriage.

We don't always boast of our afflictions, but we can definitely relate to Paul's assurance that affliction produces endurance, endurance proves our character, character sustains our hope, and our hope in God has never been disappointed. We might sometimes be confused, or frustrated, or impatient, but in that *deeply ultimate* sense of sustained, and sustaining, relationship with God, we have never been disappointed.

Once in a while, Trinity Sunday is also Father's Day. Henry has been a biological father for over forty years now, and a clergy Father for almost ten. I see the vocation to fatherhood as a very real calling from God because, as Paul says, "the love of God has been poured out into our hearts through the Holy Spirit that has been given to us."

Sometimes Henry's fatherhood has manifested in unusual ways. One autumn, Henry was ministering near the US/Mexico border in Nogales, Sonora when a twentysomething Venezuelan woman came up to him (probably because he was wearing his clergy collar) and asked where to apply for asylum. He explained that there was a long waiting list, and helped her get on that list. Then he offered to escort her to a safe house where she could find refuge while she waited.

As they walked, the young woman told him her story. Venezuela was a country in chaos, where the inflation rate hit one million percent, fertile fields lay empty, and the capitol of Caracas had the highest murder rate in the world. The president embraced a state of emergency and used his super-powers to brutally squash dissent. As a college student, she was thirsty for justice. She dared to join a dissident group, shepherding youth in active demonstrations against this police state and posting about it all on social media. As a result, she was targeted, beaten, and just managed to escape being kidnapped. Fearing for her life, she left home and traveled over 3,000 miles in hopes of finding a new and safer life in *Estados Unidos*.

Henry and his colleagues talked more with this woman as she waited her turn at the border. Because her government had targeted her, she was naturally fearful of being handed over to the US government. Henry and I talked, prayed, and agreed that, if ICE would allow it, we would be willing to host her during the asylum-seeking process.

Unfortunately, when she crossed the border, she immediately disappeared into the government system. For days, we did not know where she was. Then we learned she was in the detention center in Eloy, Arizona, a 45-minute drive from our home. We did apply to have her released into our custody, but ICE denied the request.

She ended up staying in the Eloy detention center for six long months. Talk about affliction producing endurance! We visited her as often as we could, but visitations were limited to weekends, so we saw her once a week for an hour. We were as faithful as possible, because we believed God had called us to be in relationship with this woman.

Her first court hearing was in January. She pled guilty to entering the country without a visa and requested asylum. Her second hearing was at the end of February, when she presented her paperwork, with the help of a lawyer. At that hearing, she was granted a final hearing date, for the presentation and decision on the case, on June 10. That was a tough day for her—learning that she would have to spend over three more months in what felt like prison. We went to every court hearing, so she knew she wasn't alone, but she had plenty of opportunity to develop her character through endurance.

And she took advantage of her opportunities. She applied to work in the detention center library, despite her very limited English, and convinced them she could do the job. She worked hard every day to learn English, making friends with detainees from half a dozen other countries, ranging from China to Cuba, Russia to Guatemala. She practiced her English on me every weekend, while talking with Padre Henry in Spanish by phone during the week to help keep her spirits up.

I watched her grow through these months, as a daughter of God, and as our Goddaughter. I believe God was glorified through this relationship. And our hope was not disappointed when, shortly before Trinity Sunday, she was granted asylum in the United States of America. She is now a free woman, in part because Father Henry took his role as Father seriously— and because we take our marriage vows seriously. And because, as Richard Rohr says in his book about the Trinity, our Creator, Christ, and Holy Spirit are in a divine dance. The Trinity is not some distant, static idea, but an active relationship: an eternal dance between three persons.

None of our relationships are static. They move and change as we ourselves grow—through affliction and endurance, and through grace and rest. Our bonds of relationship expand as we move out into the world, thirsting for justice through ministry and service. Our bonds contract as we return to each other for sustenance and restoration. Our relationships expand to include children—of our bodies and of our spirits. Our relationships contract as we circle the wagons in times of illness, struggle, and death.

The Holy Trinity's divine dance of relationship has, over the eons, expanded to include every element of God's amazing creation: the earth beneath our feet, the stars above, the humans around us, the plants and animals alongside us, even the mosquitos and scorpions we often struggle to accept. The Trinity's dance of relationship also contracts to the smallest unit possible: an intimate relationship with each and every one of us. We are called, daily, into a dance of transformational relationship with the Holy Trinity.

Jesus told his disciples that the Holy Spirit would take what was his and give it *to us*. Each day, the Trinity offers us love and invites us to share that love. The Trinity becomes known, through us, in the fruits of our lives. Where are you called into the divine dance of relationship? Where are you called to be father, and mother—to bring hope into the world, perhaps in new and surprising ways?

The MOST HOLY BODY *and* BLOOD *of* CHRIST

FR. JAMES MARTIN, SJ

They all ate and were satisfied.

1ST READING	2ND READING
GEN. 14:18-20	1 COR. 11:23-26
PSALM	**GOSPEL**
110:1-4	LUKE 9:11-17

IT'S COMMON AMONG SOME PEOPLE TO interpret this great miracle of Jesus as an incidence of sharing. That is, nothing miraculous happened, but instead, the fact that Jesus and the disciples had shared those few loaves and fishes encouraged others to be generous, prompting everyone in the crowd to take out all the food that they had been keeping for themselves and pass it around. Thus, as this line of thought goes, there was more than enough for everyone.

My New Testament professor, Daniel J. Harrington, SJ, once called this the "nice thought" interpretation, mainly because it tries to domesticate for us what was for the people of the time a stunning supernatural event.

Needless to say, sharing is important. But it's important to see that this was not simply an occasion of sharing, but something so dramatic that it is recorded in every single Gospel, and in two Gospels twice, as the Feeding of the 5,000 and the Feeding of the 4,000. (The Gospel writers, by the way, were not above repeating a story twice for emphasis, by slightly altering it.) The Multiplication of the Loaves and Fishes, which happened on the shoreline of the Sea of Galilee, made a profound impression, first on the many witnesses present, then on the early church, and finally on the evangelists.

The story also had deep Eucharistic overtones, which is why we hear it today, on the Solemnity of the Most Holy Body and Blood of Christ. At the Multiplication of the Loaves and Fishes, Jesus performs the same actions that happen during the Mass. Some of the same words are even repeated during the Eucharistic prayer. The familiar formula of what Jesus did is well known to liturgical theologians: take, bless, break, give. Take, bless, break, give.

But the story of this miracle goes even beyond Jesus's power to multiply food and offers us several other themes to meditate on.

First of all, hospitality. Notice what the disciples initially want to do with the crowd. They want to "dismiss" the people, send them home. Why? There's not enough food. There's not enough for all these strangers. There are not enough resources for all these people we don't know. Sound familiar?

The story should have resonances with what is going on in our country today, for much of this story is about welcoming people. The disciples, as I said, want to send the crowds of people away. What is Jesus's response? The opposite: Feed them, care for them, treat them like you would want to be treated yourself. Even if it seems hard to do. Even if it seems like you won't be able to do it. Even if it doesn't seem reasonable. Hospitality and welcoming the stranger are consistent themes in Jesus's teaching.

A second theme: There is no "us and them." In the reign of God, there is enough for everyone, not just the insiders. One of the hallmarks of Jesus's ministry is that those on the outside are brought inside. Those on the margins are brought to the center: tax collectors, centurions, women, prostitutes, those who are sick, and on and on. And he encourages those in the center— the disciples, in this case—to go out. So, it's bringing those on the inside out, and those on the outside in. It's a bringing together, a gathering.

In fact, in this Gospel story, if you read between the lines, you can see that the disciples already had food—for themselves. They tell Jesus, "Five loaves and two fish are all we have, unless we ourselves go and buy food for all these people." In other words, "We have enough for us." For Jesus, though, that makes no sense. It makes no sense that the disciples would eat when others are going hungry, because in the reign of God, when Jesus is present, there is no us and them. There is only us.

Finally, a third theme: Jesus can take what little we give and magnify it, or, here, multiply it. You don't have enough? Don't worry; start giving. You don't feel that you can love enough? Start loving.

A few years ago, I was working with a couple who was going through a terrible time in their marriage. (I'll change some details here.) The husband had cheated on the wife in the most serious way, by sleeping with several women. And the wife was, not surprisingly, furious. I'm sure that you can fill in the details in your own mind. It was a terrible situation and I ended up counseling both the husband and the wife.

After almost a year, the wife decided that she would forgive her husband. The reasons were complex: She valued her marriage, she adored her children, and, ultimately, she realized that she still loved her husband. But here's the point: She didn't think she could do it. She felt that she only had a small amount of forgiveness. She didn't think she had enough.

But when she did forgive him, in her own way, she was overwhelmed by her ability to do it. The husband was overwhelmed too, completely transformed. She felt that she had only a few loaves and fishes to give, but when she started to give, it was more than enough for him, and for her, because Jesus was with her, and him, in all of this. God can take what little love we can give and magnify it.

This stunning reading, this miracle, is, as I said, contained in all four Gospels—the only miracle outside of the Resurrection (which is something beyond a miracle) that you find in Matthew, Mark, Luke, and John. The early church found in it a bottomless source of wonder, of inspiration, of nourishment.

They understood it as a companion to the Eucharistic meals that they were already celebrating. They understood it as an invitation to hospitality for all people, including strangers. They understood it as a call to inclusion for those who seemed different. They understood it as an encouragement to love as much as they could and trust that Jesus would magnify that love.

So, as you receive the Most Holy Body and Blood today, and as you hear the words of the Mass, remember what Jesus did for the people of his time, what he does for us today, and what he asks us to do. Not only "take, bless, break, give," but welcome, include, and love.

FEAST *of* ALL SAINTS

FRAN ROSSI SZPYLCZYN

"Rejoice and be glad, for your reward will be great in heaven."

1ST READING	2ND READING
REV. 7:2–4, 9–14	1 JOHN 3:1–3
PSALM	**GOSPEL**
24:1–6	MATT. 5:1–12A

IN THE MID-1990S, SOME FRIENDS BOUGHT
me a print to hang in my home; I loved it then and today I love it still. It is
a piece of art from Brian Andreas, founder of Story People. Go look up the
website if you are unfamiliar with it; the work is wonderful. Anyway, this
print has a whimsical image with these words printed on it: "I don't know
if I really believe in all the saints, she said, but I pray to them anyway. It
makes every night feel more like a slumber party."

Of course, I absolutely believe in the saints! Don't you? The saints are
such a beautiful element of our faith practice, and they are ever-present
reminders of hope in Christ. When I was younger, I imagined the saints as
perfect, and supposed that I might never be like them, no matter how tightly
I clasped my hands in fervent prayer. Today I understand this differently, and
that is one of the reasons the "slumber party" imagery is so meaningful to me.

We celebrate All Saints' Day each year, but I know I did not always
appreciate this day for what it is. Did you hear the way the readings all lead
us deeper into the love of the saints? It is so powerful, isn't it?

Every year on the feast day, we hear the Beatitudes in the Gospel of Matthew. That is where it all hits home for me. Blessed are the poor in spirit, blessed are those who mourn, blessed are the meek, and so on. Each line reminds us that Jesus is addressing all of us! We are poor in spirit, we mourn, we are meek—at least that is how we should be.

As humans, our tendency is often to make the Gospel literal, and we think, "I'm not poor in spirit; my faith is powerful! I'm not poor or meek!" How can we see past all the social and cultural armor that we don so regularly that we mistake it for our own skin? How small and broken we all are. All children of God are this way. And in our natural state, we know that we have every promise of God behind us and therefore our blessings are numerous and assured.

We are not promised a pain-free and easy life. There are no rewards for doing the right thing. The blessing is that in following Christ Jesus and living for one another as the saints did and still do, we give it all away in the name of love.

And maybe that is the most important element of being a saint: Over time, we come to learn that we surrender all for God, give it all away, have it all stripped away, and then—and only then—can we open our arms and our hearts wide to receive God. That is sainthood! When we recognize our weakness and allow God to transform all of it into our strength and gift.

To be a saint is not perfection. To be a saint is not unattainable. To be a saint is to be open, willing, and surrendered in Jesus's name. Can we peel off our second skin to reveal the skin of God's love? Can we disarm in order to have our hearts be illumination for others? Can we live totally for God and others without hesitation?

Perhaps we cannot do this always, but we can attempt it a little bit each day. All Saints' Day reminds us of the power and potential that awaits us, and All Saints' Day invites us into the immediacy of being a saint. Come join the Kingdom, like the print on my wall. We don't really know, but it might feel like a nice party if we all decide to attend. Will you join me?

MEGAN McKENNA

"This man welcomes sinners and eats with them."

1ST READING
EZEK. 34:11–16

2ND READING
ROM. 5:5–11

PSALM
23:1–6

GOSPEL
LUKE 15:1–7

HOW'S YOUR HEART? HOW TO TALK ABOUT the heart? The Oxford American dictionary begins with the definition in physical terms: "hollow muscular organ maintaining the circulation of blood by rhythmic contraction and dilation." And yet, when we speak of "heart," we have so many other ways of describing something to do with the heart. The list is revealing in itself: heartbroken, heart-to-heart talk, bleeding heart, wearing your heart on your sleeve, heart of darkness, eat your heart out, pure of heart, heart sore, have a heart, will you? And so many other expressions.

Take this first one: How's your heart? If we move first to our heart—that is, to the organ that beats inside our body—we don't necessarily even think about it, unless there is something wrong and we are in distress, or in pain. But if we have a heart condition or are born with hereditary heart issues, then we can answer swiftly. If that is the case, we are always somewhat aware of what is happening within us and can become acutely aware at a moment's notice that something might be changing or not as it should be. And the heart describes the whole person—not just one organ, or emotions and feelings—at one time. We each bear our own heart deep with us. And then, there is the heart of God.

And what about Jesus's heart? Jesus, the child of God the Father, bears the heart of God within his own human body. In a sense, his Spirit and flesh have a hereditary heart condition. What is Jesus's heart like?

In a sense, our bodies bear a map or geography of our souls and spirits. We talk about our hearts "feeling," but for people in Asian countries, including the Middle East where Jesus lived, the heart is where the will is situated. People in Israel, at the time of Jesus and still today, consider the heart to be the place where our wills and intelligence reside.

The book of Sirach says: "God has given people a heart to think" (Sir. 17:6). A person, toward the end of their life, says in this wisdom book: "My heart has seen much" (Sir. 1:16). And in the Bible, God acts the same way: "The Lord regretted making human beings on the earth, and his heart was grieved" (Gen. 6:6).

Jesus also reveals how his heart beats and acts. When the leper comes to him and tells him, "If you wish, you can make me clean," Jesus responds strongly with the words, "I do will it" and stretches out his hand and heals him (Mk. 1:40–42). In the gospel, Jesus's heart is touched by pain, and he reacts immediately. When a father cries out to Jesus about his son's sufferings, he prays: "If you can do anything, have compassion on us and help us" (Mk. 9:22). Jesus's heart is attentive and is moved first by others' pain, distress, and lack.

Today we remember and rejoice in the heart of Jesus and our readings tell us what Jesus's own heart is like. The prophet Ezekiel, moved by God's Word, speaks of what God's heart is like. "I myself will search for my sheep and examine them. As a shepherd...himself is among his scattered sheep, so will I examine my sheep." The heart of God is a shepherd's heart. God shepherds his people. He gathers them from foreign lands, in dark times, and brings them home. He pastures them on good land, even in the mountains, with good grazing areas. And he has them "lie down on good grazing ground.... I myself will pasture my sheep; I myself will give them rest.... The lost I will search out, the strays I will bring back, the injured

I will bind up, and the sick I will heal; but the sleek and the strong I will destroy. I will shepherd them [justly]." This is the heart of our God from the beginning.

In Paul's letter to his Roman community, we are told "the love of God has been poured out into our hearts through the holy Spirit that has been given to us." This love is vast and strong, even to the point of dying with us and for us, reconciling us to God and to one another. This undying love of Jesus for all of us has been shared, poured out from his heart into our own hearts, so that we too can love others, forgiving, reconciling, and saving one another with Jesus's Spirit. As Jesus himself has told us, "Learn from me, for I am meek and humble of heart" (Mt. 11:29). Once we have been in communion with God's heart and Spirit in Jesus, we too must be intent on unity and dwelling in peace together.

The gospel brings us to Jesus seated at a table with tax collectors and sinners, all gathered around, listening to him. The Pharisees "complain" about Jesus: "This man welcomes sinners and eats with them." The heart of Jesus attracts those estranged, excluded, shunned, and demeaned, those poor and hungry, and delights in their company. And then Jesus responds, using this parable, to those who are not pleased with those who are his guests. He speaks it directly to them: "[Who] among you having a hundred sheep and losing one of them would not leave the ninety-nine in the desert and go after the lost one until he finds it? And when he does find it, he sets it on his shoulders with great joy." And then he invites everyone, friends and neighbors, to rejoice with him! The style of the story and the example force all who are listening to decide: Will they follow suit and go after the ones who are not there, the ones lost by straying or being forced to flee, or will they ignore his confrontation and go about their usual way of dealing with others?

First, it's a parable, which means Jesus is out to shock them. We sometimes miss the obvious: that the usual answer would be, "What? Leave the ninety-nine in the desert and go after that one?" The majority would be quick to say, "No, that's stupid." Yet Jesus's heart is always with those who are not there, those whom others could care less about, or, worse, despise or demean.

Jesus's heart cares more about those who need to repent, need to change, need help, need to be touched with acceptance, grace, and tender regard. The others can fend for themselves, with one another. This is not what many who consider themselves righteous, or just even okay, would instinctively say or do. Their hearts—our hearts—are a bit bent, often tightly closed and walled against many others. We often have a tendency to have stone cold hearts and places in our hearts that are mean-spirited and unloving.

The heart of our God in Jesus that beats with the Spirit's power and grace is the heart of a shepherd, the heart of a servant, the heart of one who welcomes the least and those most in need—and yet the heart of one who tells the truth to those who need to hear it and need to "take heart" from Jesus's words and life. The heart of Jesus is quick to rejoice and his heart pulses with strong life, eager to be shared with anyone else whose heart is sore and needing to be touched. Broken hearts are drawn to Jesus's heart like a magnet.

Jesus's heart seeks communion with all hearts, with all the earth, seeking to transform everything into wholeness, peace, and holiness. This heart of God can transfigure and enrapture everyone's heart. There is no limit to Jesus's reach and his will to grab ahold of our weak hearts and make us courageous, free, and as passionately devoted to others as he is.

IMMACULATE CONCEPTION

MARY SPERRY

"Behold, I am the handmaid of the Lord."

1ST READING
GEN. 3:9–15, 20

2ND READING
EPH. 1:3-6, 11-12

PSALM
98:1–4

GOSPEL
LUKE 1:26–38

I THINK IT'S A REQUIREMENT THAT EVERY homily on this feast day begin by clarifying the difference between the Immaculate Conception and the virgin birth. Put simply: The virgin birth refers to Jesus's conception without the involvement of a human male. The Immaculate Conception refers to Mary being set apart by God from the very moment of her conception, by God keeping her free from the stain of original sin.

Unfortunately, even understanding the meaning of the feast doesn't address the concerns it may raise or explain its importance in the lives of contemporary people of faith. One concern arises from the Lectionary decision to pair the Gospel reading of the Annunciation to Mary with the first reading's retelling of Adam and Eve's sin in the garden. This pairing has often led to misogynistic interpretations, assigning Eve the sole blame for the fall of all humanity and making the claim that women are saved as they model their lives on Mary's life—because being sinless from conception and being both virgin and mother isn't an impossible standard at all!

But probing more deeply into the meaning of this feast and understanding how it can and should help to shape the lives of all the faithful—men and women alike—lets us avoid this constricting interpretation. The meaning of the feast becomes clearer when we consider the context of the first reading and the Gospel.

Before today's first reading begins, Adam and Eve have committed the original sin, disobeying at the serpent's suggestion God's direct command not to eat of the fruit of the tree in the center of the garden. Adam and Eve ate the fruit out of a desire to be like God. So, the original sin is to forget that God is God, and we are not. (As today's reading begins, Adam and Eve quickly follow their first sin with the second—blaming others for their own failures.) It is from this original sin that God preserves Mary. She was always able to understand her true relationship to God, and it is this understanding that makes Mary the perfect disciple that we are called to emulate.

We see Mary's discipleship in action in the first chapter of the Gospel of Luke. When the angel Gabriel comes to Mary with the news that she is to bear God's own Son, the long-awaited Messiah, her first response is not pride that she has been chosen from among all women, but a question about her own ability. Assured that God's power and grace can overcome any obstacle, her response stands as an example for all disciples: "Behold, I am the handmaid of the Lord. May it be done to me according to your word."

In this response is the essence of Christian discipleship: to conform our will to God's will so that his will be done on earth as it is in heaven. The vestiges of original sin (called concupiscence) keep us from this goal, tempting us to obey our own selfish impulses instead of obeying God's will. Because Mary was conceived without original sin, she is able to conform her will to God's will perfectly. Understanding that she is God's servant, she chooses to live as he called her to live, embracing the challenges of bringing his Son to birth, nurturing him, and supporting his mission wholeheartedly.

But, as with today's first reading, to understand Mary's discipleship more fully, we need to look beyond these verses in Luke's Gospel to what comes next. Luke tells us that, after the angel's departure, Mary's first action is to travel to the home of her kinswoman Elizabeth. Her visit has two purposes. First, she wants to share her good news with someone who can truly understand it. After all, Elizabeth also has a miraculous pregnancy—a woman thought barren is now pregnant in her old age. Second, Mary goes to the hill country to offer support and assistance to her kinswoman. After greeting Elizabeth, Mary sings her Magnificat, a song of praise that is also a song of discipleship. She sings of the God who remembers the lowly and the vulnerable and who restores justice in an out-of-balance world.

Even for those of us not immaculately conceived—i.e., the rest of us—Mary serves as the perfect model of discipleship. But how can we, sinners that we are, learn from Mary's example? How can we become better disciples? The word "disciple" comes from a Latin root meaning "learner." The ultimate goal of any disciple is to become more and more like the teacher. A true disciple does this not as Adam and Eve did it, desiring to acquire God's knowledge and power. Instead, the true disciple is like Mary, striving to conform her will to the teacher's will, to God's will.

For each of us, conforming our will to God's will is a lifelong task, full of stops and starts, steps forward and falls backward. We begin anew each day, relying on the grace of God that filled Mary from the moment of her conception. For us, that grace comes through the sacraments, in Baptism and Confirmation, and throughout life in the Eucharist and Penance.

As disciples like Mary, we ask that God shape us according to his Word. Like Mary, we set out as missionary disciples, bearing the good news of Jesus to a world waiting for hope. We lay down our lives to serve those who need our help. And we strive with all our strength, through the gift of God's grace, to help to build the kingdom that Jesus came to announce—a world truly conformed to God's plan: a world where justice reigns, where the powerful are cast down and the humble and lowly are lifted up, where the poor and the hungry have all they need.

Though we are sinners living in a world marked all too clearly by the effects of sin, Mary reminds us that God's will works in and through us, if only we open our hearts to his grace.

FEAST *of* CHRIST *the* KING

SHIRIN McARTHUR

In [Christ] were created all things in heaven and on earth.

1ST READING	2ND READING
2 SAM 5:1-3	COL. 1:12-20
PSALM	**GOSPEL**
122:1-5	LUKE 23:35-43

TODAY IS THE CULMINATION OF THE liturgical church year. Every church year begins with Advent, with our anticipation of the Incarnation—the Eternal Christ, coming to dwell with us as a fragile human baby. Through the year, we remember Jesus's birth, growth, ministry, death, and resurrection. Over the past few weeks, many of our readings have focused on the end times and scripture's understanding of what the future would hold. All of this leads up to today. In liturgical terms, it's the pinnacle of the journey, the day toward which every other day has pointed. And, for the past century, it's also been called the *Solemnity of Our Lord Jesus Christ, King of the Universe,* or, in short form, the Feast of Christ the King.

I did some research, presuming that this feast has been celebrated in the church for centuries. Turns out, I was wrong. This feast was introduced a century ago by Pope Pius XI, in response to the movement toward secularism which was taking place in the early twentieth century.

The idea that Christ has dominion over the earth is, of course, a much older idea—although it originated, not with Jesus, but with his followers. After Jesus fed the five thousand, the gospel of John (6:14–15) records this: "When the people saw the sign he had done, they said, 'This is truly the Prophet, the one who is to come into the world.' Since Jesus knew that they were going to come and carry him off to make him king, he withdrew again to the mountain alone."

Jesus's plan for his ministry did not include a kingdom, although his disciples were slow to catch on to that fact. Remember James and John, wanting seats of power at Jesus's right and left when he came into his kingdom? It seems that—at least culturally—we don't know how to handle power except by holding it *over* others.

But Jesus had a radically different perspective on power. His model for power was clearly demonstrated in his washing of the disciples' dirty, smelly feet. In Mark 10:42–44, he says this:

> "You know that those who are recognized as rulers over the Gentiles lord it over them, and their great ones make their authority over them felt. But it shall not be so among you. Rather, whoever wishes to be great among you will be your servant; whoever wishes to be first among you will be the slave of all."

Power and dominion were distinctly, and explicitly, *disconnected* for Jesus—so how did we come to connect them so thoroughly? As the saying goes, it's complicated.

The problems started in the aftermath of the Roman Emperor Constantine's edict allowing Christianity in the year 313. The transition from an underground, upstart faith of the underclasses was, over not too long a period, coopted by the ruling class to meet their needs. As Franciscan Richard Rohr said at one of his conferences, "Emperors don't want the poor in spirit. They want loyalists."

One interesting side note in this regard is that we know *practically nothing* about Pope Sylvester I, who was consecrated bishop of Rome in 314—one year after Constantine's edict—and held that office for twenty-one years. We don't know if Sylvester was from the ruling class. We don't know what he thought or felt about this shift in the role of the Christian church—and if he was for it or against it. We have none of his writings. Was he silenced, and his writings destroyed, because he resisted change, or was he a loyalist who did his job and obediently followed Constantine's direction?

Certainly Christianity changed in the decades and centuries after Constantine. It became a religion formed and controlled by the ruling class, for the benefit of the ruling class. Those powerful people put Jesus up on a throne, declaring his dominion here on earth, and eventually over the entire universe, for the sake of their ability to maintain power.

There's great irony in that. The early Christians did want the risen Christ to rule over the kings of the earth. But my best guess is that this was *not* so that he could be coopted, but so that he could straighten them out! The poor and powerless early Christians expected Christ to return and literally make the powerful weep and mourn (see Revelation 18:9). They expected him to *overturn* the rulers and oligarchies, not align with them.

Human societies tend toward certain rhythms that I believe are inevitable. Revolutionary thinkers arise. Their radical ideas gain them adherents. Those adherents eventually seek to codify and preserve those ideas. They develop organizations to do this, which become institutions. Over time, they attract and become the powerful rulers that they initially rejected. Then a new revolutionary thinker arises in response to the calcified institution, and the cycle begins again.

A century or so ago, secularism was the radical new idea, and the institution of Roman Catholic Christianity inaugurated a Feast of Christ the King to combat it. Do you see the irony in instituting a feast that focuses attention on a *secular* idea—of Jesus as a dominating king—to combat secularism? How far we have come from the Jesus of the gospels!

So how do we return there? *Can* we even return there? None of us speak Aramaic, or Greek. We don't have Jesus's middle eastern mindset. All we have are the words, mostly of his followers, which we, by our very being in *this* time and place, must take out of context.

Fortunately, those human words point *toward* the Eternal Word. That Eternal Word did choose the radical restrictedness of coming to earth in limited human form. Unfortunately, most of the people he encountered didn't understand why. As we hear in today's gospel lesson, the rulers and the soldiers—the powerful—jeered at him as he hung on the cross. They responded to what they perceived as his threat to their power by ridiculing and dismissing his power. That sign above Jesus's head—"This is the King of the Jews"—was certainly nailed there with irony from Pilate's point of view.

But what does the letter to the Colossians tell us? It declares that all things—"whether thrones or dominions or principalities or powers"— were "created through him and for him." Jesus didn't need to be king over anything because he was already, as the eternal Christ, part of every person and element of creation. Nothing is above his reach, or beyond it—even when his hands are nailed to a cross.

Next week, we begin a new liturgical year and the season of Advent. Our scripture readings in the coming weeks will focus on both preparing for Jesus's birth and longing for a dramatic return of Christ in the "end times." Early Christians hoped that those end times would include an overturning of the structures of power and hierarchy and an end to the domination of the ruling classes. The irony for us today is that, if this were to happen, we privileged Americans would probably be considered part of the ruling classes.

What kind of kingship do you believe Christ wants for us today? Are you—or can you be—aligned with that vision? How are you called to pray and work for a world where servant leaders truly live the powerful, yet powerless, way of Christ?

Funerals

"...that the love with which you loved me may be in them."

READING
JOHN 17:20-26

BEN WAS MY BIGGEST FAN HERE IN THE congregation. I say that with only the deepest thanks to him for the love and support he gave to me and my family, and with profound gratitude to God for the privilege of being Ben's pastor for fifteen years. More than once, his effusive words about my ministry rose to the level of embarrassment. Let me read you a portion of a letter he wrote to our ruling elders several years ago.

> I will never forget the time when I was listening to David Davis as he was at the peroration pitch of deliverance. I was so engrossed, to the extent of not watching my speedometer, and ran right into a Maryland speed trap for a cost of over $200. I was not dangerous; I was just enthralled with what David was saying. It was worth the fine, but I could not persuade the cop that this fine should be put to better use in our hunger offering. When I sayeth unto him, "Verily, verily that was the case," the cop sayeth back to

> me, in clear definitive terms, that I could keep my verilys
> and Maryland would keep the money.

The purpose of the letter was to request support for a project through the chaplain's office at Princeton Hospital to make great music and my sermons available to every patient. When I tried to convince Ben that the project would have to be broader and that, at the very least, we would have to make sermons available from other ministers, priests, rabbis, and imams, he said in no uncertain terms, "Nobody would want to listen to them, and nobody need listen to anyone else."

Just when I thought I had talked him into a different twist on the project, or I mistakenly thought he had forgotten, or maybe even his ill health had derailed the effort; just when, once again, I had taken Ben's persistence too lightly, the call would come to the church office: "Now David, it's Ben. About our project." And am I the only one left on the phone at the end of a phone call with Ben? He never really said goodbye; he just sort of hung up in mid-sentence and the call was done.

When invited to Ben and Lisa's for dinner, I learned a long time ago to ask who else was invited. I learned that by trial and error, but it's too risky here to tell stories or name names. He approached a guest list like he was pairing a fine wine with the right cheese, and he wasn't apt to ask your opinion of the pairing beforehand. One of the highlights for anyone at a Ben and Lisa dinner party would come when Lisa would try to trim the length of a story by interrupting and turning Ben's name into a three-syllable word: "Now, Ben, you promised."

You all know that Ben never met a word he didn't like or a sentence that was too long. I learned so much from him about World War II, about the YMCA, about Princeton, about this congregation. More than once, he summarized his critique of the lifetime of preachers that he saw fill this pulpit. Some of that critique was downright scathing, but with that flowery language and southern accent, it sounded just beautiful.

From my spot here, I watched Ben tear up at hymns and sermons. It wasn't just the beauty of the tune or the particular rhetoric of the sermon. Ben was moved by the love of God. He was a constant reminder to me that some Sundays, most Sundays, every Sunday there is someone sitting out there who just wants to be reminded that God loves them. Ben told me many times that it was only the prayers of his family and the love of God that brought him home from the war alive.

During his last stay in the hospital, I promised Ben that I wouldn't let this service be (in his words) little more than a meeting of a book club. It was his way of asking me to make sure it felt like church. It was to be worship. God would have a prominent role here this afternoon. In order to do that, I want to share these bits of my conversations with Ben from the last month or two.

One afternoon, at their home on Palmer Square, Ben started to tell me of the debt and gratitude he felt toward God. It was a level of gratitude, he said, that came with a profound sense of responsibility—responsibility to give back, to try to be faithful, to contribute to the common good, and to offer thanks and praise in worship. Yes, there was his thought about coming home from the war. But the emphasis of his greatest thanks, his greatest gratitude to God was for his family and how he and Lisa were over-blessed with healthy children, grandchildren, and great grand-children. "I have done the math," he said. "I know the percentages out there. There is absolutely no explanation for why we would be so far ahead of the curve, except for the love and grace of God." The more his body failed, the more work was in the rearview mirror, the more he talked about his family—all of his family, telling me over and over again that, despite his error-prone efforts at being a husband and father, God blessed him with you.

At the hospital, he thoughtfully and quietly told me that he never dared consider himself on par with God. "What Presbyterian ever would?" he chuckled to himself, with a reference to John Calvin and the depravity of humankind. But he said, "There is one exception, one area where I think I am pretty close to God. One way that God and I are alike." I didn't have to ask. He told me. "It is my unconditional love for Lisa. It is the only area of my life where I might be close to the Divine." And he went on to describe Lisa to me with awe and wonder.

One more tidbit. We were sitting at the dining room table after the noontime meal just a few weeks ago. Ben had more beverages in front of him than he could drink in a week. There was a glass of water, a can of Ensure, a mug of something I couldn't see, and a glass of what I assumed was apple juice. A bit later, he offered me a sip and told me it was scotch. It was during that conversation that we talked about eternity, about heaven. "I know people get all worked up about what to believe and they have trouble with this scripture or that," Ben said. "It doesn't seem to me to be all that complicated. For me, it all comes down, the gospel all comes down to love. The promise is God's everlasting love. That's enough for me." And he finished his homily by saying, "I don't need any more than that: God's everlasting love."

You see the bit of irony, right? Here's a guy who turned in a three-page paper in graduate school that was all one sentence. He told me he got an F, but the grammar was spot-on. Here's a man who would go on for hours about innovation and investment, a man who could write about market trends and make it sound like *The Rime of the Ancient Mariner*. But, at the end of his life, at the end of one incredible, wonderful life: "God's everlasting love, that's enough for me. I don't need any more than that."

The Apostle Paul wrote, "So faith, hope, and love remain, these three; but the greatest of these is love" (1 Corinthians 13:13).

Jesus said, "I made known to them your name, and I will make it known, that the love with which you loved me may be in them and I in them" (John 17:26).

Ben said, "God's everlasting love, that's enough for me." Ben Anderson on resurrection hope, resurrection power, resurrection life.

Death for him is finished. Life, forever basking in the love of God, has now begun.

I rise before you to give thanks to God for the life of Ben Anderson!

Christ is Risen. He is Risen Indeed.

FUNERAL HOMILY *for* BOBBY HEYER

DEACON GREG KANDRA

Love never fails.

READING
1 COR. 13:4–13

I WANT TO BEGIN BY EXPRESSING MY condolences to Maureen, to Siobhan, and to all of Bobby's family and friends who are here today. This has been hard for so many of us. It is a grace, at least, to be together, to pray for him and pray with him.

A few days ago, I spoke with Maureen about what we were planning for today, and I asked her if there was anything special she wanted me to mention about Bobby. And she told me something I didn't know; she told me he had a very deep and sincere devotion to St. Thérèse of Lisieux, the Little Flower.

It's important to remember that, as a flower, Thérèse was hardly a wallflower—and maybe that was part of what attracted Bobby to her. She was spirited, courageous, dramatic, even rebellious. She had the audacity to throw herself at the feet of the pope during a visit to Rome when she was just fifteen, begging him to let her join the cloister. In his wisdom, he left it in the hands of the Carmelites—but how could they say no to someone like that?

But she was also known for her simplicity, her fervor, her quiet strength, and her deep love of the Lord. It was a love that only deepened, even as she dealt with illness and disease. She struggled with so much during her life. She battled anxiety and scrupulosity, wrestled with atheism, and even told one of the sisters that she would have committed suicide if it were not for her faith. In her final years, she lived with and fought the plague of her time, tuberculosis.

In 1895, a seminarian named Maurice Bellière wrote to the convent where she lived in Lisieux. Maurice himself was filled with doubt and uncertainty about his vocation. He asked the mother superior if there was a sister who could pray for him. The mother superior passed his letter along to Thérèse.

Across the next two years, she wrote him just ten letters—but they are extraordinary. Here we find words of encouragement and hope to a troubled young person. More than anything, they are the letters of a dear friend, reaching out to uplift and support another searching soul.

Just weeks before she died, Thérèse wrote Maurice to tell him her life was coming to an end. She was just twenty-four years old. Maurice was overwhelmed with grief. To try and comfort him, she found the strength to write him one last letter.

She addressed her words to Maurice Bellière, but this morning, I think, she offers them to Bobby and, in some ways, to all of us.

"My poor dear little Brother," she wrote.

> How I wish I could make you realize the tenderness of Jesus' heart.... As I read your letter of the fourteenth, my heart thrilled tenderly. More than ever I realized the degree to which your love is sister to mine, since it is called to go up to God by the elevator of love, not to climb the rough stairway of fear.... I am certain that I shall aid you better to walk that delightful way when I am free of my mortal envelope, and soon you will be saying with St. Augustine 'Love is the weight that draws me.'"[1]

She enclosed a photograph of herself, taken just a few days before, and added:

---

1   Michel Bettigole and James D. Childs, eds., *The Catholic Spirit: An Anthology for Discovering Faith Through Literature, Art, Film, and Music* (Notre Dame, IN: Ave Maria, 2010), 169.

If my photograph does not smile at you, my soul will never cease to smile on you when it is close by you. Goodbye, dear little Brother, be assured that for eternity I shall be your true little sister.[2]

"Love is the weight that draws me."

Love is what has drawn us here this morning, as well.

The epistle we heard a few moments ago, from St. Paul, tells us everything we need to know about love. We usually hear it at weddings. Paul was writing to the people of Corinth about the best way to love one another as friends, neighbors, family—and yes, as husband and wife.

But I think those words this morning speak of another love: God's love for each of us. He loves us in our frailty and weakness, our suffering and struggles.

He loves us, too, in our grief.

His love is patient. It is kind. It bears all things, believes all things, hopes all things, endures all things.

It is a love that never fails.

This morning, we pray that Bobby understands those words in a way we can only imagine. We pray for him, and we ask him to pray for us.

Bobby, I think, was more than a son, or a brother, or a friend. He was also a soldier. He fought enemies most of us could never see.

There are so many other soldiers like him on the battlefield this day— warriors whose names we may never know. They are fighting addiction, fear, loneliness, illness. They are battling life. Many bear the wounds of battle.

Yet they fight on.

This morning, please: remember them. Let that be Bobby's legacy, that these other soldiers are not forgotten. Pray for them. Pray that they may find help and healing and hope.

May Bobby know the embrace of God's infinite mercy, in a place where he can gaze forever at the understanding, tender face of his friend Thérèse.

And this morning, may we all know the nearness of God's love for every one of us—the love that never fails.

---

2 Bettigole and Childs, 170.

FUNERAL HOMILY *for* PATRICIA POLONEY

DEACON JIM KNIPPER

"Unless a grain of wheat falls to the ground and dies, it remains just a grain of wheat; but if it dies, it produces much fruit."

FOR SO MANY DECADES OUR FAMILY HAS gathered in this church, celebrating Baptisms, First Communions, Confirmations, Weddings, as well as so many Eucharistic celebrations. And as time moved on, we all knew that this day would come—when we would gather here together, as a family, surrounded by friends, to give thanks for the life of Mom, to mourn her death and to celebrate her new life with Christ.

I think one of the hardest lessons we learn is that life and death always, always coexist, as was witnessed this past Friday, when Mom's sixth great-grandchild was born in the south of France and, by the end of the day, Mom was called home. This paradox of life and death is woven through our lives and our faith. As we heard in the second reading, when Mom was baptized, she died to who she was and, through the waters of baptism, was reborn as a disciple of Christ—out of death came new life.

Ninety years since then—and surrounded by the same sacramental signs of baptism: the paschal candle, white cloth/pall, and water—Mom has now died to this temporary and brief life we all share and is now reborn into a new and eternal life with Christ.

This was the same message Christ was giving to his disciples in the Gospel story I just read. Listening to the Parable of the Grain of Wheat, his rural audience easily understood the principle of resurrection produced by dead seeds sown into the earth. It is a reminder that all of us will need to die to our current convictions, ideas, and egos, and then eventually our lives in this world, so that we can be reborn in the Kingdom of God.

Mom knew this, maybe better than most, as witnessed in her own version of this Gospel, in what I call the Parable of the Milkweed Seed. As you know, Mom and Dad enjoyed their summers boating and fishing in Cape May. Mom especially loved to sit on the beach and talk to her visiting friends. With Cape May being a central corridor for the migration of butterflies who feed on the milkweed, Mom decided, one day, to cast milkweed seeds in the sand and rocks of the seawall across the street from us. The terrain she chose made it difficult for growth to take place, but with patience and time, the sprouts of a milkweed plant finally began to show. But soon after, Hurricane Sandy arrived, and with it came the ocean waters rushing over the seawall for over a day, wiping out everything in their path, including the milkweed sprouts—or so we thought. For the following spring, there it was, bigger and better than ever before: the orange milkweed plant!

I doubt that one could find a better metaphor for Mom's life. For, like that milkweed plant, throughout the storms and chaos that Mom faced in life, her roots were anchored in the rock of her faith, seeing God's presence in family and friends and bringing beauty and nourishment to everyone in her life.

Perhaps the best example of how she did this was through the grace of hospitality. At home, it was said to have been a rarity to only have the family gathered for a meal, for all were welcomed. Neighbors and friends would always be joining in whatever food there was, with Mom ensuring there was always room for one more—well, at least most of the time. These past few weeks, she did admit to having prayed over most of her daughters' boyfriends in order to be rid of them—so Dave, Jim, Charlie,

Dave, and I seem to be the lucky ones who made it, despite any possible prayers that Mom may have said!

Indeed, prayers were central to Mom, as was this church we are sitting in, for it was Mom's second home as she breathed life into this community, reaching out to those who needed help. Often, we would be sitting on the beach with her, and she would announce that she had to go and get ready to head back to Annville. When we asked her why, her usual response was that she had to do the altar linens and help some "old ladies" get to the doctor...and we would remind her that she was an old lady!! But off she would go, with nary a complaint, showing her colors, feeding others, caring for those in need—anchored, like that milkweed plant, in her rock of faith.

Then, on July 9th, the diagnosis of glioblastoma was given. Unfortunately, our family already had experience with this type of cancer, so we knew what to expect—only to find out what we never expected. But before I go there, this is probably the best place to pause and acknowledge with gratitude the incredible coordination of love and service by Patrick, Annie, Teresa, Alice, Mary, and Helene, and so many loving grandchildren and great-grandchildren, as well as a bevy of caregivers who provided so much comfort to Mom and Dad and the whole family. Each with your own gifts and graces, you gave Mom the greatest demonstration of love possible—your presence.

So, once our family received the diagnosis, everyone adjusted their schedules, as flights were made and Airbnb reservations booked. We took turns gathering around Mom as we watched a steady decline in the ensuing weeks. But what we didn't expect was that as the brain cancer began to shut her mind down, it opened her up to what the Irish call the Thin Places.

The Celts say that heaven and earth are separated by only three feet. But, when you can calm your mind and listen to your heart and soul, allowing your spiritual side to come to the forefront—and thus open your eyes to God's presence—the distance between the two worlds becomes very thin. It is said that one can then walk between both worlds, where the difference is indiscernible, where something is felt instead of seen, where truth abides, love is the foundation, and one feels connected with something—someone—much greater.

Perhaps you have felt brief moments of being in a Thin Place with the birth of a child, the embrace of a loved one, or a moment of great beauty in nature. But for Mom, as the cancer continued to rob her of her daily cognitive thoughts, her stories and quips made it clear that she was spending more and more time experiencing Thin Moments.

It began with her telling us that when she was waking from sleep, she kept hearing a voice inviting her to "Come fish with me." For she had already described to us that heaven will be like a great sea, filled with plenty of fish to catch. And that when she dies, she knows that her dad, Alice Smaska, and Fr. Pantle will be there to introduce her to Jesus. But we reminded her that she will need no introduction to Christ, for she has always known and seen and shared Jesus with others. Yet, throughout her stories, you could still sense Mom's fear about dying.

But then something happened on Saturday, July 27th. As our family well knows, Alena was due to give birth to her first son around August 10th, another great-grandchild for Mom. But by the morning of the 27th, Alena was in full labor, two weeks early. Around 4:00 that afternoon, Alena gave birth to Kai and, at the same time, a few miles away, Mom was waking from her nap—from spending time in those Thin Moments—and later described to us a dream that she had. She said that she had this vision of a swaddled baby, lying on her wheelchair ramp and telling her to have courage, to not be afraid. She went on to say, "I passed him in the night and saw that he is coming, and I am going. I was afraid of my terminal cancer at first, but then so many prayers came, so God took care of that and sent Kai to help me."

If that wasn't enough, you just need to look a bit deeper at this story, and reflect on Kai's name. His full name is the Greek word Kairos, which is different from Chronos. Chronos is chronological time, time as duration, one moment after another, and that's what most of us think of as time. But Kairos time means a deep time. It represents those moments where you say, "Oh my God, this is it. I get it," or, "This is as perfect as it can be," or, "This moment is summing up the last years of my life," where time comes to a fullness, when the stars seem to be in alignment and all the dots connect. For Mom, the gift of Kai and of her Kairos moment brought a great deal of peace to her—peace that she wants us to take with us this day.

For it is a day that we mourn her passing from this life to the next, but it is also a time for us to remember her life and remember this sacred journey of these past months, where we witnessed her faith in the face of death.

Soon we will lay Mom to rest, and we will head back to our homes and our daily lives, richer for her being a part of our lives, but still carrying the loss of her physical presence. So, what do we do?

First, she wants us to smile and not to cry—and thus the poem she chose for the back of her prayer card. After that, I think we should follow the sage advice Mom wanted to be shared with everyone today through the readings she chose and her encounters with Thin Moments. Namely:

1. Be who you are and be that well. Be yourself, not who others expect or want you to be—but be who you are in Christ, as you were created by the God who loves you unconditionally, a God who has you engraved in the palm of God's hand.

2. Be gentle and kind to yourself and be at peace with God, or whatever name you want to give your Creator, and never cease to look for that Divine presence all around you by being present to the one you are with each moment of every day.

3. Be at peace with silence and stillness. Make time to quiet your mind and your body—for when you do, you may find yourself in one of those Thin Moments, where those who have gone before us and who continue to love us are still present to us, and where you just may hear a voice calling you to "Come and fish with me."

Indeed, Mom—and all of us—were blessed with many years of seeing the fruit of the seeds that she sowed her whole life come to fulfillment, in so many ways. So, let us continue to teach, love, and mentor our children and grandchildren, and all those who come into our lives, using the gifts God has given each of us—and in ways that, frankly, we may not be able to comprehend...in essence, to indeed live fully until the day we die. Then, once again, we will be united with our Patricia, our Gigi, our mom, our grandma, and our beloved, who now rests easily with a view of a newfound, fish-filled, wide open sea, embraced by God's arms...being more of God through this mutual, unfathomable, and never-ending love—a love that is always present to you and me, and the same love that now brings our Mom to the place that has been prepared for her by our good and gracious God.

FUNERAL HOMILY *for* MARIA

RICHARD G. MALLOY, SJ

"Faith is the realization of what is hoped for and evidence of things not seen."

READING
HEB. 11:1

THERE'S AN OLD SAYING THAT THERE ARE some things even the youngest, newly ordained priest cannot explain. I'm not newly ordained. I can't explain what happened here, nor why.

There are only two things of which I am absolutely sure. One is that God loves us, and the second is that people suffer. No one has ever challenged the second assertion. The truth is that God loves us and responds to our suffering. God suffers with us. God too lost a child to the pain and brutality and seeming senselessness of this world.

Everyone in this world suffers. Jesus suffered on the cross. The truth of our faith is that God responds to suffering, God saves us from suffering. God transforms pain, suffering, and death by having us share in the power of Christ's resurrection.

Today we suffer. We mourn the loss of a lovely young woman through a tragic car accident. We grieve. This hurts. This is painful, very painful.

It's much more painful for Alex and Karen, and Maria's brothers, Carmen and Alex. Is there anything more painful than losing a child? Than burying a lovely, wonderful person like Maria? Maria's grandmothers, Ann and Rosalie, mourn her, and Joe. What can we say? Alex came across a card Joe wrote to her in her room. He wrote, "Trust in God." How hard that is to do at this time. And Lenni—how lost he must feel.

So, let me try and say something about what I learned in this from Alex, something about how I got through something like this, and something about what our faith says about all this.

As I get older, I learn more and more, and realize more and more, that the only thing people really care about are their kids. This was so evident to me when I spoke with Alex on Saturday. It was so palpable over the phone: the love, the deep, real, incredible love he has for his daughter. This daughter, Maria, whom he brought into this world with Maria's mother Karen. This baby girl they had to wait five years to conceive. This wonderful person who was first touched by her father's hands. This Maria, with whom Alex spoke shortly before the horrible accident.

Friday, Maria had been having some car trouble, and, like a good dad, Alex had gotten her car fixed, got the car over to where she was working on Friday, and sent her on her way back to Scranton. He gave her some money, kissed her goodbye, and then got a call from her a while later. She was stuck in traffic. She was frustrated, as we all are when traffic gets bad. She had had a stressful day at work. Alex told her, "Maria, say a few Our Fathers and Hail Marys. Ask God to center you. Ask God to give you peace." What a beautiful final wish for a child.

One thing we learn at times like these is that God loves us the way Alex loves Maria. God loves us the way Karen and Alex love their children. God loves us the way good parents love children.

And, like good parents, God can't protect us from everything bad. God is not a thing among other things. God doesn't intervene and capriciously act to protect this person or that person from pain, suffering, and death. God brings good out of destruction and death. God works resurrection.

Maria was born in 1991. She went to St. Ann's grade school and Conwell Egan high, where she was a tennis star. She really hit her stride at the University of Scranton, where her sparkling personality, her sense of pride and service in her occupational therapy program, and her gift for leadership made her a standout among her peers.

She really was a cross between Tina Fey and Mother Teresa: a lot of Italian Philly "attytood," with a loving, caring heart. She was a great athlete and had just completed a "Tough Mudder" twelve-mile event. She was funny and fun, smart and spunky, and expressive, caring, and kind. She spent hours knitting prayer shawls. She is deeply missed by her classmates and teachers. She is also especially mourned by the folks in our Student Affairs office, where she was a student worker as an undergrad.

Ten years ago, my family faced something like this. Francine was a math professor. There was not a lot of romance in her life. At forty-one, she married a widower with five kids and then they had Kevin, a great kid, a baseball player. Kevin died of epilepsy at nineteen. Who dies of epilepsy? I was frustrated with God. I mud wrestled in prayer for months. The only thing that ever came to me was this: I was assuming Kevin would have had a great life. Maybe God knows something I don't. Maybe Kevin would have suffered something terrible. Maybe he was saved from something I wouldn't wish on my worst enemy.

What does our faith tell us about a young woman like our Maria? Like Martha, she believed in the resurrection. We believe Maria, and all of us, will be transformed. We will be given the grace, the ability, to live with God forever. "God became what we are so we might become what God is." That's not some Jesuit spin on theology. That's St. Athanasius, from the third century.

We have to believe in transformation. What's really going on is not always apparent to the naked eye. The hope for transformation runs deep and real in human hearts.

Death, for us, is a transformation. Resurrection is not the resuscitation of a corpse. Resurrection is the transformation of all we are and have been into a new creation. Eternal Life is not like a change of horses, where we ride off into a far distant sunset on another stallion. Karl Rahner, the great Jesuit theologian, taught that the resurrection means we become all we ever could have been. All the limits of this life are lifted, and we are all we could ever hope and desire to be.

We are limited in this life. It would be very difficult to be both a doctor and a lawyer. You can't be married to two people at the same time. You can't spend your whole life in California and also in Philly. You can't be an Eagles fan and a Cowboys fan; it's impossible. You can't be both a movie star and a Jesuit priest. (Well, to be honest, I really didn't have to face that choice.) Still, the truth is that there are forks in the road, and some choices eliminate other choices. But in heaven we get everything we ever wanted and desired.

The resurrection means that the Kingdom of God has arrived on this earth. Heaven means we join Jesus in his reign over the "course of world history. Heaven...is not a kind of perennial 'Old Folks Home.' It is not simply a place of retirement and celestial repose for senior citizens of the kingdom of God.... Heaven consists in the active participation in the glorified Christ's direction of history."[1]

Rahner wrote:

> The Great mistake of many people...is to imagine that those whom death has taken, leave us. They do not leave us. They remain! Where are they? In the darkness? Oh, no. It is we who are in darkness. We do not see them, but they see us. Their eyes radiant with glory, are fixed upon our eyes.... Oh, infinite consolation! Though invisible to us, our dead are not absent.... They are living near us transfigured into light and power and love.[2]

Maria has been transfigured into light and power and love. She was loving and loved. She was our sunshine, and we know that above the clouds, the sun always shines. We were lucky to have such a light and love in our lives. Her light and love will be with us always. It will be with us until we too enter into eternal life, with her, into eternal light and love.

---

1   David M. Stanley, *The Apostolic Church in the New Testament* (Westminster, MD: Newman, 1967), 282–284.

2   Karl Rahner, *On the Theology of Death*, trans. C. H. Henkey (Freiburg, Germany: Herder and Herder, 1961).

PATRICK WENRICK

He went into the tomb and saw the burial cloths there, and the cloth that had covered his head.

READING
JOHN 20:1–10

THE STONE ROLLED BACK, THE WRAPPINGS lying on the ground, the piece of cloth which had covered his head rolled up in a place by itself. These were all signs to Mary, Peter, and John that Jesus's body was taken or absent from where it was supposed to be. In the traumatic events of the past days, none of them expected to see what they saw. None expected to see a tomb without a body.

But those wrappings that covered the body and the cloth that covered the head of Jesus's body are signs, not of death, but of life. When his mother Mary saw those, I wonder if her mind wandered back to when Jesus was born and how they wrapped him in swaddling clothes and laid him in a manger. Those swaddling clothes were indicative of birth, of new life. I wonder too if these wrappings in the tomb were more indicative of a new life that we have come to know as resurrection. The tomb became the manger, though owned by another Joseph, out of which emerges Jesus, the anointed one, who has conquered death itself.

We come together today over the body of our brother. Our bodies are like those wrappings and cloth found in the tomb on the day of the resurrection of Jesus. These bodies hold our spirits for a brief period and then are left behind as we journey back home to God. I heard a priest say, about a friend who had died, "We will put his body in the ground, but we cannot bury the Spirit."

We, like the early visitors to the tomb, are still at a loss for words. Memories flood our minds about our relationship with our brother. Words and experiences shared through the years slam against the reality that he is no longer with us. He is absent. Yet, absence means presence in a paradoxical way. The wrappings could only mean one thing for those who have faith: Jesus has risen and has come to take with him the person whom we called Joe in this life.

Back during World War II, a Jewish person hiding from the Nazis summed up this paradox of faith this way: "I believe in the sun even when it is not shining. I believe in love even when feeling it not. I believe in God even when [God] is silent."[1]

> Standing on the shore, early one morning, I was fortunate to see a ship spread her white sails and start across the blue ocean. She was an object of beauty and strength. She captivated my imagination and so I stood and watched, until finally, the great ship seemed to be only a ribbon of cloud, positioned just where the sky and sea come together.
>
> I was unaware of another's presence until, at that moment, as we witnessed the tiny speck of white disappear, a person next to me said: "There. She's gone."
>
> The words sounded so final. Gone? Gone where, I wondered. Gone from my sight, that's all. I knew that somewhere on that ocean, the beautiful ship I had been watching was still just as large in mast and hull, just as

1   Jared T. Kieling, ed., *The Gift of Prayer: A Treasury of Personal Prayer from the World's Spiritual Traditions* (New York: Continuum, 1995), 59.

strong and proud and beautiful, as the first moment I saw her. I realized that her seemingly diminished size was only my perception and not reality. I realized too, that just as the stranger announced, "There. She's gone," there were others on the far shore picking up the joyous shout of, "Here she comes!"[2]

And that is dying.

We picture death as losing, but it is gaining. We think of going away, but we are called to focus on the arrival. Jesus tells us, "Do not let your hearts be troubled...I will come back again and take you to myself, so that where I am you also may be" (John 14:1-3).

Today, we give Joe back to God, who gave him to us. As God did not lose him in giving, we do not lose him by his return.

As we gathered today at the entrance of this church, we greeted the body of our brother's remains by the sprinkling of holy water and the clothing of the casket with a pall—reminiscent of his baptism some time ago. The physical body and the pall are the wrappings left behind, indicative, we believe, that Jesus has taken our brother home. Until we meet again, we pray the words of the Antiphon:

May the angels lead you into paradise.
May the martyrs come to welcome you
and take you to the holy city,
the new and eternal Jerusalem.

---

2 Author unknown.

HOMILIST BIOGRAPHIES

WILLIAM J. BAUSCH is a retired parish priest of the diocese of Trenton, New Jersey. He is the award-winning author of numerous books on church life, parish ministry, storytelling, and several books of homiletics. He has lectured widely in the United States and abroad, and currently resides in Freehold, New Jersey.

MARGARET BLACKIE, PHD is a senior lecturer in the Department of Chemistry and Polymer Science at Stellenbosch University in South Africa. She researches in the areas of medicinal chemistry and tertiary science education. In addition, she also teaches spiritual direction and Ignatian spirituality, working primarily in ecumenical groups. She is the author of *Rooted in Love: Integrating Ignatian Spirituality into Daily Life* and *The Grace of Forgiveness.*

GREGORY BOYLE, SJ is a Jesuit priest and the founder of Homeboy Industries in Los Angeles, the largest gang-intervention, rehabilitation, and re-entry program in the world.

Born and raised in Los Angeles, Father Boyle served as pastor of Dolores Mission Church in Boyle Heights from 1986 to 1992. Dolores Mission was the poorest Catholic parish in Los Angeles that also had the highest concentration of gang activity in the city. Father Boyle witnessed the devastating impact of gang violence on his community during the so-called "decade of death" that began in the late 1980s and peaked at 1,000 gang-related killings in 1992. In the face of law enforcement tactics and criminal justice policies of suppression and mass incarceration as the means to end gang violence, he and parish and community members adopted what was a radical approach at the time: treat gang members as human beings. In 1988, they started what would eventually become Homeboy Industries, which employs and trains former gang members in a range of social enterprises, as well as provides critical services to thousands of men and women who walk through its doors every year seeking a better life.

Father Boyle is the author of the 2010 New York Times-bestseller *Tattoos on the Heart: The Power of Boundless Compassion.* His second book, *Barking to the Choir: The Power of Radical Kinship,* was published in 2017. His third book, *The Whole Language: The Power of Extravagant Tenderness,* was published in October 2021. He has received the California Peace Prize and been inducted into the California Hall of Fame. In 2014, President Obama named Father Boyle a *Champion of Change.* He received the University of Notre Dame's 2017 Laetare Medal, the oldest honor given to American Catholics. In 2020, he served as a committee member of California Governor Gavin Newsom's Economic and Job Recovery Task Force as a response to COVID-19 crisis. In the same year, Homeboy Industries was the recipient of the 2020 Hilton Humanitarian Prize.

REV. DR. MARK BOZZUTI-JONES, DMIN is an Episcopal priest with Trinity Church Wall Street in New York City. He serves as the Priest and Director of Spiritual Formation of Trinity's Retreat Center in West Cornwall, Connecticut.

A former Jesuit priest from Jamaica, Mark has missionary experience in Belize, Brazil, and Guyana. He believes that prayer, silence, and rest deepen our connection to God. Prayer and silence help us to name the pain, face the realities of our time, and claim the Way of Love for all people. At the Retreat Center, Father Mark fosters an environment suited to prayer, silence, meditation, rest, and reveling in the beauty of nature.

He is an avid reader, award-winning author and international speaker, and has taught at the elementary and university levels. He has a passion for the cultures of Latin America and the Caribbean. Father Mark's intellectual interests include the impact of social issues on faith and spirituality, racism, and the impact of poverty. He is passionate about the inculturation of religion. Mark loves flowers, Brazilian and Reggae music, and is currently working on a book of poetry.

He is an award-winning author; recent books for children include *God Thought of You, God Created, Jesus the Word, The Gospel of Barack Hussein Obama According to Mark, Never Said a Mumbalin' Word, The Womb of Advent,* and *The Rastafari Book of Common Prayer.* Two new books in 2021 include *Absalom Jones: Leader and Guide* (CPG) and one on the Spirituals: *Face to the Rising Sun: Reflections on Spirituals and Justice* (Forward Movement). Father Mark is married to the Rev. Dr. Kathy Bozzuti-Jones (Interfaith). Mark Anthony is their son, the Beloved, the Negus.

REV. DR. MARGARET BULLITT-JONAS is an Episcopal priest, author, retreat leader, and climate activist. Her latest book, *Rooted and Rising: Voices of Courage in a Time of Climate Crisis,* is an anthology of essays co-edited with Leah Schade. She serves as Missioner for Creation Care (Episcopal Diocese of Western Massachusetts; Southern New England Conference, United Church of Christ) and Creation Care Advisor (Episcopal Diocese of Massachusetts). She preaches and leads retreats in the USA and Canada on spiritual resilience and resistance in the midst of a climate emergency. She has been a lead organizer of many Christian and interfaith events about care for the Earth, and has been arrested in Washington, DC and elsewhere to protest the expanded use of fossil fuels. She is a graduate of Stanford (BA, Russian Literature), Harvard (PhD, Comparative Literature), and Episcopal Divinity School (MDiv). Her website, RevivingCreation.org, includes blog posts, sermons, multimedia, and articles.

L. PATRICK CARROLL was a Jesuit for forty-four years, then worked twenty years for Providence Health and Services, serving the poor and vulnerable. He has published eight books: six on spirituality, one collection of poems, and one memoir. Now retired, married, and living in his Seattle hometown, he offers the collected wisdom of his 85 years, hoping others will join him in struggling to know, love, and follow Jesus.

JOHN CHAFFEE is a Director of Youth Ministries and Adjunct Professor of Christian Spirituality just outside of Philadelphia. With an MDiv from Palmer Seminary and a ThM from Princeton Theological School, he writes and teaches on developmental theories and frameworks as they interact with Christian spiritual formation. He hiked the entirety of the Appalachian Trail in 2015, enjoys the Philly scene, and hosts the *Begin Again* Podcast.

RORY COONEY has served for twenty-seven years as director of liturgy and music at St. Anne Catholic Community in Barrington, Illinois. Since 1984, he has composed or contributed to nearly twenty collections of music for worship with his wife, Theresa Donohoo, and friend Gary Daigle. A contributor to several periodicals including *Pastoral Music*, *Today's Parish*, and *GIA Quarterly*, he was the recipient of the 2014 Pastoral Musician of the Year award from the National Association of Pastoral Musicians. He served for six years on the steering committee for the Liturgical Composers Forum, three as chair. Rory is the author of *Change Our Hearts*, a book of Lenten reflections from Liguori Publications, and contributes several times a year to "Sixty-Second Sermons" on the *PrayTell* blog. He is the father of six and grandfather of five.

DAVID A. DAVIS is currently the senior pastor of the Nassau Presbyterian Church in Princeton, New Jersey. He has served that congregation since 2000. David earned his PhD in Homiletics from Princeton Theological Seminary, where he continues to teach as a visiting lecturer. His academic work has focused on preaching as a corporate act and the active role of the listener in the preaching event.

Before arriving in Princeton, he served for fourteen years as the pastor of the First Presbyterian Church, Blackwood, New Jersey. David grew up in Pittsburgh and did his undergraduate work at Harvard University, where he was a member of the University Choir, singing weekly in Memorial Church and listening to the preaching of Professor Peter Gomes. David is married to Cathy Cook, a Presbyterian Minister who is currently Associate Dean of Students and Director of Senior Placement at Princeton Seminary. They have a son, Ben, and their daughter Hannah is married to Henry, with whom they have a child, Franny.

He has published two sermon collections, *A Kingdom You Can Taste* and *Lord, Teach Us to Pray*. He has served on the Board of Directors of the Presbyterian Foundation and the local Princeton YMCA. In addition to preaching in Presbyterian congregations around the country, David has preached to congregations in South Africa, Scotland, the Samuel Proctor Child Advocacy Conference of the Children's Defense Fund, the Calvin Symposium for Worship, and on the campuses of Harvard and Duke Universities.

BECKY ELDREDGE is an Ignatian-trained spiritual director, retreat facilitator, and author of two books: *The Inner Chapel* (Loyola Press, 2020) and *Busy Lives & Restless Souls* (Loyola Press, 2017). She leads a ministry that offers spiritual direction, resources, and retreats (virtual and in-person) rooted in the Spiritual Exercises of St. Ignatius. Passionate about Ignatian spirituality and teaching people how to pray and discern, Becky draws from over twenty years of ministry experience to help people make room for God in the busyness and invite them deeper in their walk with Christ. She holds an MPS from Loyola University in New Orleans and an MEd from Louisiana State University. You can learn more about her ministry at www.beckyeldredge.com.

ROBERT ELLSBERG is the publisher of Orbis Books and the author of many books about saints, including *All Saints* and *A Living Gospel: Reading God's Story in Holy Lives*. For ten years he has written a daily feature on saints, "Blessed Among Us," for *Give Us This Day*. A former managing editor of *The Catholic Worker*, he has also edited several volumes of the writings of Dorothy Day, including her diaries and letters, and most recently *On Pilgrimage: The Sixties* and *On Pilgrimage: The Seventies*. He is active on twitter: @RobertEllsberg.

JOHN FISHER, OSFS made first profession for the Oblates of St. Francis de Sales in 1980. Ordained in 1988, he spent thirty years in various Oblate high schools and their university. He is currently in his sixth year as the rector of the Cathedral of the Immaculate Conception for the Diocese of Camden. He has written for *Review for Religious, Homiletic and Pastoral Review* and *The Priest Magazine*. He is unabashedly the proudest uncle of twelve wonderful and good nieces and nephews.

MICHELLE FRANCL-DONNAY is a professor of chemistry and an adjunct scholar at the Vatican Observatory. When not doing research on quantum mechanics, she writes on the joys and struggles of attempting to live a contemplative life in the midst of the everyday chaos that being a wife, mother, and scientist brings. She is an occasional contributor to *Give Us This Day* and a regular columnist for the science journal *Nature Chemistry*. Her most recent book is *Prayer: Biblical Widsom for Seeking God*. Michelle gives the occasional retreat and blogs about prayer, God, and laundry at Quantum Theology (quantumtheology.blogspot.com). More of her writing can be found at www.michellefrancldonnay.com.

KYLE HADEN, OFM, PhD is a Franciscan priest. He received his doctorate in Historical Theology and is an Associate Professor and chair in the department of Theology and Franciscan Studies at St. Bonaventure University. His interests are church history and studying and applying the theories of René Girard in his writing. He is the author of two books, the second of which was published in 2020 by Lexington Books and is titled *Embodied Idolatry: A Critique of Christian Nationalism*.

CASSIDY HALL is an author, filmmaker, podcaster, student, and holds a MA in Counseling. She works as a Teaching Assistant at Christian Theological Seminary in Indianapolis, where she is studying for her MDiv and MTS degrees. She is currently pursuing ordination as a Member in Discernment with the United Church of Christ. For the past four years, Cassidy has served as the secretary of the International Thomas Merton Society. More recently, Cassidy began serving on the board of Enfleshed, an organization focused on spiritual nourishment for collective liberation. She worked as a producer on the award-winning film *In Pursuit of Silence*, and her directorial debut is a short film about Thomas Merton's hermitage years, *Day of a Stranger*. She is a co-host of the podcast *Encountering Silence* and recently created a podcast about the intersection of contemplation and social justice, titled *Contemplating Now*, which is featured on Christian Century.

LUKE HANSEN is a campus minister and religious studies teacher at St. Ignatius College Preparatory in San Francisco. He has a master's degree in social philosophy from Loyola University Chicago, a Master of Divinity degree from the Jesuit School of Theology in Berkeley, and a Licentiate in Sacred Theology from the Pontifical Gregorian University in Rome. Luke has served as a co-director of the Discerning Deacons project, which engages Catholics in the question of women and diaconate, and he has worked as an editor for the Jesuit journals *America* and *La Civiltà Cattolica*. He has won several awards from the Catholic Press Association for his writing. A native of Wisconsin, Luke enjoys running, playing basketball, and cheering for his favorite sports teams.

FR. JAN MICHAEL JONCAS was ordained in 1980 as a priest of the Archdiocese of St. Paul and Minneapolis, and holds degrees in English from the (then) College of St. Thomas in St. Paul, Minnesota, and in liturgical studies from the University of Notre Dame and the Pontificio Istituto Liturgico of the Ateneo S. Anselmo in Rome. He has served as a parochial vicar, a campus minister, and a parochial administrator (pastor). He is the author of six books and more than two hundred fifty articles and reviews in journals such as *Worship*, *Ecclesia Orans*, and *Questions Liturgiques*. He has composed and arranged more than 300 pieces of liturgical music. He is currently Artist in Residence and Research Fellow in Catholic Studies at the University of St. Thomas, St. Paul, Minnesota.

DEACON GREG KANDRA is the creator of *The Deacon's Bench* blog, which has garnered some 20 million readers from around the world since its inception in 2007. Additionally, he serves as Senior Writer for Catholic Near East Welfare Association (CNEWA), a pontifical association founded by Pope Pius XI in 1926.

Deacon Greg has received every major award in broadcasting, including three Emmys, two Peabody Awards, and four awards from the Writer's Guild of America. His spiritual writing and essays have been honored multiple times with awards by the Catholic Press Association. He's one of seventy-six New Yorkers—including Dorothy Day and Fulton Sheen—profiled in the 2014 book *New York Catholics*. He also travels the country directing retreats and parish missions. In May 2016, at the invitation of the Vatican, Deacon Greg was one of the featured speakers at the international Jubilee for Deacons in Rome. In 2017, he became the first deacon to be honored as Clergy of the Year by the Catholic Guild at Our Lady of the Skies Chapel at John F. Kennedy Airport. He was one of the speakers at the 2018 diaconate Congress in New Orleans, marking the fiftieth anniversary of the restoration of the diaconate as a permanent order.

A Maryland native, Deacon Greg graduated from the University of Maryland with a BA in English in 1982. He was ordained a deacon for the Diocese of Brooklyn in 2007. He and his wife live in Forest Hills, New York, where he serves at Our Lady Queen of Martyrs parish.

ANNA KEATING is writer, speaker, and former college chaplain. She is the co-author of *The Catholic Catalogue: A Field Guide to the Daily Acts that Make Up a*

Catholic Life (Image) and the owner of Keating Woodworks, a handmade furniture studio in Colorado.

DEACON JIM KNIPPER is the publisher of Clear Faith Publishing, which is focused on publishing books with a spiritual foundation. Their first four books, consisting of homilies, have received several awards by that industry. In addition, the books have raised over $100,000 for various charities.

Deacon Jim graduated from the University of Scranton with a degree in chemistry and in 1984 he received a Master's in Business in the Pharmaceutical Industry from Fairleigh Dickinson University. He received a Master's in Theology from Georgian Court University in May of 2015 and an honorary degree from that institution in May 2017. He is currently a member of the Board of Trustees for the Basilica of the National Shrine of the Immaculate Conception in Washington DC.

Today, he divides his time between Marco Island, Florida and Washington Crossing, Pennyslvania with his wife Teresa. He is the proud father of four sons and six grandchildren. He is a member of St. Paul's Catholic Church, Princeton, New Jersey, where he serves as a deacon to the parish. You can follow him and his preaching at teachbelief.blogspot.com.

MICHAEL LEACH, publisher emeritus of Orbis Books, has edited and published more than three thousand books over a fifty-year career that is still in progress. He was awarded a Lifetime Achievement Award from the Catholic Book Publishers Association in 2003.

FATHER RICHARD G. MALLOY, SJ, aka "Mugs," was born at Temple University Hospital in Philadelphia, the friendly city of brotherly shove. He studied Cultural Anthropology at Temple, so he didn't go far in life. From 1988–2003, he lived and worked as a member of the Jesuit Urban Service team in Camden, New Jersey. During those years, he also taught at St. Joseph's University in Philadelphia, and from 2010–2019 at the University of Scranton, teaching anthropology, sociology, and theology. He lived for fifteen years in first-year dorms (anthropological fieldwork!). In 2019, he began serving as director of Mission and Ministry at Cristo Rey Jesuit High School in Baltimore, Maryland.

Fishing is his passion in life. He is convinced that catching a ten-pound trout, the Eagles winning (another!!!) Super Bowl, or the Phillies beating the Yankees in the World Series are all sure signs that the second coming of Jesus is imminent. His books from Orbis, *A Faith that Frees: Catholic Matters for the 21st Century*, *Being on Fire: The Top Ten Essentials of Catholic Faith*, and *Spiritual Direction: A Beginner's Guide*, have all been recognized with awards by the Catholic Press Association. Follow him @FrMalloy.

JAMES MARTIN, SJ is a Jesuit priest, editor at large of *America*, consultor to the Vatican's Dicastery for Communication, and the author of many books, including the *New York Times* bestsellers *The Jesuit Guide*, *Jesus: A Pilgrimage*, and *Learning to Pray*.

SHIRIN McARTHUR is an Episcopal laywoman, spiritual guide, retreat leader, writer, and editor who ponders the sacred through prayer, poetry, dance, photography, nature, and contemplation. She holds an MDiv from Boston University School of Theology and a Certificate in Spiritual Guidance from the Shalem Institute in Washington, DC. Shirin has been leading retreats since the early 1990s and offering spiritual guidance since 1995. She also serves on the faculty of the Hesychia School of Spiritual Direction. Raised in New Mexico, she spent two decades in Massachusetts and now lives near Tucson, Arizona with her husband, the Rev. Henry Hoffman. Shirin copyedited this volume of *Homilists for the Homeless*. You can learn more about her at shirinmcarthur.com.

MEGAN MCKENNA is a native of New York City, but has lived in New Mexico for more than three decades. She is a theologian, storyteller, poet and scribe of the Scriptures, a teacher, preacher, and minor prophet. She has authored more than fifty books, drawn from her missionary work in Latin America, Southeast Asia, and Africa. Her focus is on peace, reconciliation, and restorative justice among Indigenous peoples worldwide, with Native Americans and with First Nations of Canada.

Most groups she works with struggle with poverty, violence, forgiveness, peacemaking, and community organizing in the face of change, trauma and shifting ways of life with multi-cultural and multi-religious groups. She seeks to pass on the wisdom of the universal Church and of human communities using the Word of God and stories from all people through retreats, parish missions, and transitional conferences for religious communities and groups that do justice in Europe and the US.

She has authored more than fifty books, including *And Morning Came: Scriptures of the Resurrection*, *Praying the Rosary*, *Send My Roots Rain*, *The New Stations of the Cross*, *On Your Mark: Reading Mark in the Shadow of the Cross*, and the recently released, *The Poor Will Save Us*.

BRIAN McLAREN is an author, speaker, activist, and public theologian. A former college English teacher and pastor, he is a passionate advocate for "a new kind of Christianity"—just, generous, and working with people of all faiths for the common good. He is a faculty member of The Living School at the Center for Action and Contemplation and an Auburn Senior Fellow. His most recent book is *Faith After Doubt* (2021), and his next release, *Do I Stay Christian?* will be available in May 2022.

THE REV. PENNY A. NASH is a priest living in the Episcopal Diocese of Virginia. After twelve years of "regular" parish ministry in parishes in both Georgia (where she was ordained in 2007) and Virginia, Penny became certified as an intentional interim minister and now serves in the capacity of interim rector, guiding parishes through the time of wilderness between settled pastors as they rediscover who they are, who their neighbors are, and what God is calling them to in their next life as a beloved community.

Penny loves to travel, and the beach (pretty much any beach) is her happy place. An avid photographer, she showcases her photography as sermon illustrations and occasional other posts on her blog: penelopepiscopal.blogspot.com. She and her husband, Tom Cox, are the parents of three wonderful adult children. They live in Richmond, Virginia, with their two cats, Sally and Bella.

THE REV. JAN RICHARDSON is an artist, writer, and ordained minister in the United Methodist Church. She serves as director of The Wellspring Studio, LLC, and has traveled widely as a retreat leader and conference speaker. With work described by the *Chicago Tribune* as "breathtaking," she has attracted an international audience drawn to the spaces of welcome, imagination, and solace that she creates in both word and image. Jan's books include *The Cure for Sorrow, Night Visions, In the Sanctuary of Women,* and her latest book, *Sparrow: A Book of Life and Death and Life.* She makes her home in Florida. For more about her work, visit janrichardson.com.

FATHER RICHARD ROHR is a Franciscan priest and ecumenical teacher who bears witness to the deep wisdom of Christian mysticism and traditions of action and contemplation. He is the founder of the Center for Action and Contemplation and Academic Dean of the Living School in Albuquerque, New Mexico, where he has lived since 1986.

For over fifty years, Father Richard's personal experience of God's infinite and transforming love has inspired his lifelong work of helping to remove the barriers that keep people from knowing God's love for themselves.

He is the author of numerous books, including *The Universal Christ, The Wisdom Pattern, Just This, Everything Belongs, Adam's Return, The Naked Now, Breathing Under Water, Falling Upward, Immortal Diamond, Dancing Standing Still,* and *Eager to Love.*

THE REV. TIM SCHENCK is rector of the Episcopal Parish of St. John the Evangelist in Hingham, Massachusetts, and the creator of the wildly popular online devotion Lent Madness. The author of five books full of faith and humor, his most recent is *Holy Grounds: The Surprising Connection Between Coffee and Faith—From Dancing Goats to Satan's Drink* (Fortress Press). Tim writes a syndicated monthly column titled "In Good Faith," blogs at *Clergy Confidential,* and is active on social media where you can follow him on Twitter @FatherTim. He lives in the St. John's rectory on the South Shore of Boston with his wife Bryna, rescue dogs Delilah and Cooper, and on occasion their twenty-something adult children.

ANNIE SELAK, PhD is a Roman Catholic systematic theologian and lay minister. She earned her PhD in systematic theology from Boston College with a dissertation entitled, "Toward an Ecclesial Vision in the Shadow of Wounds." Her theological research focuses on ecclesiology, authority in the church, feminist theologies, theological anthropology, Karl Rahner, and racism and sexism in the Roman Catholic Church. Annie is also a graduate of Santa Clara University (BA/BS) and the Jesuit School of Theology at Berkeley (MDiv). She has a wealth of experience in Catholic Higher Education, focusing on gender on college campuses, alternative break trips, mission integration, and diversity, equity, and inclusion. Her writing has appeared in *Modern Theology*, *Journal for Catholic Social Thought*, *The Washington Post*, *Commonweal Magazine*, *National Catholic Reporter*, and *America* media. Originally from California, Annie lives in Washington, DC with her spouse and children.

TIMOTHY SHRIVER is married, a father of five, the Chairman of Special Olympics International, and co-founder of UNITE, an initiative to promote national unity and solidarity across differences. Tim began his career as an educator and subsequently cofounded and currently chairs the Collaborative for Academic, Social, and Emotional Learning (CASEL), the leading school reform organization in the field of social and emotional learning. Shriver earned his undergraduate degree from Yale University, a master's degree from Catholic University, and a Doctorate in Education from the University of Connecticut. He has produced six films, is the author of the *New York Times* bestseller *Fully Alive: Discovering What Matters Most*, and co-editor of a new book, *The Call to Unite: Voices of Hope and Awakening*.

MARY ELIZABETH SPERRY holds a master's degree in liturgical studies from the Catholic University of America and a master's degree in political science from the University of California, Los Angeles. She is the author of *Bible Top Tens* (Our Sunday Visitor), *Ten: How the Commandments Can Change Your Life* (Franciscan Media), *Scripture in the Parish: A Guide for Catholic Ministry* (Liturgical Press), *Real Life Faith: Bible Companions for Catholic Teens* (Liguori), and *Making Room for God: Decluttering and the Spiritual Life* (Ave Maria Press).

FRAN ROSSI SZPYLCZYN is a former corporate executive turned writer and church worker. She graduated from St. Bernard's School of Theology and Ministry in May of 2013 with a Master of Arts in Pastoral Studies. By day she is the Pastoral Associate for Administration at the Church of the Immaculate Conception in Glen-ville, New York. Fran has extensive experience facilitating faith formation for both teenagers and adults, directing retreats, and public speaking. In 2016, she fulfilled a life dream when she walked the 500-mile route of the Camino de Santiago.

A published writer, her work has appeared in numerous books, online forums, and publications. She was a charter contributor to the *Homilists for the Homeless*. Fran has also been published in the *National Catholic Reporter*, *New Ways Ministry Blog*, *The Evangelist*, the *Albany Times Union*, and *America Magazine*, and is a regular contributor to *Give Us This Day*. A longtime social media advocate, she has a blog called *There Will Be Bread*. Originally from the New York City area, Fran moved to Clifton Park, New York in 2007 to be with her spouse Mark.

THE REV. PATRICK J. WENRICK graduated with an MDiv in Mission Specialization from Catholic Theological Union in 1982 and was ordained a priest in October of the same year. Since that time, he has been in various ministries within the Roman Catholic Tradition, including being a Vocation Director and Assistant Pastor of two churches in New Jersey as well as an Assistant Rector of a Religious community. Graduating from LaSalle University in Philadelphia with a master's degree in Pastoral Counseling, Pat went to work first as a therapist and later as Program Director for a drug and alcohol outpatient facility in Bucks County, Pennsylvania. While Program Director, he also taught world religions as an adjunct faculty member at Bucks County Community College. In 1998, he also established a clinical practice as a New Jersey licensed professional counselor.

In July 2003, Rev. Wenrick married his lovely wife Susan in Princeton, New Jersey, and relocated to the Tampa area with their daughter, Allyson. In the Tampa area, Rev. Wenrick has served as a chaplain with hospice in Lakeland, Florida and given numerous workshops and talks on lifespan development, spirituality, and bereavement issues, weaving a healthy spiritual-psychological approach to the problems that confront contemporary society. He continues to witness marriages, perform baptisms, and to be available for visiting the sick and dying in hospitals and nursing homes as part of CITI Ministries. Rev. Wenrick and his wife participate in the faith life of St. Francis Ecumenical Catholic Community in Largo, Florida and support charitable causes in and around where they live and work.

FATHER JOHN D. WHITNEY, SJ grew up in Northern California, but in 1983 entered the Jesuits of the Oregon Province following time as a Jesuit Volunteer in far-western Alaska. Ordained to the priesthood in 1994, with degrees in philosophy and English from Georgetown and a licentiate in philosophy from St. Michael's Institute in Spokane, John has spent much of his ministerial life in Seattle, where he worked in various roles at Seattle University—including instructor in philosophy, Campus Minister for Liturgy and Sacraments, and Alumni Chaplain—and taught at Seattle Prep, until he was named Provincial Superior and moved to Portland in 2002. During his six years as Provincial, the sexual crisis in the Church erupted in the Northwest, and John spent much of his time seeking to work with survivors of abuse, always trying to find a route by which both justice and healing could be found. In 2009, John became pastor of St. Joseph Church in Seattle, where he was known for his preaching and writing, as well as his encouragement of the LGBT community and support of immigrants and refugees. In 2021, he moved from Seattle to San Francisco, where he currently serves as Associate Pastor at St. Ignatius Church.

DR. PHYLLIS ZAGANO is an internationally acclaimed Catholic scholar who has lectured throughout the United States, and in Canada, Europe, and Australia. Her many awards include the 2014 Isaac Hecker Award for Social Justice from the Paulist Center Community in Boston for "her prolific body of work that has constantly echoed the cry of the poorest of our society for dignity and for justice both inside and outside the church...specifically the dignity of all women." Her groundbreaking work on women in the diaconate led to her appointment to the Pontifical Commission for the Study of the Diaconate of Women in 2016. She has taught at Fordham, Boston, and Yale Universities, and currently holds a research appointment at Hofstra University, Hempstead, New York. Her newest book, *Women: Icons of Christ* (Paulist, 2020) received a Catholic Media Association 2021 Book Award.

CHARITIES

THIRST PROJECT

Thirst Project is a non-profit organization that exists to end the global water crisis and the fact that over 785 million people on the planet do not have access to safe, clean water. They travel across the world to educate individuals about the global water crisis and challenge them to fundraise to build freshwater wells in developing nations and impoverished communities. They guarantee that 100% of all public donations go directly toward their well projects. Over the last decade, Thirst Project has raised more than $11 million, which has given over 500,000 people in thirteen countries safe, clean water for life.

www.thirstproject.org

WATER FOR PEOPLE

Whether it's a drink from the tap, a toilet that works, or a place to wash our hands, having water is a basic necessity that many of us take for granted. But in many parts of the world, women and children spend more than four hours each day walking for water, and nearly 1 in 3 people still lack access to safe drinking water.

Water For People believes that everyone should have access to clean water and sanitation services, forever. They know that improved water, sanitation, and hygiene change everything, which is why they are committed to making sure these services are sustainable for the long term, not just for today. They partner with local leaders and communities to implement the solutions that are right for them, then provide the tools to make sure water, sanitation, and hygiene services last for generations to come.

Water For People works in nine countries across Latin America, Africa, and Asia, changing lives, communities, and countries—making clean water available to Everyone Forever. They have impacted 1.54 million people with their sanitation services and created 2,436 permanent jobs through their work.

www.waterforpeople.org

CHARITY: WATER

charity: water believes that sustainable work is locally led. Along with implementing community-owned water projects, their local partners help facilitate comprehensive water, sanitation, and hygiene (WASH) programming to protect everyone's long-term health. During the past fifteen years, they have funded over 79,000 water projects in 29 countries.

www.charitywater.org

CLEAN WATER FUND

Clean Water Fund's mission is to develop strong grassroots environmental leadership and to bring together diverse constituencies to work cooperatively for changes that improve their lives, focused on health, consumer, environmental and community problems. Based in Washington, DC, Clean Water Fund operates locally staffed environmental and health protection programs serving communities in more than fifteen US states.

www.cleanwaterfund.org

ACKNOWLEDGMENTS

As with all things in life, it takes many people coming together and supporting each other for true success to be achieved. Therefore, I am most grateful to the expanding group of people in my life who all have supported our work on this and our other books that gift spiritual wisdom to our readers and make it possible to help, in a small way, to feed the hungry and give drink to those who thirst. So, my deepest thanks to...

- **ALL OF OUR CONTRIBUTORS**, some who have been with us for all of our volumes and some who have joined us for the first time. Your talented words, opening our eyes and hearts and souls to the Gospel, are a true gift to all of us.

- **BROTHER MICKEY McGRATH**, whose inspiring art throughout the book visually brings life to the words on the page.

- **DOUG CORDES**, who continues to give beautiful style and design to the works we publish.

- **SHIRIN McARTHUR**, who has an incredibly keen eye in technically editing the works of such a variety of authors, keeping to their individual styles, while enhancing the ability of the words to reach our readers.

- **MAUREEN EDORE**, who keeps me on track and helps bring order to my life and my ministry.

- **SERGIO HERNANDEZ** and **FRAN ROSSI SZPYLCZYN**, who support our social media presence each day.

- For my sons, **TIM**, **JON**, **PETER**, and **JACOB**, and their wives, who are always there to support my work.

- For my beautiful grandchildren: **BODHI**, **BLOOM**, **OLIVER**, **HENRY** and soon-to-be one more grandson who remind me how to see Christ through the eyes of a child.

- In memory of my beloved grandson, **JULIAN**, who will never be forgotten, and who, through every moment of his short life, reminded me how to love others.

- And for my wife, **TERESA**, who for over thirty years has endlessly provided me with love and support and spiritual wisdom.

And for you, **OUR READERS**, who support our work and thus support our charities. May you be blessed in all that you do as you remember to live with love for others so that, together, we can continue our call to welcome the stranger, to give food to those who hunger, drink to those who thirst, and to care for all those who live on the margins.

Made in United States
North Haven, CT
08 December 2021

12216160R00183